Best wishes for success in your life

Jim Owen

GOVERNING METROPOLITAN INDIANAPOLIS

The Politics of Unigov

A publication of the Franklin K. Lane Memorial Fund, Institute of Governmental Studies, University of California, Berkeley

The Franklin K. Lane Memorial Fund takes its name from Franklin Knight Lane (1864–1921), a distinguished Californian who was successively New York correspondent for the San Francisco *Chronicle*, City and County Attorney of San Francisco, member and later chairman of the United States Interstate Commerce Commission, and Secretary of the Interior in the cabinet of President Woodrow Wilson.

The general purposes of the endowment are to promote "better understanding of the nature and working of the American system of democratic government, particularly in its political, economic and social aspects," and the "study and development of the most suitable methods for its improvement in the light of experience."

Lane Studies in Regional Government:

Metropolitan Winnipeg: Politics and Reform of Local Government, by Meyer Brownstone and T. J. Plunkett

New York: The Politics of Urban Regional Development, by Michael N. Danielson and Jameson W. Doig

Governing the London Region: Reorganization and Planning in the 1960s, by Donald L. Foley

Governing Metropolitan Toronto: A Social and Policy Analysis, by Albert Rose

Governing Greater Stockholm: Policy Development and Urban Change in Stockholm, by Thomas J. Anton

GOVERNING METROPOLITAN INDIANAPOLIS

The Politics of Unigov

C. James Owen

York Willbern

Published for the Institute of Governmental Studies
and the Institute of International Studies
University of California, Berkeley

UNIVERSITY OF CALIFORNIA PRESS
BERKELEY LOS ANGELES LONDON

University of California Press
Berkeley and Los Angeles, California

University of California Press, Ltd.
London, England

© 1985 by
The Regents of the University of California

1   2   3   4   5   6   7   8   9

Library of Congress Cataloging in Publication Data

Owen, C. James (Carroll James)
    Governing metropolitan Indianapolis.

    (Lane studies in regional government)
    "Published for the Institute of Governmental Studies
and the Institute of International Studies, University of
California, Berkeley."
    Includes index.
    1. Indianapolis Metropolitan Area (Ind.)—Politics and
government.   I. Willbern, York Y. II. University of
California, Berkeley. Institute of Governmental Studies.
III. University of California, Berkeley. Institute of
International Studies.   IV. Title.   V. Series.
JS943.A8094 1985   320.8'09772'52   85-2776
ISBN 0-520-05147-5

To our wives,
Susan Poplett Owen and
Johnne Bryant Willbern

Contents

Illustrations

Maps

Charts

Photographs

Tables

Foreword

Five years after the City of Indianapolis and Marion County had been consolidated by an act of the Indiana legislature, Mayor Richard Lugar said: "Modernizers and reformers of the municipal government must approach each opportunity with seemingly boundless enthusiasm, moral fervor, and careful definition of the grounds on which they expect to win."[1] After reading this book, one can understand the complex process whose outcome at times seemed doubtful and why Mayor Lugar considered it important to capitalize on every opportunity with at least the appearance of "boundless enthusiasm."

The Indianapolis Story

James Owen and York Willbern, in the seventh volume of the Franklin K. Lane series on the governance of major metropolitan areas, have reconstructed the history of the only consolidation of a large city and county to occur in the United States without a popular referendum since the creation of Greater New York in 1897.[2] It is the story of how Mayor Lugar convinced the Republican Party leaders and other influential citizens of Marion County that unifying the city and county would be "good politics" and that a consolidated government with a mayor and council could provide the public leadership that Indianapolis had lacked for years. He persuaded the Republicans that

1. Richard G. Lugar, "A Few Comments on Local Government Modernization," proceedings of the Advisory Commission on Intergovernmental Relation's National Conference on Federalism in Action, Washington, DC, February 21, 1975.
2. An advisory referendum not binding on the New York legislature was held in 1894 in New York City, Brooklyn, and the rest of Kings County, Queens and Richmond counties, and the southeastern portion of Westchester County. The result was favorable to consolidation, with a close vote only in Brooklyn and one of the Westchester towns. Four years elapsed before final action was taken by the legislature; see David C. Hammack, *Power and Society: Greater New York at the Turn of the Century* (New York: Basic Books, 1982); Barry Jerome Kaplan, "A Study in the Politics of Metropolitanization: The Greater New York City Charter of 1897," Ph.D. dissertation, State University of New York, Buffalo, 1975, pp. 151–155. The city and county of Honolulu were consolidated without referendum in 1904, but at that time the population of each was very small.

they would benefit from the move. Consolidation was facilitated by a rather unusual coincidence: simultaneous Republican control of the mayor's office, the governorship, and the state legislature. This is also the story of how Mayor Lugar led his team of advisers in putting together a legislative package that could attract the wide support—or at least the acquiescence—of most city and county officials, the press, and legislative leaders. He compromised when compromise was politically essential, but he also managed to protect his main objectives: consolidating the policymaking structures of the city and the county.

Even after responsibility for the consolidation effort shifted from the mayor to the legislative leaders, Lugar still exercised influence. For example, he spoke at various county and congressional district meetings gathered to celebrate the memory of Abraham Lincoln, reminding Republicans of their unique opportunity to "unstick the gears of an archaic, expensive and overlapping Model-T form of government."[3]

Mayor Lugar was talking from his own experience when he responded in 1973 to a question about the dynamics of a consolidation movement. His reply emphasized the importance of a few active dedicated leaders: "It seems to me that probably someone or a very small group of people active in the political life of Montgomery County, Dayton, Ohio, will need to determine their own plan of action. It may be assisted by a citizens' study group. But I think a number of people, or maybe a single person will need to put his political life on the line."[4]

It is difficult to overstate the importance of Mayor Lugar's leadership. He was that "single person" who played for high stakes and won. In fact, he managed to ride the issue into the US Senate, in the face of conclusions in the prevailing literature that such efforts are no-win or even losing propositions for the leaders involved.[5] Mayor Lugar's experience demonstrates that there *can* be political gain from such efforts, depending on state-local circumstances that predispose for or against success, as well as on the quality of leadership displayed. Moreover, political parties as well as strategically positioned political leaders elsewhere may gain or lose from metropolitan reorganization, or believe that they will. In another volume of this series,

3. "Lugar Intends to Lobby for Unigov," *Indianapolis Star*, January 5, 1969, p. 12.

4. National Association of Counties, *Consolidation: Partial or Total*, transcript of the National Conference (Washington, DC, 1973), p. 15.

5. Marilyn Gittell, "Metropolitan Mayor: Dead End," *Public Administration Review* 23 (March 1963). Although leadership in metropolitan reform does not often result in election to higher offices, as it did for Senator Lugar, local officials nevertheless frequently perceive the proposed reforms as supporting their ambitions; see John C. Bollens and Henry J. Schmandt, *The Metropolis: Its People, Politics, and Economic Life*, 4th ed. (New York: Harper & Row, 1982), p. 384.

Metropolitan Winnipeg, Meyer Brownstone and T. J. Plunkett discuss the combination of "public interest" and "partisan advantage" in developing and enacting the proposal to consolidate all the local governments in the Winnipeg region.[6] Contrary to what happened in Indianapolis, the sponsor of Winnipeg's reform, the Manitoba New Democratic Party, has not benefited from the consolidated city's electoral politics the way it had hoped to.

Of course, Mayor Lugar did not work alone. Owen and Willbern show how a succession of informal organizations came into play. Each had a core of largely the same people, plus additional persons with such technical or symbolic qualifications as the occasion required. But Mayor Lugar and his key associates never allowed an independent organization to determine strategies or tactics. Procedure in Indianapolis thus differed significantly from the usual reform effort in the United States where moves to consolidate a city and county are typically sponsored by citizens' groups without the leadership of influential and ambitious public officials.[7]

Only after the basic elements of a plan for Unigov—the popular term for the proposed reorganization—had been put into draft bill form by Lugar and his close associates did the mayor appoint the Task Force on Improved Government Structure for Indianapolis and Marion County. The task force consisted of 23 business leaders, a Presbyterian minister (later mayor), a member of a carpenters' apprenticeship program, a member of the League of Women Voters, and ex officio the 23 members of the all-Republican Marion County delegation to the state legislature. As Owen and Willbern observe: "Perhaps the task force members were most effective in promoting Unigov simply because of who they were. . . . Mayor Lugar's original task force instructions omitted any suggestion that it had the option of turning

6. Meyer Brownstone and T. J. Plunkett, *Metropolitan Winnipeg: Politics and Reform of Local Government* (Berkeley: University of California Press, 1983). See also Frank Smallwood, *Greater London: The Politics of Metropolitan Reform* (Indianapolis: Bobbs-Merrill, 1965), pp. 102–103:

> The London Labour Party was flatly opposed to any reform that would lead to the abolition of its local political prize, the London County Council, and dilute its central area strength in a sea of Conservative suburban votes. The Conservative position, on the other hand, was not quite this precise. While many Conservatives cast covetous eyes on precisely the political prospect Labour feared (i.e., the swamping of central London's Labourites within a sea of Conservative suburbia), some of the powerful Conservative county council leaders, especially in Surrey and Kent, were adamant against any reform that would result in the metropolitan fringes of their own home counties being wrested away from their local control and turned over to a new Greater London authority.

7. See, e.g., Henry Schmandt, *The Milwaukee Metropolitan Study Commission* (Bloomington: Indiana University Press, 1965); and Government Affairs Foundation, *Metropolitan Surveys* (Chicago: Public Administration Service, 1958).

down the whole plan. . . . The overriding effect was that the Unigov's principals successfully got the approval of an important segment of the community while retaining effective control over the Unigov effort." In short, the mayor used the task force to legitimize consolidation rather than to make major changes in the proposal. A well-informed student of metropolitan governance has remarked that nowhere else have citizen task forces been used with such political skill.[8]

Indianapolis and Winnipeg: No Referendums

The prevailing practice in the United States requires that any major (and often minor) metropolitan governmental reorganizations of the kind discussed in this book must be approved in a referendum. In Indiana, however, lacking a strong tradition of local home rule, astute Indianapolis leaders were able to capitalize on their party's control of the governorship and both houses of the legislature, pushing through legislation that consolidated the city and Marion County without a referendum. The near-simultaneous creation of Greater Winnipeg's Unicity—as the consolidated government was popularly known—in Canada's prairie province of Manitoba meant that two of North America's three largest consolidations of this century were achieved without a referendum vote.[9]

---

8. Letter from Vincent L. Marando, University of Maryland, to Stanley Scott, December 8, 1982. The unique features of the political process by which the Unigov reorganization was put together should not blind us to the complex political nature of almost any reorganization as well as the skillful maneuvering required to put it into effect and make it work. Note, e.g., Beatrice Webb's astonishment at the "intrigue" she and Sidney Webb found necessary to achieve Fabian Socialist goals through the London County Council and other institutions at the turn of the century. She wrote in 1903:

> It is a tiresome fact that, to get things done in what one considers the best way, entails so much—to speak plainly—of intrigue. There is no such thing as spontaneous public opinion; it all has to be manufactured from a Centre of Conviction and Energy radiating through persons, sometimes losing itself in an unsympathetic medium, at other times gaining additional force in such an agent as the Bishop of Stepney or the *Daily Mail*. Of course there is always the element of "sport" in this life of agitation, watching the ideas one starts, like, for instance, "the dominance of the N.U.T. [National Union of Teachers] over borough councils," wending their ways through all sorts of sources to all sorts of places and turning up quite unexpectedly as allies in overthrowing counter interests and arguments. (Quoted in Ronald Clark's review of *The Diary of Beatrice Webb*, vol. 2: *1892–1905: All Good Things of Life*, ed. Norman MacKenzie and Jeanne MacKenzie [Cambridge, Mass.: Belknap Press/Harvard University Press, 1983], in *New York Times Book Review*, January 29, 1984).

9. Indianapolis–Marion County had a 1970 population of 800,000, and Greater Winnipeg, 500,000. The third large consolidation, which did involve a referendum, brought together Jacksonville and Duval County, Florida. This area had a 1970 popula-

The two nonreferendum consolidations, however, took place in distinctly different political and constitutional circumstances: Indiana operates under a constitutional separation of powers dividing the executive and legislative branches, whereas Manitoba operates under a parliamentary system. Readers can compare this Indianapolis volume with the Brownstone and Plunkett account of Winnipeg's consolidation, given in another of the Franklin K. Lane volumes.[10] The two books help highlight the differing limitations and opportunities under the two systems as well as the corresponding strategies and tactics of consolidation's opponents and proponents in the two metropolises.

Parliamentary Versus Nonparliamentary Systems

To most observers from the United States, it looks much easier to reorganize local governments in parliamentary systems (e.g., as in the province of Manitoba) than in the United States with its nonparliamentary system, written national and state constitutions, and separation of powers between legislative and executive branches. Canada's provinces have neither written constitutions nor separation of powers, and Canadian political parties are comparatively strong and well disciplined. In those circumstances the cabinet of a provincial government, particularly a government with a respectable majority in parliament, is in a strong position to effect reorganizations. In the United States, by contrast, consolidation statutes—either generally permissive or individual special acts (as in the case of Indianapolis)—must get the assent of two legislative houses and the governor. In addition, one or more referendum majorities from the local citizenry living within the areas to be reorganized are usually required.

One of our Canadian reader-critics urged that we emphasize the importance of these effects of the parliamentary system, *as a system,* in facilitating successful reorganization. He acknowledged that absence of a referendum requirement is perhaps a necessary condition of effective local reorganization, but he also observed that lack of a referendum is not in itself a sufficient explanation. Several features of the

---

tion of 529,000. Another proposal, to consolidate Louisville and Jefferson County, Kentucky (population 685,000), went to a referendum in November 1982, losing by a hairline margin of 0.08 percent; see D. A. Gilbert, "Louisville Merger Goes to Voters," *National Civic Review* 71(9):468–469 (October 1982); and 72(1):52–53 (January 1983); Joseph F. Zimmerman, "City-County Mergers: Voters Say Yes and No," *Public Administration Times* 5(22) (November 15, 1982). In November 1983 voters rejected a consolidation proposal for the second time in the same year by an even larger margin than in November 1982; see D. A. Gilbert, "Louisville Voters Reject Merger Proposal—Again," *Public Administration Times* 6(23) (December 1, 1983).

10. Brownstone and Plunkett, *Metropolitan Winnipeg.*

parliamentary system also contribute. His succinct description of the workings of the parliamentary system follows:

> The norms of cabinet secrecy, collective responsibility and party discipline make it much easier for political parties of any stripe to make dramatic changes in the status quo. Internal opposition to proposals for local government reorganization are discussed privately in the cabinet and in the caucus of the governing party. After the cabinet has acquired the support of the caucus, or at least its acquiescence, the cabinet can proceed to ask the legislature to pass the required legislation, with the assurance that it will pass (assuming the governing party has a majority in the legislature). To be sure, the opposition can attempt to mobilize public opinion against the proposal, but if the governing party is willing to face the political consequences, passage of the legislation is almost assured. Moreover, there is no executive veto to fear, as there is in the United States.[11]

Referendums and Multiple Majorities

In addition to lacking the political-organizational "clout" of the parliamentary system, many US states are further limited by their written constitutions, which often protect local governments from abolition by statute or sometimes even from actions by the electorate, short of an actual state constitutional amendment. The most common protection is the requirement that local consolidations be approved by referendums, often by multiple majorities. Thus, at the very least, separate majorities are required in both the central city and the remainder of the county.[12] But the protection in some state constitutions is even more formidable. For instance, Article IX of New York's constitution requires double or triple concurrent majorities to transfer a function to the county from a subcounty unit. If a city or town func-

11. This comment was made to the editors by a knowledgeable reviewer with the Canadian government who requested anonymity.

12. From 1933 to 1957 the constitution of Ohio required that the transfer of municipal functions to the county be approved by three separate majorities—in the entire county, in the largest municipality, and in the county outside the largest municipality. For counties of more than 500,000, an additional set of majorities was required—a majority vote in enough individual municipalities and townships to comprise a majority of the units; see Ohio Constitution, Art. X, sec. 3. An extreme case of multiple and preponderant majorities stymied the 1929 attempt to adopt a metropolitan charter in the Pittsburgh area. Pittsburgh demonstrated that it is possible to lose while securing approval by a majority vote in a majority of municipalities and townships (82 of the 129 subdivisions approved the proposed charter). The relevant constitutional provision required a two-thirds majority vote in each of a majority of municipalities and townships; see Paul Studenski, *The Government of Metropolitan Areas in the United States* (New York: National Municipal League, 1930), pp. 376–383. For Cleveland, see Victor Jones, *Metropolitan Government* (Chicago: University of Chicago Press, 1942), pp. 236–247.

tion is involved, city voters cast ballots as one unit, and town voters cast ballots as a second unit. If a village function is involved, separate affirmative majorities of city, town, and village voters are required before the function can be shifted. Village voters, of course, vote twice since they also are town voters.[13]

Since 1961, at least four attempted city-county consolidations in the United States would have succeeded if similar special majorities had not been constitutionally required. Thus, despite a 54 percent favorable vote in 1961, the consolidation plan for the city of Richmond and Henrico County, Virginia, was rejected when it did not meet a multiple-majority test. Such requirements also defeated Virginia's Roanoke–Roanoke County consolidation proposal in 1969 (66.4 percent yes), Georgia's Savannah–Chatham County proposal in 1973 (58.3 percent yes), and another Georgia proposal in Augusta–Richmond County in 1974 (51.8 percent yes).

The Referendum: Sources and Consequences

In the United States, popular-vote approval of reorganizations that change local boundaries and/or eliminate general purpose local units has come to be considered a virtually obligatory convention, even when not constitutionally required. By contrast, the local referendum is rarely used elsewhere. The recent history of substantial

---

13. In 1977 the US Supreme Court held that the state requirement of such multiple majorities does not violate the equal protection clause of the US Constitution; see *Town of Lockport, NY, et al. v. Citizens for Community Action at the Local Level et al.,* 430 US-259 (1977). The lower court had held such requirements unconstitutional because they violate the one-man, one-vote principle. The Supreme Court, however, reversed the judgment, holding that whereas all voters have "an equal interest in representative democracy," not all voters in a "single-shot" referendum on county government reorganization have the same interests in or will be affected in the same manner by the reorganization of the county government.

> The challenged provisions of the New York law rest on the state's identification of the distinctive interests of the residents of the cities and towns within a county rather than their interests as residents of the county as a homogeneous unit. This identification is based in the realities of the distribution of governmental powers in New York, and is consistent with our cases that recognize both the wide discretion the States have in forming and allocating governmental tasks to local subdivisions, *and the discrete interests that such local governmental units may have qua units* [emphasis added]. (*Town of Lockport v. Citizens,* pp. 268–269)

> In terms of recognizing constituencies with separate and potentially opposing interests . . . separate voter approval requirements are based on the perception that the real and long-term impact of a restructuring of local government is felt quite differently by the different county constituent units that in a sense compete to provide similar governmental services. Voters in these constituent units are directly and differentially affected by the restructuring of county governments, which may make the providers of public services more remote and less subject to the voters' individual influence. (*Town of Lockport v. Citizens,* pp. 271–272)

local government reorganizations in Canada, Great Britain, West Germany, Austria, Denmark, Norway, and Sweden shows how major restructuring is carried out by national (or state) legislative act, usually without provision for approval by either local voters or the governing bodies of the local authorities affected.[14] Arthur Gunlicks notes: "In no other country [except the United States] did we encounter the concept of volunteerism, the idea that it is somehow illegitimate to change local government boundaries or create regional substate special-purpose authorities without the consent of the local governments or local inhabitants concerned."[15]

Why has the United States adopted the seemingly eccentric course of placing such heavy reliance on referendums to approve governmental reorganizations? The roots of the referendum in the United States are traceable as far back as the late 1700s when constitutional conventions and legislatures drafted state constitutions and hinged their adoption on the results of plebiscites, reasoning that voter validation was appropriate for such basic laws. Later, toward the end of the nineteenth century and at the beginning of the twentieth century, as the concept of municipal or local home rule developed in some states, the resulting city and county charters were typically voted on by the electorates—probably because they seemed similar to state con-

14. In Canada the 1955–1965 study by Harlan Hahn found local referendums used much more frequently than usually supposed and for a variety of issues. Generally, such votes are held on the initiative of local councils that want to "get off the hook" on divisive issues, not because of a mandatory constitutional requirement. The referendum topics included such matters as "blue laws," sports or recreational facilities, hospitals, utility and other public improvements, liquor control, suffrage expansion, transportation systems, daylight saving time, and utility regulation. City government reforms were the subject of 20 of the 450 referendums included, and municipal annexation or amalgamation figured in 18. In short, referendums *were* held on a few local reforms and boundary changes, but the numbers and proportions were relatively small—only 8.4 percent of the total; see Harlan Hahn, "Voting in Canadian Communities: A Taxonomy of Referendum Issues," *Canadian Journal of Political Science* 1:462–469 (December 1968).

Significant for our discussion here, voters were *not* asked to pass on the creation of the seven metropolitan and regional governments in Ontario, the three urban communities in Quebec, Unicity in Winnipeg, or the regional districts created in British Columbia. All were established by provincial statutes and without local referendum votes. For a detailed discussion of provincial laws authorizing or requiring referendums in Canadian municipalities, see J. Patrick Boyer, *Lawmaking by the People: Referendums and Plebiscites in Canada* (Toronto: Butterworth, 1982). Whereas the vast majority of state and local referendums in the United States are final and self-executing, almost all of the Canadian referendums are advisory only.

15. Arthur B. Gunlicks, "The United States in Cross-National Comparison," in *Local Government Reform and Reorganization*, ed. Arthur B. Gunlicks (Port Washington, N.Y.: Kennikat Press, 1981), pp. 205–215. Austin Ranney points out that Switzerland makes substantial use of the referendum, including, in at least some circumstances, to approve boundary changes (letter to Stanley Scott, May 24, 1983).

stitutions. Austin Ranney suggests the analogy among local, state, and national levels:

> The big plus for referendums is that on most issues they acquire a degree of legitimacy that no other form of democratic decision-making can achieve. . . . Presumably that is why most states and many nations require popular approval of constitutional amendments before they become effective. Perhaps it is also why most changes in the political status of national units—the formation of new states, the dissolution of old states, and so on—are usually done after that special version of referendums now generally called "plebiscites." . . . Indeed . . . in some respects referendums on local-unit consolidations . . . have some resemblances to changes in the international status of former colonies, established states, and the like.[16]

From shortly before the turn of the century until World War I, the Progressive movement pushed hard on behalf of the initiative, referendum, and recall, which were employed to reduce the influence in local and state legislatures of the political machines or special interests that often dominated them—for example, in California, the Southern Pacific Railroad—and to take decisions on certain issues out of the hands of legislative bodies. In any event, many influences prevailing at the time—for example, accepted styles of constitution validation, Progressivism, populism, moves for local home rule, and strong distrust of legislatures and political machines—produced long ballots in many states. These ballots included referendums to approve local charter amendments, governmental boundary alterations, and other structural changes. Such use of the referendum has now become an integral part of the written and unwritten constitutional system in the United States.

The relative success of the Canadian and European structural reform efforts is largely explained by the lack of such vote requirements. Robert Morlan considers their absence "of central importance" because referendum requirements would presumably have defeated most of the Canadian and European proposals. "Experience with referenda in Europe and North America has clearly indicated that, short of the most extreme financial exigency, the public is strongly resistant to amalgamations."[17]

In short, restructuring by provincial, state, or national legislative action without a popular referendum is a key feature of most reform

16. Letter from Austin Ranney to Stanley Scott, May 24, 1983.

17. Robert L. Morlan, "Local Government Reorganization: The Components of Success," *National Civic Review* 70(8):404–409 (September 1981); see also Gunlicks, ed., *Local Government Reform*, chs. 2, 3.

adoptions outside the United States. Conversely, the nearly universal referendum requirement is the principal reason for the failure of most reorganization proposals in the United States. Marando noted in 1979 that of 68 efforts in the last three decades, three-fourths were turned down in referendum elections.[18] Furthermore, as we have noted, the referendum often extended well beyond requiring a simple areawide majority, calling for separate majorities in the central city and the remainder of the county or even for multiple majorities in several local units.

Noting the high failure rate of reorganization efforts under a referendum formula, Marando reminds us that the states have both the authority and potential for reorganizing local government and suggests that the "political constraints upon consolidation may well create circumstances in which states may be drawn more directly into metropolitan area governing processes." He comments further: "States continue to consider changes in the 'rules of the game' in order to facilitate metropolitan reorganization. One of the areas where the 'rules of the game' will be changed is ending the referenda requirement for approval of local government reorganization."[19] Certainly the stresses and pressures on state and local governments attributable to our contemporary economic and fiscal environment are likely to accelerate demands for more effective governmental processes. Will this also promote or even force a basic reconsideration of conventional wisdom and of requirements for referendum votes on at least some forms of structural change?

In any event, many kinds of responses—short of comprehensive governmental reorganization—are possible in the quest for more effective government. Moreover, state and local officials see few constitutional impediments to such alternative courses. For example, a recent Advisory Commission on Intergovernmental Relations survey of governors, attorneys general, departments of community affairs, legislative research bureaus, state municipal leagues, and state associations

---

18. Vincent L. Marando, "City-County Consolidation: Reform, Regionalism, Referenda, and Requiem," *Western Political Quarterly* 32(4):409–421 (December 1979).

19. Ibid., p. 421. In addition to Indiana, Nevada, and Montana, mentioned by Marando, Minnesota acted without a referendum when in 1967 the legislature created one of the most successful recent examples of a regional government in a major metropolitan area, the Metropolitan Council of the Twin Cities (Minneapolis–St. Paul). The Twin Cities Council is basically an umbrella agency, all the preexisting governments having been left intact. While the council has less far-reaching authority than most other reorganizations, it has more power than the typical regional council of governments (COG) in the United States. For this reason the Twin Cities formula has been called "metropolitan policymaking with teeth"; see John J. Harrigan, *Political Change in the Metropolis*, 2nd ed. (Boston: Little, Brown, 1981), pp. 334–338. See also John J. Harrigan and William C. Johnson, *Governing the Twin Cities Region* (Minneapolis: University of Minnesota Press, 1978).

of counties found that 70 percent did not consider the ability of state legislatures to solve "metropolitan and other areawide problems" to be "inhibited" by constitutional grants of local discretionary authority or by constitutional prohibitions against special legislation.[20] Of course, the respondents may have differed widely on the definition of a "metropolitan problem" or on legislative actions adequate to solve them. Nevertheless, the evidence of state inaction suggests a wide difference between constitutional *authority* to act and the apparently much more limited *political will* to act.[21]

Critiques of the Referendum

When Unigov was successfully established without a referendum, opponents of reform in other parts of Indiana were in effect forewarned by the Indianapolis experience. Owen and Willbern note how other subsequent Indiana urban reform efforts were guided by Unigov's example but also "inherited a share of its 'negative' legacy." "Consolidation opponents across the state—feeling they had been caught unaware in 1969 when Unigov passed without requiring a referendum—were now vigilant and insisted on a referendum. They would undoubtedly try to add a referendum requirement to any future consolidation bills. Local officials in Indiana are aware of the typical fate of referendums. Accordingly, subsequent local reform proposals have been much less comprehensive."

Unless the United States' reliance on the referendum can be reduced, past experience suggests that few structural reorganizations will succeed. Moreover, most of them will be limited to small or middle-sized urban areas or to single-county situations where there are relatively few other governmental units to act as a focus for opposition.

In contrast to the United States' experience, a major component of the European reform efforts' success is a "general public commitment to the *representative* government concept" (emphasis added). This rests on the belief that legislative bodies made up of elected representatives should make judgments on complex policy matters

20. See Joseph F. Zimmerman, *Measuring Local Discretionary Authority* (Washington, DC: Advisory Commission on Intergovernmental Relations, 1981), pp. 31, 77.

21. In a letter dated November 19, 1982, Henry Schmandt emphasized this last point: "State legislatures have historically demonstrated an unwillingness to intervene in metropolitan reorganization matters, in the absence of some consensus among local politicos, and seldom has such consensus existed. I also wonder whether special interests would be less effective in influencing legislative bodies in reorganization issues than they are in influencing popular referenda. These doubts lead me to be somewhat more tentative with respect to the greater likelihood of metropolitan reorganization success in the United States under the representative as against the referendum approach."

but without a referendum. Public participation is often sought through public hearings. Furthermore, the deliberations of special investigative bodies are often accompanied by widespread public discussion and debate. In this way the leadership can try out proposals, reviewing and evaluating the response from interested sectors of the public, as well as from key officials whose interests might be affected. Policymakers thus retain their leadership while getting feedback from the public.

Reasoning from such grounds, Scott and Nathan concluded: "Holding referenda . . . is not central to representative democracy, and indeed has not worked well. A referendum vote does not reflect the depth of information, perception, or issue awareness that may be essential to an appropriate decision on a policy issue. These added qualitative values, however, need not be lost when voting operates in its primary function: *electing legislators* to a representative government" (emphasis added).[22] But the United States has a widespread distrust of political parties and of interest groups that operate through legislatures to make or influence public policy. As David Butler and Austin Ranney observed:

> The Progressives . . . believed that truly democratic government consists of all the John and Jane Q. Publics observing, discussing, pondering, deciding, and, finally voting . . . any organization that seeks to interpose itself between the people and their government—that is, any intermediate organization—is bound to subvert democracy *and* the public interest to some degree. . . . Even popularly elected legislatures and municipal councils are bad because they are so easily purchased by special interests and dominated by party bosses.[23]

On the other hand, there are various ways of organizing democratic processes. The best procedure is not necessarily to insist on elections where voters are expected to decide large numbers of ballot propositions. Regardless of how well or poorly the referendum may have fulfilled its Progressive proponents' fond hopes in the early days, many subsequent changes affect its performance today. Among the many developments the Progressives could hardly have foreseen is the great and growing influence of special interests with demonstrated abilities to collect large sums of money for direct mailings and to buy time from the pervasive electronic media. This gives such well-financed groups direct access to voters, facilitating the use of public

22. Stanley Scott and Harriet Nathan, "Public Referenda: A Critical Reappraisal," *Urban Affairs Quarterly* 5(3):314–328 (March 1970).

23. David Butler and Austin Ranney, "Theory," in *Referendums: A Comparative Study of Practice and Theory*, ed. David Butler and Austin Ranney (Washington, DC: American Enterprise Institute, 1978), pp. 28–29.

relations methods to plead causes and frequently cloud issues as well as deliberately misinform. The influence on US elections of the media and of highly committed, if not fanatical, single-interest groups now justifies serious concern for its effects on the electoral process. While money spent in such campaigns does not necessarily always determine election results, it nevertheless has great influence.[24]

Over twenty years ago Frank Smallwood argued eloquently that Anglo-Canadian policymaking is in important respects more democratic than our own: "By subordinating the prerogatives of widespread public participation to those of forceful political leadership, the English and Canadians have added a number of democratic elements to their decisionmaking process that are usually conspicuously missing from our own."[25] While acknowledging that direct public participation in policymaking is far more restricted in England and Canada than in the United States, Smallwood points to several "democratic elements" that we lack. First, he maintains that the Anglo-Canadian processes reduce the stalemate that clogs the processes here where our system has "a built-in bias sharply favoring those interests which support the status quo." He points out that stalemate or the inability to take any action "does not mean that no party has won the contest but, rather, that those who did not want such action in the first place are the victors." Because it minimizes this bias, Smallwood considers the Anglo-Canadian system more responsive to the democratic ideal than our own.[26]

Second, Smallwood believes that our system—especially the referendum—risks "overloading the decisionmaking process to accommodate the feelings of basically disinterested and often unknowledgeable individuals, while assigning less weight to the views of those who are intensely interested." Again, he prefers the Anglo-Canadian

24. Edwin M. Epstein, "PACs and the Modern Political Process," paper delivered at the Conference on the Impact of the Modern Corporation, November 12–13, 1982, Columbia University School of Law; Epstein is a professor at the School of Business, University of California, Berkeley.

25. Frank Smallwood, "Guiding Urban Change," *National Civic Review* 54(4): 191–197 (April 1965), p. 197.

26. Ibid., p. 195. A carefully reasoned article by L. J. Sharpe strongly supports Smallwood's conclusion. Moreover, Sharpe points to difficulty in changing the status quo as a deficiency in American government:

> Two kinds of responsiveness must be distinguished. The first is responsiveness to those who wish government to maintain the *status quo*. The second is responsiveness to those who wish government to change the *status quo*. The deficiency of the American tradition is its strong tendency to equate the responsiveness of government solely with the first kind of responsiveness, with the result that government may be incapable of being responsive in the second sense. Yet it is the second kind of responsiveness that is more vital to democracy. (Sharpe, "American Democracy Reconsidered," *British Journal of Political Science* 3:129– 167 [1973], p. 140)

approach, which gives a hearing to interested individuals and groups but reserves the final decision on matters of local institutional change to referees or "brokers" drawn from the Canadian provincial or British central government.[27]

Third, Smallwood argues that many policymakers in the United States have used the referendum as a loophole, a way "to avoid or dodge responsible commitment on issues of vital public concern." He writes: "Other leaders have tended to fuzz referenda issues so completely through the use of emotional symbols that the issues have become meaningless . . . in actual practice the referendum has often confused alternatives and allowed officials to escape the commitments of responsible leadership accepted by the English and Canadians."[28] Smallwood also notes that public interest and voter participation in local referendum issues have often been very low, and he questions the role of the referendum in "dealing with complex issues of institutional reform in highly developed urban societies." He concludes that "the referendum procedure is so highly unstructured, diffuse and susceptible to distortion, it is very questionable whether we have actually been able to exercise as meaningful a degree of democratic control over local policy-making as the English and Canadians."[29]

27. Smallwood, "Guiding Urban Change," p. 195. Harold Kaplan also emphasizes Canadian

> deference to authority and leadership . . . [which] appears to stem from a more general Canadian political culture, which in turn is an adaptation to North American experiences of the British political culture. . . . These aspects of culture may produce in Canada, as they do in Great Britain, a willingness to let public policy matters be determined by the officials' greater understanding of the issues and to rely on the officials' self-restraint for the protection of one's rights. (Kaplan, *Urban Political Systems: A Functional Analysis of Metro Toronto* [New York: Columbia University Press, 1967], pp. 209–210)

However, see also Sharpe's questioning of the allegation that Americans are less deferential and therefore more egalitarian than the British, in "American Democracy Reconsidered," pp. 9–17.

For another example of metropolitan governance under a political culture different from the American, see Thomas J. Anton, *Governing Greater Stockholm* (Berkeley: University of California Press, 1975), pp. 15–36, 185–188. Anton emphasized that the Swedish system is "one of elite interaction. While the number of elite participants for any given decision is likely to be large, neither participants nor common citizens expect any interference from outside citizen groups" (p. 30).

28. Smallwood, "Guiding Urban Change," p. 196.

29. Ibid., p. 197. The themes featured in Smallwood's critique can also be found in more recent writings on the referendum, e.g., Butler and Ranney, eds., *Referendums*; Austin Ranney, ed., *The Referendum Device* (Washington, DC: American Enterprise Institute, 1981); and David B. Magleby, *Direct Legislation: Voting on Ballot Propositions in the United States* (Baltimore: Johns Hopkins University Press, 1984).

Effect on Reform Processes

The story of Unigov's creation, as told by Owen and Willbern, highlights other contrasts between reform processes using referendum votes and those not using them. For example, the referendum not only greatly reduces the chances of success but also intimidates the sponsors of reform and influences the character of the proposals they put forth, which are more modest than they might otherwise have been. In fact, inclusion of a referendum alters the very process of reform in highly significant ways, shifting the arenas and sequence of debate, as well as foreclosing prematurely (in our view) the possibility of negotiations and of mutually acceptable compromises whereby policymakers can exercise effective political leadership in practising "the art of the possible." Instead, as soon as the text of the ballot proposition has been determined, the referendum requirement largely sets the character of the discussion, "freezing" the debate into a litany of arguments for or against the single, fixed reform proposal, which has passed beyond the point of flexibility and compromise. Finally, it is natural that opponents of reorganization use the referendum as a deliberate strategy to defeat reform.

The referendum-influenced process clearly contrasts with Unigov's process, which featured virtuoso performances by Mayor Lugar and other city, county, and legislative leaders, who negotiated and compromised in working toward ultimate legislative approval. At various stages, the sponsors were willing to accept many changes, including some that significantly reduced the executive power they had hoped to assemble under the mayor's umbrella. Yet they still were able to go "down to the wire," negotiating their way to a reorganization plan that was acceptable to the county's legislative delegation and to the statewide legislative leadership. The result was successful implementation of a new governmental structure that has since accomplished a good deal of what the sponsors had hoped for and that the citizenry has apparently found satisfactory.

The process would necessarily be substantially different under a referendum since the electorate would be the final judge of the outcome. Anticipating the referendum, the proponents (and the legislature) presumably would further modify the proposal in ways considered likely to improve its acceptability to the electorate. The end result would probably be an appreciably different reorganization from the one that could be put in effect by legislative act alone.

Moreover, as noted above, after a reorganization proposal is finally agreed on and accepted for a referendum, there is then no longer any opportunity for change despite the continuation of the debate. Weeks or even months before the campaign, the negotiators would have been forced to try "psyching out" the probable response of an electorate that might at the time be largely uninformed and indifferent. The greatest effort would be devoted to the campaign, trying to reach and convince voters who have little or no knowledge about the proposal, who do not have the skills and sophistication to judge it, and who are predisposed to react negatively to change. During the campaign many of the issues might be debated vigorously, but this could no longer influence the proposal's content. Instead, the electorate could only respond by accepting or rejecting a "frozen" and perhaps already superseded reorganization scheme. By contrast, Owen and Willbern demonstrate how the Indiana legislature debated and modified the Unigov bill until its final passage.

We can never be sure what would have happened if the referendum requirement had applied to the 1971 reform of Indianapolis and Marion County. The local Jaycees did conduct a telephone survey in trying to determine support and opposition. They found four-fifths of the respondents to be unfamiliar with the Unigov proposal and eliminated them from their survey. The remaining one-fifth, a small minority of presumably well-informed voters, indicated strong support. In an actual referendum, of course, a good proportion of the eliminated respondents would in fact have voted, with a high probability that many would be ignorant of the details even after a referendum campaign.

Potential voters confronted by strange issues are likely to vote against them and are susceptible to well-publicized opposition regardless of its merits. In short, if a referendum had been held on Unigov, a substantial portion of the 80 percent who were unfamiliar would probably have voted against Unigov. The remainder who were polled—the knowledgeable one-fifth—were 69 percent for it. But in an actual referendum, their strong favorable showing would very likely have been overwhelmed by the four-fifths who were not aware.[30] In short, we can speculate that Unigov would have had very tough sledding under a referendum and probably would have failed.

Leadership in a Pluralistic Structure

Calling Unigov "a city-county consolidation" implies a much more unitary structure than Unigov actually is. In fact, few such consolidation proposals call for monolithic structures. In Indianapolis, preexisting suburban municipalities were not consolidated, and

---

30. In California, at least, the prevailing pattern is for voters to make up their minds on ballot proposals at the last minute. Thus, Eugene C. Lee reports that "nine out of ten voters who cast a ballot on initiative measures often make up their minds how to vote on the eve of the election, particularly in the case of complex, technical issues"; see Lee, "California," in *Referendums*, ed. Butler and Ranney, p. 110.

neither were the schools. Under Unigov, individual services continue to be provided in different areas with wide variations in geography and continue to be financed by special taxes applying only to the areas served. Some important functions are still in the hands of special purpose boards, and most traditional elective offices have been retained. Owen and Willbern acknowledge that "the name Unigov may be an almost absurdly inexact description of the new *legal* entity."

But the authors also emphasize that the term, with all its unitary connotations, "is a meaningful and useful characterization of *political* realities." They note: "Political leadership and responsibility are now clearly and unquestionably held by the elected mayor, and the City-County Council is, at least potentially, a deliberating, appropriating, and policy-determining body of preeminent significance."

The prestige and influence of the mayor and the city-county government have been enhanced. Unigov mayors Richard G. Lugar and William H. Hudnut have both led the list of the community's most powerful and influential people, whereas in pre-Unigov times the topmost community power positions were occupied by private sector leaders to the exclusion of city or county officials. In short, while the Unigov reform is pluralistic, not monolithic, it nevertheless seems to have done what the sponsors wanted, that is, provide the countywide region with greater coherence in policy formulation. This appears to have been their main goal rather than a simple unitary integration of all local governments.

In light of the Indianapolis experience, readers may find it curious that some critics—especially those identified with the public-choice school—seem to argue that metropolitan reforms typically propose unitary consolidation of entire metropolitan areas under single units of local government.[31] Their evaluation rests on two unjustified assumptions: (1) that monolithic consolidations are usually involved, and (2) that the principal purpose of metropolitan reform is improved provision of local services. In fact, however, few if any reorganizations are unitary, and most reforms do not principally seek better or cheaper local services.

Obviously, neither of these assumptions is justified in Unigov's case. First, it was not unitary. Second, instead of worrying about individual services, the Unigov reformers wanted to strengthen the mayor's role and create a policymaking structure for the county that could move ahead with major programs. While some old inefficiencies were reduced after the reorganization, this was a welcome side benefit, not the principal objective of the reform.

31. Robert L. Bish and Vincent Ostrom, *Understanding Urban Government: Metropolitan Reform Reconsidered* (Washington, DC: American Enterprise Institute, 1973), pp. 48–49. See also Elinor Ostrom, "Metropolitan Reform: Propositions Derived from Two Traditions," *Social Science Quarterly* 53:474–493 (December 1972).

Getting Things Done Under Unigov:
The Federal Connection

Although the *structural* change that Unigov represented was undoubtedly crucial to the creation of an effective power center that
could get things moving, the influence of federal programs and money
was also essential. Four months after the inauguration of Unigov, at
Mayor Lugar's request, a federal technical assistance team from the US
Office of Management and Budget and the Department of Housing and
Urban Development reviewed the budgetary and planning activities of
the new government and recommended many changes in organization
and procedures.[32] Owen and Willbern note how "the formation of
Unigov and the vigorous search for federal funds complemented and
reinforced each other," pointing out that "the federal funds and the
accompanying conditions—especially the requirement of review and
comment—further enhanced the mayor's position."

Not only was the mayor's position strengthened, but also the
very nature of the programs undertaken was powerfully influenced by
federal policies and money. In fact, without Mayor Lugar's ingenious
use of the federal aid programs, Unigov would have been known primarily for its "hardware" projects, that is, the building of highways
and downtown structures principally benefiting the business community. Instead, by emphasizing community services, the Comprehensive Employment and Training Act (CETA), and community development and by focusing on social services rather than only on physical
development, Unigov helped counterbalance such local influences as
the property-tax freeze, the tax earmarking and other inflexibilities
retained under Unigov, and the reluctance of the suburbs to support
the central city. Otherwise, the concerns expressed by some blacks
and Democrats about Unigov's potential disadvantages to them would
have been realized to a much greater extent.

Ironically, under Unigov a rather conservative Republican
mayor made extensive and extremely effective use of programs inherited from Roosevelt's New Deal, Kennedy's Fair Deal, and Johnson's
Great Society. Apparently, middle-of-the-road to conservative Repub-
licanism—as expressed at the city-county level—does not necessarily mean rejection of either metropolitan reform or federally funded
social programs. One wonders what will happen now that federal
efforts have been drastically reduced. Will the cutbacks weaken the
abilities of mayors and other urban leaders to influence events in
their communities?

32. US Office of Management and Budget, Federal Technical Assistance Team,
"Improving Program, Planning, Evaluation Budgetary Functions in the Consolidated
Government of Indianapolis," Washington, DC, May 1, 1970.

The Future

We seem unlikely to have other Indianapolis-type reorganizations adopted without referendum votes. Accepted convention would very likely force a referendum on the prevalent assumption that "it's the proper thing to do" when local boundaries are changed. Moreover, the Indianapolis experience has helped establish this component of political culture in Indiana and, perhaps, intensify it elsewhere.

In any event, the widely recognized difficulty of effecting local boundary change is a significant reason why other kinds of adaptation in metropolitan governance are being explored. Even these "nonstructural" alternatives, however, can run afoul of the referendum ethos. A California example is the succession of bills sponsored by Assemblyman John Knox in the early 1970s. These would have changed no local boundaries but would have created a limited multipurpose regional agency in the nine-county San Francisco Bay Area. Any of the Knox bills could have been enacted if the author had accepted the inclusion of a referendum requirement, which he refused to do.

Under the referendum, the future of city-county consolidation looks dim. Bollens and Schmandt realistically predict that "isolated instances of such consolidation will continue, particularly in the South and West," but they expect little more.[33] The process that created Unigov may prove virtually unique. Regardless of limitations on the future role of city-county consolidation, however, or of the particular character of the circumstances that contributed to Unigov's creation, the themes and major findings of Owen and Willbern add significantly to our understanding of the way different approaches to the legitimation of governmental changes affect the outcome of reform efforts. They also provide a valuable perspective for judging developments in metropolitan governance and for evaluating attempts to deal with metropolitan problems by structural or nonstructural means. We believe the authors have made a substantial contribution to the literature of metropolitan studies.

Stanley Scott
Editor, Lane Fund
Publications

Victor Jones
Coeditor, Lane Studies in
Regional Government

33. Bollens and Schmandt, *Metropolis*, p. 344.

1

Governmental Reform in Indianapolis

Major reorganizations to adapt governmental structure to changing social and economic circumstances have been considered seriously in most of the nation's 250 metropolitan areas, but in only a
handful has substantial and comprehensive structural change actually been achieved during this century. Indianapolis is the largest of
these and the only successful effort in the nation's northern portion,
including most of the country's old urban centers. Moreover, the
Indianapolis reorganization was accomplished quickly and with substantially less apparent controversy than elsewhere.

Essentially unknown in Indianapolis were the better-known elements of conventional municipal reform, for example, a home-rule
charter, merit systems, nonpartisanship, and a city manager. Indianapolis was considered a "traditionally" governed city, without a
strong reform heritage, and having no record of developing progressive governmental institutions. In *Inside USA* John Gunther characterized the city's appearance and proclivities: "Indianapolis is an un-
kempt city, unswept, raw, a terrific place for basketball and auto
racing, a former pivot of the Ku-Kluxers, and in it you may see the
second ugliest monument in the world."[1]

Indianapolis Unigov: A Subject of Study

In early 1969, a sweeping legislative act consolidated elements of
the city government of Indianapolis with those of Marion County, a
much larger geographical area that included Indianapolis, nearly two
dozen other municipalities, plus a large unincorporated suburban
population. With this action Indianapolis soared in the national ranking of cities, from twenty-sixth place in 1960 to ninth place in 1970,
and from 476,215 persons in 82 square miles to 793,590 people in an
area of more than 400 square miles.[2] While the new consolidated gov-

---

1. John Gunther, *Inside USA* (New York: Harper & Brothers, 1947), p. 387.
2. It dropped to eleventh place in 1981, with 704,045 people, when four small
communities, which were included for some purposes but not for others, were not
counted; see *World Almanac* (New York: Newspaper Enterprise Association, 1981),

ernment is far from being a completely integrated and unitary arrangement, it provides a single executive and a central policymaking council with dominant power over what had previously been many largely independent and autonomous governmental units and agencies.

With the passage of the Unigov Act, Indianapolis became the focus of a great deal of interest in the way the bill was passed and in its essential elements. A month after the law went into effect on January 1, 1970, with the formation of an interim government, Don Campbell, a reporter for the *Times* (Hartford), returned to Connecticut from a visit to Indianapolis and wrote: "It seems a little strange that a city like Hartford, with its reputation for progress in so many areas, could be so far behind in its approach to local government. You have to go to some corn pone town like Indianapolis to find innovation in government, and then you realize that Indianapolis is anything but corn pone, and that Hartford is anything but progressive."[3] A year later, after Richard Lugar, mayor of the former city, had been elected as first mayor of the consolidated City of Indianapolis, an article appeared with the same theme: "Some time ago an urban magazine story on innovation in Indianapolis asked the question, 'Why Indianapolis of all places?' The implication was clear: why should urbanologists and others concerned with the plight of cities turn to Indianapolis, allegedly surrounded by a cornstalk curtain and commonly believed to offer little beyond the 'Indianapolis 500'?"[4]

How *did* Indianapolis become a proving ground for local government innovation? Except for its conservative "corn pone" image, in 1968 Indianapolis resembled many large northeastern cities in the United States. Its population was still growing, although much more slowly than its suburban fringe areas. Its economy was stable, and new industries were being attracted, although most were locating outside the city limits. Its property-tax income was increasing, but not rapidly enough to keep pace with increasing demands.

What Indianapolis shared most with other large cities was its problems. Indianapolis had its share of crime, pollution, racial strife, central-city decay, suburban sprawl, and other urban maladies. Like most large old American cities, it had neither the financial wherewithal nor the governmental capacity to cope with these problems.

Annexation programs to extend the city's boundaries nearly always met interminable delays or were defeated in the courts. Al-

---

p. 110. The communities whose populations had been counted in the previous national ranking were Lawrence, 25,591; Speedway, 12,641; Beech Grove, 13,196; and Southport, 2,266.

3. " 'Unigov' in Indianapolis," *Times* (Hartford, Conn.), February 9, 1970.

4. US Department of Housing and Urban Development, "Unigov," *HUD Challenge* 2(5):4 (May 1971).

though there was some success in enlarging jurisdiction over certain programs through the creation of single-purpose special districts, this also often compounded matters by adding new layers of government to an already complex governmental system. Furthermore, having already extended its most-demanded services to areas beyond its boundaries, Indianapolis denied itself important bargaining leverage in annexation proceedings.

Circumstances and Scope of Reform

In any event, Indianapolis had its share of the problems that prompted many other areas to consider metropolitan reorganization. Attempts usually failed because the forces resisting change were too strong. In Indianapolis, special circumstances facilitated a successful reorganization effort. Moreover, the reorganization itself, while enhancing the political leadership and community cohesiveness, also preserved a substantial degree of organizational complexity and structural pluralism.

What did happen in Indianapolis? An orthodox, reasonable answer is that the area's people or leaders became so frustrated with divided and fragmented government that they decided to streamline and unify it, Unigov being the result. While there is much truth to this answer, there were also special circumstances that are crucial to understanding what happened.

Special Circumstances.   A combination of forces at a particular time led to the Indianapolis metropolitan reorganization. Some of these forces, but not all, are found in other cities. Moreover, they do not all "come together" in quite the same way. For example, although Indianapolis was the state's largest city by far, it did not have its own legal "charter," and its governmental structure was regularly modified by special state legislative acts applying only to Indianapolis. Over the years such special laws had already made a large number of adjustments in individual governmental functions and services. A basic thrust of the Unigov Act was to subject the existing institutional structures to a greater degree of central political control.

The strong entrenchment of partisan politics in Indiana government provided the discipline and cohesiveness that made Unigov's enactment possible, and the prospect of partisan advantage provided much of the motivation. The emergence of a political leadership with a sophisticated interest in governmental structure and with the will to use available political power to effect structural change was what got the law passed.

Scope of Reform.   While Unigov clearly represented a centralizing move, it was nevertheless probably even more complicated legally

The Indianapolis–Marion County combined government building was constructed by a countywide building authority in 1963. This was one of a number of ad hoc intergovernmental cooperative ventures that led to the more comprehensive Unigov reform of 1969.
From: Division of Planning and Zoning, Indianapolis–Marion County.

and structurally than the setup it replaced. For example, the city and county were continued as legal entities, along with the townships and all of the previously existing municipalities. Under Unigov the geographical areas of individual governmental functions and services vary widely, can be changed in a variety of ways, and are financed by earmarked taxes applying only to the particular areas involved. The school districts remain independent and unconsolidated. Some other functions are also still run by boards under complex formulas governing appointments and responsibilities. Most of the traditional elective offices have continued. Some regional units have responsibility for several counties. Finally, there was an abortive attempt to establish an underlying set of small community governments in much of the metropolitan area.

In short, Unigov's reformed, "consolidated" governmental system is still quite complex. On the other hand, Unigov *was* created and is an operating reality. Thus, to a substantial degree, a single reasonably coherent political community exists now and did not before. This kind of coherence characterizes few of the nation's other sprawling metropolitan areas.

A National Perspective

Unigov's passage in 1969 came at a pivotal time in the running debate throughout the country over the merits of city-county consolidation as a reform measure. For proponents of consolidation the decade of the 1960s was a time of considerable activity and promise but also a time of defeat and rejection. With marked successes at Nashville and Jacksonville and philosophical support from the Committee for Economic Development (CED) and the National Commission on Urban Problems, city-county consolidation received a great deal of attention in metropolitan areas throughout the United States, especially in the South. Despite this growing interest, however, there was mounting frustration as voters in 10 cities turned down consolidation proposals between 1959 and 1969. The fact that so many cities attempted consolidation had bolstered expectations among consolidationists, but anticipation outweighed accomplishment. Bollens and Schmandt summarized the feelings of many at the time with their comment: "In general the one-government approach to areawide problems has passed its heyday."[5]

In these circumstances the creation of Unigov aroused widespread interest both as a rare event (creation of a metropolitan government) and for the unique reform politics that lay behind its establishment. Furthermore, various aspects of the reorganization effort in Indianapo-

5. John C. Bollens and Henry J. Schmandt, *The Metropolis: Its People, Politics, and Economic Life*, 2nd ed. (New York: Harper & Row, 1970), p. 311.

lis were related to other themes in the national literature and debates about metropolitan governance, such as regional planning, neighborhood government, and polycentricity. Countywide planning and land-use control arrangements had been among the antecedents of Unigov, and although political forces limited Unigov itself to the central county of the metropolitan region, the Unigov administration had a major role in the creation of a multicounty regional planning agency. Some of the proponents of Unigov wanted to accompany it with a "minigov" arrangement so that regional and neighborhood governments could be simultaneously strengthened, a combination of centralization and decentralization. And while the reorganization clearly vested increased power in an enlarged political entity, remaining units in their variety and complexity comprised a political system that could certainly be characterized as "polycentric." While the Indianapolis reorganization may not have provided clear and simple answers in the debates about metropolitan government, it had many strands that were receiving national attention.

The Reform Process.   Unigov is one of the few city-county consolidations to become effective without a referendum, and it is perhaps unique in the dominant role the elected political leadership played in its inception and creation. These key features are central concerns in this study. Unigov was important for the innovation it brought to the consolidation debate, but, in addition, we are interested in the features it shares with reform efforts elsewhere. Despite acknowledged differences, the similarities may in fact make Unigov a more important case study than do its unique features.

Like other North American metropolitan consolidations, Unigov was a compromise solution that departed from the more comprehensive plan originally proposed by reform proponents. The Indianapolis decisionmaking process dealt with the same merger issues that were encountered elsewhere, and the resulting document incorporates structural and functional arrangements reflecting the political currents that determined the outcome. Although powerful political forces pressed successfully for a nonreferendum decision on Unigov—and a pattern of lawmaking that favored the nonreferendum alternative—the end result is no more "comprehensive" than consolidations achieved elsewhere under different circumstances.

Traditional antimerger arguments were raised during the Unigov debate: merger would mean higher taxes, citizens would be denied a voice in the bigger government, the black vote would be diluted, and existing community and neighborhood lifestyles would be disrupted. Certain government officials opposed Unigov because the mayor would be too powerful or the City-County Council unrepresentative. After the Unigov law's passage, opponents argued that it was less a

reform measure than a Republican Party takeover. Some called it unconstitutional while others maintained that it lacked voter support.

One of our purposes is to review the debate and suggest its impact on the Unigov Act. We are also interested in effects of the legal
environment on the reform process and on the resulting law. As
noted, Indiana's constitutional and statutory provisions were generally advantageous to passage of the reform bill, while at the same time
other legal provisions posed formidable barriers to a comprehensive
merger. Welfare and education services, for example, are state functions in Indiana, administered locally by independent governmental
agencies. The independent status of these functions was responsible
for their omission from the new government. Similarly, several
elected county officers and other governmental entities retained their
independent legal status. Unigov's principal proponents—especially
the attorneys who drafted the bill—knew that to tackle these independent entities would have involved a lengthy approval process, seriously jeopardizing the entire reform.

By skirting such legally sensitive matters, Indianapolis also
avoided the lengthy court battles that followed similar reforms in
Baton Rouge and Miami. While Unigov itself has not faced any substantial court challenges, Indianapolis officials were involved in a
10-year lawsuit in federal court, questioning the omission of the
schools from Unigov. This case will be considered below in detail.

Structure and Function.   Once they determined to seek a comprehensive metropolitan areawide form of government, the Unigov
principals could choose among three basic models. (1) A two-tier federated form of government can be based on a reallocation of powers
and functions between the city and county levels of government, essentially shifting some municipal authority from the city level to the
county. The Miami–Dade County plan is a good example. (2) A three-
tier government, for example, the one adopted in the Minneapolis–St.
Paul area, retains the existing city and county arrangement and creates
a regional multiservice district as the third tier. (3) City-county consolidation combines local units into one government. Indianapolis
chose city-county consolidation, as did Nashville, Tennessee, and
Jacksonville, Florida. In Indianapolis, no extensive consideration was
given to the federated two-tier or three-tier forms. The Twin Cities'
pattern was quickly dismissed as politically unattainable in Indiana
where antiregional government feelings run high. The two-tier form
(e.g., Miami–Dade County) would conflict with the Unigov planners'
goal of extending the mayor's administrative jurisdiction countywide.
Moreover, making a Republican mayor a countywide figure appealed
to some Unigov proponents who saw advantages in a countywide
electoral constituency. Nor was the existing county government seen

as adequate to the task of administering a comprehensive municipal government, such as the two-tier plan would call for.

Perhaps another important consideration was Nashville's proximity to Indianapolis. While Mayor Lugar knew about other mergers, he was most familiar with the Nashville–Davidson County experience. He had studied Nashville Metro and invited Nashville officials to Indianapolis as consultants during the early Unigov discussions. Accordingly, similarities between Nashville and Indianapolis are to be expected. For example, the idea of creating a special urban service district for certain service and taxing functions was based on the Nashville model. Both metropolitan governments were restructured at the county level, essentially merging the former city and county policymaking and administrative units. Both were strong mayor-council governments, giving the mayor substantial administrative powers.

Despite these similarities, Unigov has many structural and functional features that are not based on the Nashville model. (See tables 1 and 2 for similarities and differences between Unigov and five other metropolitan governments.) Just as Unigov is not an exact replica of Nashville Metro, it cannot be closely likened to any of the other metropolitan governments. Despite its uniqueness, however, Unigov does conform to the general definition of a city-county consolidation in the 1980 *Municipal Yearbook:* "The National Association of Counties . . . defines city-county consolidation as the unification of the governments of one or more cities with the surrounding county. Boundary lines of the jurisdictions become coterminous. Some incorporated jurisdictions may be excluded from the consolidation. Political considerations often dictate exempting smaller suburban governments from the initial consolidation."[6]

Indianapolis, Nashville, Jacksonville, and Lexington (Kentucky) all unified city and county governments into one basic unit. On the other hand, Miami and Toronto retained the existing units while shifting certain limited functions to the areawide government. Even their functional mergers, however, were less comprehensive than those of the four city-county consolidations. Toronto with three functional mergers and Miami with seven are less comprehensive than the consolidations that range from ten to thirteen in the number of functional agencies merged (see Table 2).

Political considerations dictated the exemption of several smaller suburban governments from Unigov, which was true elsewhere, with the notable exception of Lexington. Such considerations also caused some important functions to be excluded from Unigov.

6. Parris N. Glendening and Patricia S. Atkins, "City-County Consolidations: New Views for the Eighties," *The Municipal Yearbook 1980*, vol. 47 (Chicago: International City Managers Association, 1980), p. 68.

Table 1– Characteristics of Selected Metropolitan Governments

Merged City-County	Miami–Dade	Nashville–Davidson	Indianapolis–Marion	Jacksonville–Duval	Lexington–Fayette	Toronto–Ontario
YEAR OF MERGER	1957	1962	1969	1967	1972	1953, rev. 1967
City area prior to metro. govt.	32 sq. mi.	72.5 sq. mi.	82 sq. mi.	39 sq. mi.	23 sq. mi.	32.5 sq. mi.
Area of metro. govt.	2,042 sq. mi.	533.0 sq. mi.	402 sq. mi.	841 sq. mi.	280 sq. mi.	240.0 sq. mi.
City population before metro. govt.	291,688	255,000	476,215	198,200	108,137	678,600
County population before metro. govt.	703,777	410,000	793,590	507,200	174,323	1,170,000
No. of municipalities in county not incorporated in new govt.	26	6	4	4	none	6
No. of special districts (excluding school districts) within city and county before consolidation	3	city 1 county 5	city 16 county 0	city 1 county 3	city 1 county 3	NA

Table 1 *(cont.)*

Merged City-County	Miami–Dade	Nashville–Davidson	Indianapolis–Marion	Jacksonville–Duval	Lexington–Fayette	Toronto–Ontario
YEAR OF MERGER	1957	1962	1969	1967	1972	1953, rev. 1967
No. of special districts (excluding school districts) within consolidated govt.	3	4	11	0	3	NA
Executive form	county-manager	mayor-council	mayor-council	mayor-council	mayor-council	chair elected by council
Other elected administrators	yes	yes	yes	no	no	yes
Size of metro. legislative body	9	41	29	19	15	33
No. elected by district	0	35	25	14	12	NA
No. elected at large	9 council members	mayor + 5 council members	4	5	3	NA
No. of city and county depts. before metro. govt.	NA	40 city depts. 37 county depts.	20 city depts. 8 county depts.	23 city depts. 26 county depts.	4 city depts. 15 county depts.	NA
No. of depts. after metro. govt.	6	9	6	10	7	13

Source: Adapted from National Association of Counties, *Consolidation: Partial or Total,* transcript of the National Conference (Washington, DC, 1973). Appendix.

Table 2– Arrangement of Functions in Selected Metropolitan Reorganizations

	Education	Welfare	Water	Sewer	Highways	Police	Fire	Hospitals	Housing/Urban Renewal	Parks/ Recreation	Health	Planning	Library	Sanitation	Total Merged Functions
Miami	M	M	ML	ML	M	ML	L	M	M	M	M	ML	L	ML	7
Nashville	M	M	L	M	M	M	ML	M	M	M	M	M	M	M	12
Indianapolis	L	M	L	M	M	L	L	M	M	M	M	M	M	M	10
Jacksonville	M	M	ML	M	M	M	M	M	M	M	M	M	M	M	13
Lexington	M	M	M	M	M	M	M	L	M	M	M	M	M	M	13
Toronto	M	ML	ML	ML	ML	M	L	M	ML	ML	L	ML	L	ML	3

Note: M = Merged Metropolitan Areawide; L = Local; ML = Metropolitan and Local.

The refurbished Monument Circle at the center of the Indianapolis downtown area is symbolic of comprehensive central business district developments in the 1970s and a public refutation of John Gunther's derogatory description 38 years ago.

From: Division of Planning and Zoning, Indianapolis–Marion County.

Thus, Indianapolis differs from other metropolitan reorganizations in omitting schools (see Table 2). Other plans also merge part or all of police functions, whereas Indianapolis kept both the existing county sheriff and city police departments.

To sum up, Unigov extended municipal authority, but in a more modest way than Nashville's Metro, the Lexington–Fayette County plan, or the Jacksonville–Duval County merger. In functional realignments, Unigov is not much more comprehensive than the federated systems of Miami and Toronto. Schools and townships were not included, nor were the courts. There was no new grant of home-rule authority. The major distinction between Unigov's consolidation and the two-tier arrangement was the merger of city and county policy making and administration into a unified government. As our discussion will show, successes enjoyed under Unigov depended heavily on the centralization of authority in the new mayor's office.

Recognizing the political and legal limits, Indianapolis's reform proponents sought only the changes they considered essential to provide a basic mechanism that would "get things done." They did not view the 1969 bill as a finished product, reasoning that other reforms would follow in time, eventually bringing about the more comprehensive government they envisioned.

As to getting things done, the reader will see from our account that many of Indianapolis's substantial accomplishments during the 1970s are attributed to Unigov. One of these—a $2 million revitalization of Monument Circle—tells a great deal about the motivation and hopes that lay behind the Unigov Act's passage and the subsequent pride and sense of accomplishment it has brought to the city. Prior to Unigov, the Indianapolis leadership seemed weighed down by the city's "Indian-No-Place" image, and little had been done to create a new image. The Unigov proponents clearly saw the reform proposal as a break with the past and as a catalyst for the city's development. They recognized the need for dynamic changes and were convinced that an improved government structure was essential.

What they probably did not anticipate was the revived community spirit that the reform produced. Community leaders now approach new undertakings with a confidence that was lacking before Unigov. They acknowledge Indianapolis as a city of accomplishment. They view the refurbished monument with special pride as a symbolic capstone of their efforts and as an effective refutation of John Gunther's 38-year-old taunt.

2

Characteristics of Metropolitan Indianapolis

Indiana's capital and largest city is situated in a fertile farm belt near the state's geographic center. Founded as the future site for a new capital, on land secured by an Indian treaty, Indianapolis was first settled in 1821. The capital was moved from Corydon to Indianapolis in 1824, some 23 years before the latter became an incorporated city.[1] The fact that it was the state capital before it was even legally a city may suggest the state government's historically major role in the development of Indianapolis.

Growth of the City

During the new capital's formative years growth was not dynamic. The first substantial population increases came with the opening of the National Road—now US Highway 40—in the early 1830s when the first large German and Irish settlements were established there. Blacks from the South first appeared in appreciable numbers at about the same time, settling in an area around Indiana Avenue—the northwest diagonal of the city's baroque street plan.

The growth of Indianapolis as a business and industrial community is unusual because it is one of the few metropolitan areas not located on navigable water. Nevertheless, transportation made Indianapolis prosper and gave it the nickname "Crossroads of America." The National Road and the Michigan Road (now US Highway 31) were completed through Indianapolis by 1835, and by 1855 eight railroads crisscrossed downtown. Since the early establishment of these trade routes, for over a century Indianapolis has served as a major regional and interregional market and distribution center.

Indianapolis was recognized as a major city during the Civil War when it was an important manufacturing center and troop-marshaling site for the Union. During the Civil War decade its population in-

---

1. Edward A. Leary, *Indianapolis: Story of a City* (Indianapolis: Bobbs-Merrill, 1979), p. 61.

creased from 18,611 to 48,244, while manufacturing investment increased more than 10 times, from $647,650 at the beginning of the decade to $8,420,614 in 1870.[2] Principal items of production were farm machinery, cotton and woolen goods, pork packing, foundries, and spokes and wheels, especially iron wheels for railroad cars.

Except for a slight decline in its growth rate during a recession in the 1870s, Indianapolis continued its rapid population rise for the remainder of the century. By 1890 it passed the 100,000 mark, reaching 169,164 inhabitants in 1900. The arrival of more Germans and Irish from eastern states and Europe, and blacks and restless young people from the nation's rural areas, especially the South, reaffirmed the demographic trend started in the 1830s, the results of which characterize present-day Indianapolis.

An Emerging Metropolis

The city's population continued its very rapid growth—far more than that of the surrounding area—until 1920. After 1920, growth of the city proper diminished while the suburban area grew much faster. The pattern of suburban growth was firmly established in the 1920s when the three suburban communities destined to be the largest began to gain prominence. Beech Grove, a small community of 568 persons in 1910, counted 3,552 residents in 1930; Speedway and Lawrence, not even included in earlier census reports, showed 1920 populations of 1,420 and 840, respectively. The 1930 census also marked the first listing of eight smaller towns, for example, Crows Nest (population 79), Rocky Ripple (population 133), and Shooters Hill (population 11).

Convenient city-suburban transportation was provided by the electric-powered interurban railroads that flourished throughout Indiana from 1900 to 1940. Indianapolis was the center of a regional transportation network, and by 1910 over 400 interurban "electrics"— one- or two-unit intercity streetcars—delivered passengers and freight in and out of Indianapolis each day.

The automobile also began to play a prominent role in the city's development at this time, both as a means of transportation and as a major local industry. More than 60 different makes of cars and trucks were manufactured in Indianapolis. Three of the most popular—the Duesenberg, the Marmon, and the Stutz (especially the Bearcat)—were produced there until the 1930s; the Duesenberg was the last to go out of production, in 1937. Indianapolis's affection for the automobile gained lasting recognition with the opening of the Indianapolis Motor Speedway in 1910. The "500 Mile Race," first held in 1911, subsequently became an annual Memorial Day weekend event, with a month-long festival attracting drivers and fans from throughout the world.

2. Ibid., p. 117.

Although automobile manufacturing was relatively short-lived in Indianapolis, it had a lasting impact on the local economy. Several personal fortunes from the automobile boom were a major source of investment in the city, and the descendants of those who operated the city's pioneer auto industry are some of Indianapolis's major employers today.

Economic growth in Indianapolis has been stable and diversified. While its balanced economy has not given Indianapolis the spectacular growth that the aircraft industry and tourism have given other cities of comparable size, its growth has been steady. A study published the year Unigov was passed showed a balanced diversification in its labor force, with 38 percent of its workers employed in manufacturing and construction, 34 percent in wholesale-retail trade and services, and 28 percent in government and finance, insurance, and real estate. When compared with 14 other metropolitan areas, only one showed a more even weighting of the three basic sectors. Indianapolis is somewhat more prosperous than the rest of Indiana—or the nation—with higher per capita income and lower rates of unemployment than state or national figures.[3] Among the 50 largest cities in the United States, the 1970 census ranked Indianapolis fourth in median family income.

During the following 10 years, Indianapolis followed the national trend with fewer employees involved in manufacturing (23 percent) and significantly increased employment in trade and services (43 percent). Although employment in government and finance increased in magnitude from 99,100 in 1970 to 126,000 in 1980, the proportion dropped to 24 percent. Approximately 10 percent of the work force was unemployed in 1980, matching the national figures for the period but lower than the state's average of 12.5 percent. Personal family income in Indianapolis remains one of the highest for large cities in the United States.

Major industries include electronics, metal fabrication, chemicals, and transportation parts and equipment. All three major US automobile producers have plants in Indianapolis; the Allison Division of General Motors is the city's largest single employer, with 14,000 workers. Eli Lilly and Company, the firm most widely associated with Indianapolis, employs 7,000 workers in the pharmaceutical industry.

In the post-World War II period, the Indianapolis area's most rapid advances in employment have been in nonmanufacturing, particularly insurance and government. The insurance industry is one of Indianapolis's largest employers; over 70 insurance companies maintain home offices there. As the state's political center, Indianapolis

---

3. Hammer, Green, Siler Associates, *Public Policy Issues in the Economic Development of the Indianapolis–Marion County Area* (Washington, DC, 1969), pp. 1–19.

has naturally experienced increases in government employment. Government employees comprised 9.2 percent of the total labor force in 1950, increasing to 14.6 percent in 1970. The number of government employees rose from 30,200 in 1950 to 48,200 in 1960 and to 66,500 in 1970. In 1981 government employees numbered 87,600—16 percent of the established work force.

Indianapolis continues as the state's major retail center, although most retail growth has been in the suburban area. The largest shopping malls and centers are located near the outer belt of the interstate highway system. Moreover, some regional shopping facilities are now being located outside the boundaries of Marion County.

Recent Population Changes

Indianapolis had 90 percent of the county's population in 1920, dropping to 77 percent in 1950 and to 68 percent by 1960. By 1970 the city had only a little over 60 percent of the county population. The 1950–1960 growth rate showed an Indianapolis city increase of 49,085 (11.5 percent) and an increase outside the city of 96,705 (77.6 percent), giving a total county increase of 145,709 (26.4 percent). The city's population rise in this decade was, however, due almost entirely to the annexation of 47,449 people, actual population growth in the city's 1950 area per se being only 1,636.

The 1960 census put the population of Indianapolis at 476,258 and the combined population of Indianapolis and Marion County at 697,567 (see Table 3). Although Indianapolis had been defined as a single-county standard metropolitan statistical area (SMSA) at the beginning of the 1960s, the increased population of the surrounding counties and their relationships to Marion County prompted the Bureau of the Budget to redefine the SMSA, making Marion County the central county and Indianapolis the central city of an eight-county SMSA.[4]

The 1970 census, the first to enumerate the expanded Unigov population, shows a consolidated city figure of 745,739, up 260,659 from 1960. The area of pre-Unigov Indianapolis, however, saw only a slight population increase, up 8,882 (1.8 percent) from 1960. During the 1970s the county's population decreased from 793,769 to 765,233 (−3.6 percent). Between 1970 and 1980 the county dropped 28,357 in population. The decline occurred in Center Township—located, as its name indicates, squarely in the center of the city and county—which lost 65,010 people in 1970–1980. In contrast, the remainder of the county gained over 36,000 people, and the surrounding counties gained even more.[5]

4. US Executive Office of the President, Bureau of the Budget, *Standard Metropolitan Statistical Areas* (Washington, DC, 1967), p. 47.

5. US Department of Commerce, Bureau of the Census, *1980 Census Population and Housing: Advanced Report*, Series Phc 80-V-16, Ind. (Washington, DC, 1975).

Table 3– Comparison of Total Population by Township/Marion County: 1960, 1970, 1980

Township	1960 Population		1970 Population		1980 Population		Change 1960–1970		Change 1970–1980	
	NO.	(% DIS.)	NO.	(% DIS.)	NO.	(% DIS.)	NO.	(%)	NO.	(%)
Center	333,351	(47.8)	273,598	(34.5)	208,624	(27.2)	−59,753	(−17.9)	−64,974	(−23.7)
Decatur	11,310	(1.6)	15,187	(1.9)	19,426	(2.5)	+3,877	(+34.3)	+4,234	(+27.9)
Franklin	7,357	(1.1)	10,293	(1.3)	16,477	(2.2)	+2,936	(+39.9)	+6,184	(+60.0)
Lawrence	34,405	(4.9)	66,296	(8.4)	75,860	(10.0)	+31,891	(+92.7)	+9,564	(+14.4)
Perry	46,555	(6.7)	73,650	(9.3)	78,485	(10.2)	+27,095	(+58.2)	+4,835	(+6.5)
Pike	6,662	(1.0)	14,962	(1.9)	25,336	(3.3)	+8,300	(+124.6)	+10,374	(+69.3)
Warren	60,344	(8.6)	87,128[a]	(10.8)	89,208	(11.7)	+26,784	(+44.3)	+2,080	(+2.3)
Washington	97,861	(14.0)	126,136	(15.9)	129,008	(16.9)	+28,275	(+28.9)	+2,872	(+2.2)
Wayne	99,722	(14.3)	126,340	(16.0)	122,809	(16.0)	+26,618	(+26.7)	−3,531	(−2.7)
All	697,567	(100.0)	793,590	(100.0)	765,233	(100.0)	+96,023	(+13.6)	−28,362	(−3.6)

Source: Adapted from *Data Development 100: Demographic and Economic Analysis of the Unified Planning Program, 1970–1972* (Indianapolis: Indianapolis–Marion County, Division of Planning and Zoning, 1972), pp. 19, 20. Population figures for 1980 from US Department of Commerce, Bureau of the Census, *World Almanac* 1981 (Washington, DC: Government Printing Office, 1981).

[a]Adjusted population total.

Indianapolis is the largest of Indiana's 11 SMSAs (see Map 1), with a population of 1,156,200, ranking thirty-third among US SMSAs in 1980, a drop from twenty-ninth place in 1970.[6] The decline in national ranking is the combined result of the spectacular growth of four sunbelt cities and a declining rate of growth within the Indianapolis SMSA. The eight-county Indianapolis area experienced a net migration loss of 15,000 persons from 1970 to 1975. This, subtracted from the excess of births over deaths, gave a total population increase of 36,100 persons in those five years because gains of nearly 48,000 in the outlying counties outweighed Marion County's loss of nearly 12,000.

Despite its recent slight drop in national standing, the Indianapolis SMSA remains Indiana's fastest growing area; in the 1970s 30 percent of the state's total growth occurred there. Hamilton, Hancock, Hendricks, and Johnson, four of the state's fastest growing counties, are in the Indianapolis SMSA. Each grew more than 25 percent during this period, compared with a statewide growth of 5.9 percent (see Map 1). Of the outlying counties, only Shelby, with a growth rate of 5.5 percent, was below the state figure. Marion County (−3.6 percent), as noted above, lost population in the 1970s.

The trend toward increased suburban growth and a declining central-city population became even more pronounced in the 1970s. Marion County was the only county in the SMSA to lose population between 1970 and 1980. Growth is most intense in and around the Hamilton County community of Carmel, located directly north of Indianapolis on US Highway 31, just three miles above the outer belt of the interstate highway system. Carmel nearly tripled its 6,691 population in 1970 to 18,272 in 1980.[7]

Changing Patterns of Wealth and Growth

Along with its population growth, Hamilton County has also experienced the SMSA's most rapid rise in per capita income, with a 1969-to-1974 increase of 50.7 percent. Marion County showed the smallest proportionate increase (41.2 percent). Johnson County, second to Hamilton County in population growth rate, is also second in per capita income growth, with a 48.2 percent increase.[8] Slightly more than half of the workers in the seven outlying counties earn their living in Marion County so that much of the increased income in the suburban counties is actually earned in Marion County. Commuter

6. US Department of Commerce, Bureau of the Census, *World Almanac 1981* (Washington, DC, 1981), p. 113.

7. US Department of Commerce, Bureau of the Census, *Current Population Reports: Population Estimates and Projections*, Series P-25, 16 Ind. (Washington, DC, 1975), p. 16; and *1980 Census of Population and Housing*, pp. 4–20.

8. *Current Population Reports*, pp. 16, 19, 22.

Map 1.

Percent Change in Population in Indianapolis, Eight-County Standard Metropolitan Statistical Area, 1970–1980

Source: Based on 1980 census data. Prepared by Department of Metropolitan Development, Indianapolis.

traffic to the suburbs outside Marion County is still minimal; thus, of the 290,250 workers who reside in the county, 283,994 work there.[9]

Center Township is contained almost entirely within the pre-Unigov boundaries of the City of Indianapolis (see Map 2); it covers the entire central business district, plus the immediately adjacent area of old residential housing and some commercial and manufacturing buildings, many of them abandoned. It is the county's only township to show a net population loss in recent years, a trend that continues.

Nearly 79 percent of Marion County's 134,486 blacks resided in Center Township in 1970. Housing values in Center Township are consistently lower than those elsewhere in the county, and the unemployment rate is generally higher. The 1975 per capita income of $3,581 was the lowest in the county and the SMSA.

By contrast, Washington Township, immediately north of Center Township, had the highest per capita income of the county and the SMSA, with $7,027, nearly twice Center Township's. Hamilton County's Clay Township is a distant second, with $6,091 per capita income. Unemployment in Washington Township was less than 2 percent, whereas Center Township's was more than 4 percent. Needless to say, neither Center Township nor Washington Township is the norm for Marion County, the median being in between.

Because of its declining population and deteriorating residential and commercial areas, Center Township has been the focus of a considerable amount of development and rehabilitation activity under the Unigov administration in the 1970s (see Chapter 8).

Population Characteristics

While noticeable, ethnic groupings among the white population of Indianapolis are probably much less significant than in most cities of the East and Midwest. Less than 2 percent of the population is foreign-born. Of the 42,757 persons of foreign stock (persons foreign-born plus first-generation Americans with one or more foreign-born parent) in 1970, Germans represented the largest national group with a population of 9,271, followed by persons from the United Kingdom (4,802), Canada (3,355), and Ireland (2,752). Persons with Spanish surnames numbered 6,211. Many of the people who came to Indianapolis in both the nineteenth and early twentieth centuries came from south of the Ohio River. As one writer put it: "Indianapolis was a northern town, but it was southern in its style and the inflection of its voice."[10]

9. The source of this material is the Indiana Information Retrieval System (INDIRS), a computerized data bank sponsored by Indiana University and the Indiana State Library.

10. Leary, *Indianapolis*, p. 39.

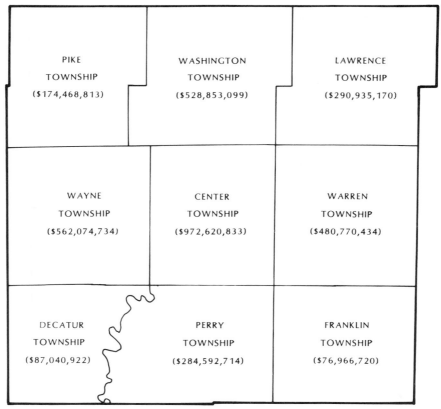

Map 2.

Marion County Townships with Assessed Valuations
    Source: City of Indianapolis, *Annual Report*, December 31, 1980.

Emigration from the city to the suburbs by many persons who usually voted Republican, coupled with an immigration to the city of a growing labor force, many from Democratic areas of the South, has made Indianapolis (like many other eastern and midwestern areas) a normally Democratic city ringed by a Republican county. During the 40 years prior to the 1968 election, the Republicans captured the mayor's office only twice, for a total of eight years.

Whichever party has been in control, Indianapolis, the national home of the American Legion and founding place of the John Birch Society, traditionally has been a conservative city.[11] When many other cities were clamoring for more federal aid, Indianapolis often chose to go ahead without outside assistance. Perhaps Paul Friggens said it

11. John Fenton, *Midwest Politics* (New York: Holt, Rinehart & Winston, 1966), pp. 177–178.

best: "Indianapolis is a solid conservative community of half a million people in a historically conservative state."[12]

Blacks in Indianapolis

Historically, the status of blacks in the Indianapolis community has taken a dual course. While certain legal and political rights were attained early, holding promise of greater freedoms, a begrudging social acceptance by the majority white community usually relegated blacks to second-class citizenship, at best, forcing them to rely almost wholly on the resources of their own communities for personal advancement.

Early Arrivals.   There is some debate as to who was the city's first permanent black resident, but blacks clearly have been a part of the city from the outset. One of the earliest to arrive was Chiney Lively, who came as a housekeeper to Alexander Ralston, the surveyor who laid out the city's original mile-square plan in 1820.[13] Although records indicate that several blacks assisted in clearing the wilderness for the new capital, the first count was not taken until 1827. A Sunday school census in that year showed 529 white and 34 "colored" males and 479 white and 24 "colored" females, for a total 1827 population of 1,069 inhabitants,[14] suggesting a black population of between 5 and 6 percent of the total.

A Growing Population.   Black population growth generally kept pace with white population increases, that is, approximately 5 percent of the total, until the decade before the Civil War. From 1850 to 1860 the black population increased from only 405 to 498, bringing the black share of the overall population down to 2.7 percent by the war's outbreak. This relative decline can be attributed to changes in the legal status of blacks in Indiana. Passage of the fugitive slave law alarmed many of Indiana's blacks, and fearing that they might be returned to slavery, they emigrated to Canada. A provision in the 1851 Indiana constitution, Article XIII, forbidding the immigration of blacks into the state, also deterred blacks from coming. The Civil War, however, soon rendered Article XIII ineffective. Indianapolis needed to bolster its work force, and black immigrants began filling the jobs of whites who had gone to war or taken better jobs.

12. Paul Friggens, "Without Federal Aid," *National Civic Review* 52(5):247 (May 1963).

13. Ralston, who as an assistant to Major Pierre Charles L'Enfant had helped lay the plans for Washington, DC, incorporated that city's radial street design into the original plan for Indianapolis.

14. Ignatius Brown, *Logan's History of Indianapolis from 1818* (Indianapolis: Logan & Company, 1868), p. 19.

By 1870 the black population had reached 2,931, nearly six times the 1860 count. It grew to 6,504 in 1880, 9,133 in 1890, and 15,931 in 1900. During the century's last three decades, the black share of the city's population rose gradually to approximately 10 percent.

Political and Civil Rights.   Carved out of the Northwest Territory, Indiana came under the Ordinance of 1787, which outlawed slavery and involuntary servitude. Frequent noncompliance with the law prompted the first state constitutional convention to include an antislavery provision in the 1816 constitution's Bill of Rights. In any event, while slavery had thus been legally barred from the territory and the state before Indianapolis's founding in 1820, other rights of blacks were not similarly protected. There was no black suffrage; blacks could not serve in the militia; they were barred from testifying in court; marriage between races was forbidden by law; and blacks were prohibited by law from attending public schools.

The economic and population growth that established Indianapolis as a major city after the Civil War also made the black community an important distinct subgroup within the city. In addition to their rapidly increasing numbers and impact on the city, the blacks' presence was dramatized by their part in the war effort. These changes brought them a number of legal and political advancements before the turn of the century.

Education, Employment, and Politics.   The education and employment of blacks in the nineteenth century followed a line of loosely defined segregation. The statutes were revised in 1869 to permit blacks to obtain public education in segregated schools—the nineteenth century form of segregation then prevalent was caused more by residential patterns than by established school policies. The standard practice was to draw school boundaries so that children could attend the school nearest their home. Thus, black children living in all-black neighborhoods attended all-black elementary schools, whereas some other blacks attended predominantly white elementary schools. Those few blacks who went beyond the elementary grades attended Indianapolis High School, the only one available.

Black employment in Indianapolis resembled the situation in other large northern cities. Thus, most blacks filled the ranks of unskilled workers. Some farmed small patches of ground on the city's fringe, and a few purchased small businesses, but most worked as hod carriers, waiters, teamsters, porters, and janitors, and many black women worked as domestics. Business opportunities for blacks were limited, and those who were successful nearly always became so with limited capital and black clientele.

Passage of the Fourteenth and Fifteenth amendments to the US

Constitution added significantly to the blacks' political presence in Indianapolis. This was particularly true of the suffrage amendment, nullifying the state constitutional provision limiting suffrage to whites. The ballot was of immediate importance to the black community, many of whose members quickly assumed the responsibilities of active citizenship.

While politics provided a ladder to success for a few individuals, many of the political rewards available to other ethnic groups still eluded blacks. Only a few blacks were elected to office, generally to the state General Assembly or the City Council. Nomination of blacks for executive office was unheard of, and patronage positions were few and restricted to the least desirable jobs. Perhaps the most direct beneficiary of black suffrage in Indianapolis was the Republican Party, which used large black electoral majorities to help control Indianapolis politics and government until the 1930s.

Population Growth in the Twentieth Century. Census figures for the present century show the city's black community to have grown steadily and more rapidly than the white community. A very noticeable increase occurred between the 1910 and 1920 census years when the black population grew from 21,816 to 34,678, a 59 percent increase. Just as in the Civil War period, blacks were attracted to fill war production labor needs during World War I.

The black population growth rate declined somewhat during the 1920s when the Ku Klux Klan was most active in Indianapolis and during the Depression in the 1930s. Nevertheless, their increases still slightly outpaced white population growth. This was true in part because of the white migration to the suburbs beginning in the 1920s.

Black population increases were even more dramatic after the beginning of World War II. From 1940 to 1950 the black population increased from 51,142 to 63,867 (12,725), and the black proportion rose from 13 percent to 15 percent. A 54 percent growth rate in the 1950s raised the city's black population to nearly 100,000 persons, bringing their share to 21 percent.

The heaviest concentration of the black population continues to be found in the old city's west to northwest side, although many of the new arrivals have located on the near east side of downtown. This initiated a certain rivalry between the west side's old timers and the east side's newcomers, which diminished during the 1960s, however, as both communities expanded to meet on the near north side at Meridian Street. In order to go from the city's center to the upper-class white areas on the north side, it is now necessary to traverse areas of heavy black population.

Almost no blacks were found in the suburban areas in 1960; Beech Grove with a population of almost 10,000 counted only one black resident, and Speedway, also with about 10,000 residents, had three blacks. Only Lawrence, the largest incorporated suburban city, had a sizable minority population of 1,196 (1.81 percent) by 1970.

In 1980 the nonwhite population was slightly more than 13 percent of the eight-county metropolitan area total, slightly over 20 percent in Marion County, approximately 30 percent in the area previously included in the City of Indianapolis, and about 41 percent in Center Township, the geographical center of the city and the county. These percentages had increased from 1970 figures of 17 for Marion County, 21 for the old city of Indianapolis, and 39 for Center Township.

As the figures indicate, the black population of the metropolitan area resides almost entirely in Marion County; only about 2,000 of more than 400,000 people in the other seven SMSA counties were black. In Marion County blacks are concentrated overwhelmingly in the old city area of Indianapolis, largely in Center Township.

Klan-Related Setbacks, and New Gains.   Pressured by Ku Klux Klan members and several civic groups, including the Chamber of Commerce, the Board of School Commissioners authorized construction in 1927 of Crispus Attucks High School for blacks and redrew elementary school districts to correspond to the all-black neighborhoods.

The school segregation was essentially total and remained so until after World War II when returning veterans, the NAACP, and church, labor, and civic groups pressed for change. Following passage of a state statute outlawing school segregation in 1949, the Indianapolis Board of School Commissioners undertook a deliberate program to desegregate Indianapolis schools. Within a decade black students were attending all of the city's high schools; junior high and elementary schools accepted students regardless of race; and the all-black teaching staffs that had taught in the black schools were broken up and assigned to teach white students.

Even so, sharply segregated residential patterns have made it extremely difficult to desegregate schools. In fact, as many white residents have moved to the suburbs and send their children to predominantly white suburban schools, the concentration of blacks in the city school districts has grown. Because for decades the city's schools were clearly and deliberately segregated as official policy, the federal courts have found a positive obligation to desegregate, and the litigation concerning this obligation has been protracted and complex.

The Klan was also influential in other political circles. During the 1924 election, when Republican candidates included a number of Klan members, many blacks voted Democratic for the first time in their lives. Although most of these returned to the Republican ranks at the following election, others remained Democrats, providing a nucleus for the massive switch of blacks to the Democratic Party 10 years later. Klan influence also effectively increased segregation in real estate, job opportunities, public recreation, entertainment, and elsewhere.

The formidable influence of the Ku Klux Klan in Indianapolis was not broken until the end of World War II. Extensive civil rights progress has been made since 1945. Relying on federal programs and local initiative, Indianapolis's leadership, both black and white, has made notable advances in providing equal opportunities in housing, public programs, jobs, business, education, and politics.

Despite the long period of strong Klan influence, in the postwar years there has been less overt tension between the races than has existed in many other cities. For example, in 1978 *Ebony* magazine rated Indianapolis among the nation's 10 top cities in terms of desirability for blacks to live in. Admittedly, *Ebony* added some qualifications, cautioning prospective black residents about the continued presence of the Ku Klux Klan, the John Birch Society, and the American Nazi Party. It also noted that black political power had been diluted by the new regional government.[15] Nevertheless, Indianapolis's overall high rating as a place for blacks to live is the underlying reason why blacks have not seriously opposed the unified government.

While opportunities for blacks clearly lag behind those of whites, the Klan no longer dominates the public sector in Indianapolis, and the white leadership seems committed to bettering race relationships. There is increasing strength among the black leadership that builds on a long tradition of Indianapolis blacks using their personal status to improve the situation of the black community. Unquestionably, Indianapolis still has problems of discrimination, but it has not experienced the racial upheavals that have characterized many other major US cities in recent years.

15. "Cities for Blacks," *Ebony*, February 1978, pp. 95–101.

3

Government Before Unigov

The 1967 census of governments identified 60 governmental units in Marion County: (1) nine townships (all of Indiana's territory is included within a township just as it is within a county), (2) 23 cities and towns (in Indiana the distinction between a city and a town depends largely on size), and (3) the county itself. None of the suburban municipalities was large compared with Indianapolis; only three (Beech Grove, Lawrence, and Speedway) had 1970 populations over 10,000, and none had reached 20,000 (see Map 3).

The county was divided into 11 school districts. One essentially served the area of the City of Indianapolis but was considered to be a distinct governmental unit. Two others corresponded to two of the other municipalities (Beech Grove and Speedway). The other eight school districts served areas outside the three municipal school systems. In addition to schools, the 1967 census also noted 16 other special districts, some coinciding with general purpose units.[1]

The Basic Units of Government

As with most states, Indiana's counties are considered primarily subdivisions of the state government, their structure being heavily influenced by the ideas and practices prevalent in the Jacksonian frontier era. Strictly prescribed and rather limited powers are vested in a board of county commissioners, comprising three members elected from districts by both city and noncity voters. In addition, there are eight other directly elected county officials: clerk, auditor, recorder, treasurer, sheriff, coroner, surveyor, and assessor. All of these save one are provided for by the state constitution, only the office of assessor being created by statute. A County Council of five members (reduced from seven in 1967) concerns itself almost entirely with matters of budget and finance.

A civil township government has even fewer functions than a

---

1. It is sometimes difficult to distinguish between *separate* governmental units and autonomous agencies *within* a general purpose unit, although the Bureau of the Census tries to make its criteria for such distinctions explicit.

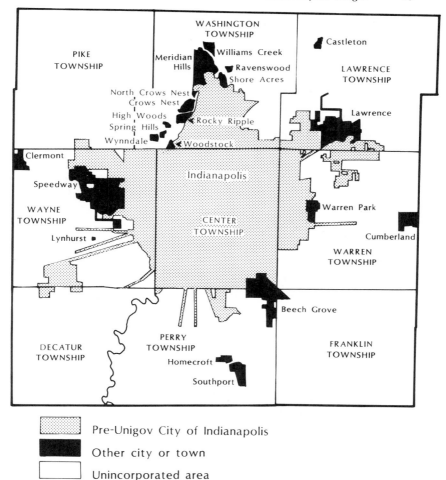

Pre-Unigov City of Indianapolis

Other city or town

Unincorporated area

Map 3.

Trends in Local Government, Indianapolis–Marion County Prior to Implementation of Unigov in 1971

Source: Indianapolis Chamber of Commerce, Governmental Affairs Department.

county. A township trustee, township assessor, and a three-member township advisory board are elected in each township. Townships continued to have some role in administering "poor relief," although most of the real responsibility for this function was transferred to county departments of public welfare in the 1930s. Property-tax assessment is done by the township assessor under the county assessor's supervision. By the time of the Unigov reorganization, Marion County's suburban townships were beginning to provide a few rudimentary urban-type services, for example, volunteer fire and ambulance departments.

Before Unigov, Indianapolis had a mayor-council government (see Chart 1). The mayor, elected for four-year terms, was the city's chief executive officer, performing administrative, ceremonial, and political duties commonly associated with a strong-mayor system. The city clerk (also secretary to the City Council), elected for a four-year term, maintained the municipal records, documents, and ordinances.

A nine-member elected City Council, officially named the Common Council, was the local legislative body for Indianapolis. The council's jurisdiction, prescribed by state law, included a wide range of powers over municipal regulations and finance. The system of electing councilmembers was unique. Each of the two parties could nominate a candidate from each of the six council districts. In the general election, the nine candidates with the most votes were elected. This formula ensured seating at least three members of the minority party.

The facilitation of borrowing was an important reason for the formation of special purpose units of government in Indiana, sometimes with boundaries identical to those of an existing general purpose unit. The state constitution does not permit a municipal corporation to incur debts exceeding 2 percent of its assessed property valuation, whereas a newly created unit, even if in the same area, could borrow up to its own limit. Special purpose units are also established to provide some particular governmental service in a territory different from and ordinarily larger than existing units. These are the two principal reasons why 16 semiautonomous units of government were added to the basic governmental pattern in the 20 years prior to 1968. Some of these units will be discussed later in reviewing steps taken to accommodate preexisting governmental structure to metropolitan growth.

A Multiplicity of Governments

The quest for Unigov did not originate with a detailed inquiry into the need for consolidated government in Marion County. No comprehensive study/charter commission preceded the reform. No outside consultant was retained, and no local university was brought in to study metropolitan problems. The issue was decided by a politically powerful group of experienced local government operatives. These men were keenly aware that the conventional wisdom of merger proposals emphasized economy, efficiency, and effectiveness in local government. While economic issues and increased productivity were important to Unigov proponents, the deciding issue for them lay in the need to devise a governmental structure in which they could get things done. They were aided by growing community concern over the ineffectiveness of government in Indianapolis—Marion County.

The governmental arrangement in Indianapolis and Marion County was seen by most of the community opinion leaders as an

Chart 1

Indianapolis City Government Before Consolidation

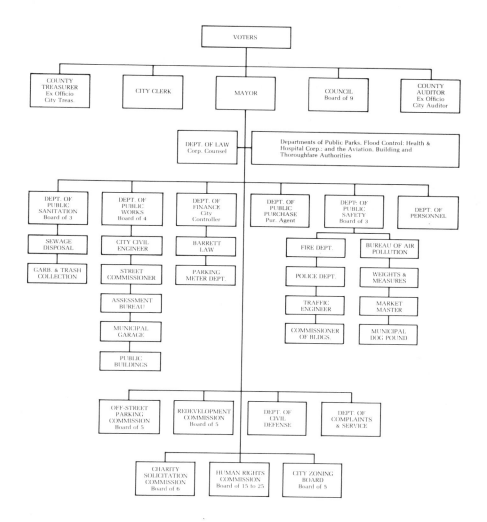

Source: Indianapolis Chamber of Commerce, Governmental Research Department, *A Primer of Local Government in Marion County* (Indianapolis, 1964), p. 43.

array of overlapping jurisdictions with functional duplication of certain services (see Chart 2). Each of the 60 units duplicated in some measure the executive and legislative offices of the others and presented the citizens and voters an often bewildering list of elected and appointed officials. The *Indianapolis News* editorialized: "The compartmental and conflicting governmental units of city, county and township are suitable no more. They were set up for a simpler era."[2] The League of Women Voters made a similar point by giving their local government study the title *Who's in Charge Here?*[3]

Functional Duplication. Many functions—purchasing, welfare, fire protection, and garbage collection—were handled by several different jurisdictions, but law enforcement was the most noticeable example of a function provided by a large number of separate units. Thus, police protection was provided by 24 different units in Marion County, including the sheriff's office, constables in six townships, full-time police forces in three cities, a park department, and marshals in 13 incorporated towns. Moreover, the FBI and the state police were always on call. In a plea for *metropol*—a term the local press coined for a proposed countywide police force—a local newspaper commented: "Included in this checkerboard of police authority are six radio broadcasting stations, five major police headquarters, with the two best equipped one block from each other, four police chiefs, a sheriff and two police garages."[4]

Ironically, despite the apparent duplication, some built-up areas were left unpatrolled. For example, new shopping centers sometimes hired private police to patrol their premises, thus in effect creating still more units of law enforcement, albeit private.

Overlapping Jurisdictions. Overlapping jurisdictions were most evident in transportation. Five separate governmental entities built and maintained highways, streets, and bridges in Indianapolis. Meridian Street, the main thoroughfare through the center of the city, also US Highway 31, was under the aegis of the State Highway Commission, like all the other federal and state highways traversing the city. Certain boulevards, for example, Kessler and Fall Creek, were under the Metropolitan Park Department. The County Highway Department also had jurisdiction in Indianapolis, although its activities were generally limited to noncity areas, except for bridge building. The newly created regional Metropolitan Transportation Authority had jurisdiction over all streets defined as thoroughfares by the Metropolitan

2. Editorial: "Census and Sense," *Indianapolis News*, June 9, 1960, p. 8.

3. League of Women Voters of Indianapolis, *Who's in Charge Here?* (Indianapolis, 1960).

4. "A Plan for Metropol," *Indianapolis Times*, March 1, 1964, sec. 2, p. 1.

Chart 2

Overlapping Layers of Local Government:
Three Typical Examples Before Unigov

In Washington Township (outside cities or towns)	In the City of Indianapolis (in Center Township)	In the City of Lawrence
	Housing Authority	
	Utility District	
	Off-Street Parking Authority	
	Redevelopment District	
	Sanitary District	Utility Board of Lawrence
	Center Township	Civil City of Lawrence
Washington Township	Civil City of Indianapolis	Lawrence Township
Metro. School District	School City of Indianapolis	Metro. School District
Indianapolis Park District		
Indianapolis–Marion County Building Authority		
Metro. Thoroughfare Authority		
Airport Authority District		
Marion County Fair Board		
Marion County Flood Control Board		
Health and Hospital Corporation of Marion County		
Government of Marion County		

Source: Indianapolis Chamber of Commerce, Governmental Research Department, *A Primer of Local Government in Marion County* (Indianapolis, 1964), p. 60.

Plan Commission. But the most important agency—in miles of streets built and maintained—was the city's own Board of Works. Outside the city, the State Highway Department, the county, the Metropolitan Transportation Authority, and the smaller municipalities all had transportation responsibilities.

Summary. The idea for Unigov resulted from the convergence of two conflicting forces—one a political movement of recent vintage, the other a governmental malaise of long standing. When the new Republican mayoral team took control of the city government after a long Democratic dominance, they were inspired by optimism and an ambition to do something dynamic and visible for their community— to make their political mark. But each of their preliminary plans was frustrated by the counsel of the more experienced members of the group, who pointed out that the governmental arrangement did not provide the mayor with enough authority to take the decisive and coordinated action needed to get things done.

Although no one had undertaken an in-depth study of local government in Marion County specifically in preparation for Unigov, a number of legislative committee hearings, civic group papers, and media inquiries in recent years had expressed a growing community sentiment of frustration and apathy over local government. The League of Women Voters publication *Who's in Charge Here?* was one of many that pointed out the inadequacy of local government structure and authority. Implicit in the report's title was the idea that the confusing array of overlapping and duplicating governmental units resulted in a situation where no one actually was "in charge."

Most of the groups that had pointed out the problems of multiple governments had also proposed city-county consolidation as an appropriate method of reform. Most of the Unigov principals had participated in the community discussions and, as active government officials, were acutely aware of the problems. Thus, when they obtained enough political leverage to change things, the move for consolidation followed almost predictably.

No "Home Rule."   All local government structures, powers, and processes are prescribed by state law in Indiana, the concept of city or county charter being absent from the state constitution and "home rule" a subject only for wistful discussion by local officials.[5] The constitution requires state laws applying to local government to be general in character but permits classification of local units according to size. Indianapolis has long been the only city in the first class, permitting legislation that is general in form to be passed applying only to Indianapolis or to Marion County (the latter often through the device of a general law applying to "any county containing a city of the first class"). A growing body of this legislation has been passed.

Adapting Government to Metropolitan Problems

The city's failure to grow by annexation left fringe-area residents without urban services unless they sought them from other sources. The county lacked authority to provide the needed services, prompting suburban builders and dwellers to incorporate towns for the task. A commission appointed to study the matter reported: "Adding to this problem [of increased service demands] is the fact that as certain localities in the unincorporated areas become more densely populated and the need for providing these localities with municipal services becomes urgent, additional towns are incorporated in an effort to sat-

---

5. A home-rule law passed after Unigov's implementation is largely ineffectual in providing new or strengthened powers to local units of government (see ch. 6).

isfy these requirements."[6] Before 1963 when Marion County's small towns were formed, it was relatively easy to set up new municipal corporations, but a 1963 law prohibited the incorporation of towns within four miles of a first-class city (Indianapolis).

Various ad hoc efforts to provide urban services in the fringe areas were also undertaken. Over a considerable period of years, significant efforts were made to enlarge the governmental areas within which particular services and functions were conducted. Most of these efforts focused on Marion County, since Indianapolis was entirely within the county, which was considered to be a single-county metropolitan area until the middle of the 1960s (see Chart 3).

Growing interest in governmental arrangements for the Indianapolis metropolitan area prompted no small number of studies and reports on the subject, but without any major effort at comprehensive reorganization before 1965. On the other hand, there were a number of attempts—some successful—to extend the jurisdiction for several individual municipal functions (discussed below).

Special Service Districts

After World War II, nearly every state legislative session passed acts to adjust the allocation of local government functions in relation to the Indianapolis metropolitan area. Usually each piece of legislation (proposed or enacted) dealt with only one particular function.[7]

As early as 1929, the city's public utility board was authorized to operate "within and outside" the city and to hold property up to five miles from the corporate limits if necessary to provide service to the city and the "community contiguous thereto."[8] Indianapolis operates a gas utility that is not subsidized by taxation. Water and electric power are provided by private corporations.

Ten additional special service districts were established during the ensuing 40 years,[9] all with extraterritorial jurisdiction beyond the

6. Metropolitan Area Study Commission of Marion County, *Report and Recommendations for the Eighty-Eighth Session of the General Assembly, State of Indiana* (Indianapolis, 1952), p. 4.

7. The history of these efforts to adapt function to area was clearly and succinctly summarized by Carl Dortch in a paper presented to the Governmental Research Association in January 1971. Dortch, retired executive vice-president of the chamber, has worked from time to time for local governments and has been associated with these efforts for years.

8. Indiana Legislative Council, Indiana Code 19–4–23 (Indianapolis: West Publishing Co., 1973).

9. The 10 additional special service districts established between 1929 and 1969 were the Board of Aviation, Capital Improvement Board, County Planning Board, City-County Library Board, Indianapolis Flood Control District, Indianapolis Housing Authority, Marion County Health and Hospital Corporation, Metropolitan Park Board, Metropolitan Thoroughfare Authority, and the Sewer and Sanitation Department.

Chart 3

Marion County Government Organization Before Consolidation

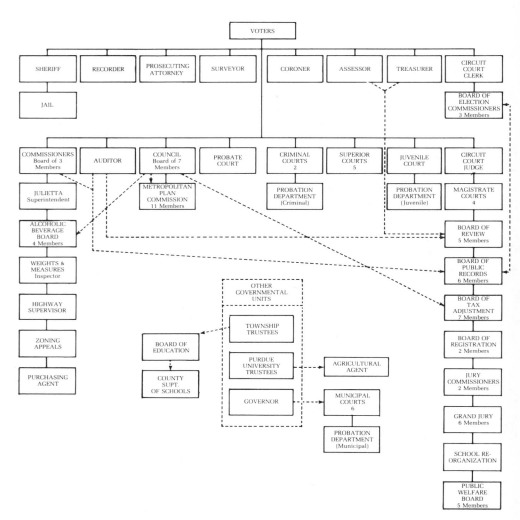

Source: Indianapolis Chamber of Commerce, Governmental Research Department, *A Primer of Local Government in Marion County* (Indianapolis, 1964), p. 25.

city limits and operating under independent boards or commissions with various degrees of fiscal autonomy. Four of these units had particularly significant effects on Unigov:

1. The Health and Hospital Corporation was supported by a powerful political block and was partially excluded from the Unigov structure.
2. The Sewer and Sanitation Department provided services beyond the city limits long before Unigov. Its service area and tax base were extended after Unigov. In 1978, the tax base for its capital program was extended to nearly the entire county.
3. The County Planning Board, formed in 1955, was the base unit in the formation of a formidable Department of Metropolitan Development.
4. The Metropolitan Thoroughfare Authority was authorized in 1963 but in 1969 was still struggling to get off the ground. It became one of Unigov's most powerful departments.

Unsuccessful Reorganization Attempts

Some major unsuccessful efforts were made to establish larger territorial bases for particular functions. In 1959, an official study commission was created to make proposals concerning Marion County school districts. (This was part of a general statewide effort for the reorganization of school districts.) The commission unanimously recommended a county unit school system, consolidating the 12 independent school districts into one. But the public response was so vehemently negative that the commission withdrew its recommendation. In 1967, a recommendation of the Greater Indianapolis Progress Committee (to be discussed later) resulted in legislative proposals for a countywide consolidated police force. But when sheriffs and other sources voiced stronger opposition than had been anticipated, the mayor did not support the proposal, and the effort collapsed.

4

The Reorganization Proposal:
Background and Drafting

Governmental reform had been debated in Indianapolis for 50 years, and 16 special purpose units had been established in the preceding 20 years. The push for major reorganization intensified in the five years immediately preceding Unigov. The Democrats and Republicans consecutively gained political ascendancy statewide, which gave them confidence to pursue major reform proposals.

The Mounting Complexity of Change

By 1968, responding to urban and metropolitan growth, the Indianapolis metropolitan community had taken major steps, one function at a time, to adjust the territorial base of most of the important functions of local government. The base most often used was the county, which had about five times the city's geographic area and about 60 percent more people. Sometimes a smaller base was used, but one still substantially larger than the city.

In any event, the areas and the mechanisms employed were those that seemed appropriate for the service needs or that recognized the political realities of the particular function. While other metropolitan areas were making similar adjustments, the shifts in Indianapolis even before 1968 were probably more numerous and significant than most of those elsewhere, although they had not attracted much attention, either national or local. Of the major local functions, only police and fire services were administered by the Indianapolis government entirely within the municipal boundaries, and even with these there were occasional extraterritorial activities.

The base-widening actions had been ad hoc and function by function, with little or no attention to coordination or integration and only limited concern with political responsibility. The motives behind the various shifts were usually mixed. In part, the moves were made in the interest of the fiscal autonomy that came with increased borrowing power and earmarked revenues for functions. But often equally important was the proponents' desire to separate a particular function from the partisan politics and the spoils system that prevailed in the general purpose governments. Where these problems seemed somewhat less pressing, for example, with schools, the reorganization effort was unsuccessful.

The base-widening move usually gave the function to a board, appointed partly by the mayor or City Council and partly by county officials. Sometimes there was ex officio membership. Most of the board members had overlapping terms, and powers of removal were often vague or nonexistent. The creation of these single-purpose special districts alleviated some problems but often compounded others by adding governments to an already complex pattern. Political and governmental power were widely dispersed among these functional agencies.

Annexation

Meanwhile, by effectively extending its most-demanded services beyond the city boundaries via the special purpose agencies, Indianapolis lost a bargaining position that would have otherwise been useful in annexation proceedings. The upshot, as Deputy Mayor John W. Walls saw it, was the economic and political isolation of the city from the rest of the county. Thus, the city had no place to grow. "The old City of Indianapolis had literally put its back to the wall through all the metropolitan reorganizations. It had really nothing to offer through annexation. It was stymied."[1]

Moreover the growing social differences between the central city and the suburbs also made central-city annexation increasingly difficult. *The Municipal Yearbook,* which lists annexations of "one-fourth square mile or more" each year, included Indianapolis only twice from 1960 to 1968, for a total annexed area of 5.16 square miles.[2]

In any event, the city government did not pursue annexation aggressively. Its approach was succinctly stated in the words of Mayor Al G. Feeney: "We feel we ought to go slow on annexation. . . . It's difficult, sometimes impossible, to give people in annexed areas the services they have a right to expect for their taxes. We don't want to be like other cities that have to overextend themselves just to make population figures look good."[3] Expansion efforts were also limited by several other factors. Thus, a state statute called for municipal annexa-

---

1. John W. Walls, interview with James Owen, Indianapolis, April 20, 1972.
2. "Metropolitan Area Developments," *The Municipal Yearbook,* vols. 23–29 (Chicago: International City Managers Association, 1962–1966).
3. "Annex Cautiously Feeney Urges," *Indianapolis Times,* September 15, 1950, p. 1.

tions to be accompanied by extension of the school boundaries so that the two would be coterminous. But suburban residents, proud of their own institutions and dubious about the city schools with large black enrollments, fought bitterly against inclusion in the city school district from which they may have only recently moved away. Contested annexations were heard in court, and the city was reluctant to risk drawn-out, expensive litigation with angry citizens on both sides. Furthermore, the Democratic mayors of Indianapolis may not have been enthusiastic about bringing the largely Republican suburban voters into city elections.

General Reform Discussions

One irony in Unigov's success is its occurrence in a city without a recognized record of reform. Admittedly, Indianapolis did have a long record of reform *discussions*, which now in retrospect appear to have been far more important than they seemed at the time. Thus, when the Unigov debate was initiated, consolidation had already been debated and commented on for over 50 years. For example, 52 years before the Unigov statute was passed, a study by the New York Bureau of Municipal Research recommended the "consolidation of city, township and county governments in Indianapolis and Marion County."[4] More than a decade later, in 1930, Paul Studenski also wrote of Indianapolis as a city that had already seen decades of consolidation efforts.[5] But these moves lost much of their impetus after several unsuccessful attempts to reform city government. For example, a highly spirited campaign for a council-manager form of government was particularly responsible for drowning out the voices for consolidation in the late 1920s. This issue, along with home rule, superseded consolidation as a reform issue in Indianapolis. (Indianapolis actually got legislative approval for a city-manager government, only to have it declared unconstitutional by the Indiana Supreme Court.)

Attention was understandably diverted to other matters during the Depression years and World War II. After the war, provoked in part by John Gunther's taunt, in 1947 Mayor Robert H. Tyndall appointed a citizens' committee to study the problems of Indianapolis. This committee was the forerunner of others formed in the subsequent two decades, with varying kinds of sponsorship, to consider the problems of government in Marion County.

Many of these recommended some form of consolidated govern-

4. "Consolidated Local Governments," *Indianapolis Star*, December 1, 1917, p. 21.

5. Paul Studenski, *The Government of Metropolitan Areas in the United States* (New York: National Municipal League, 1930), p. 171.

ment,[6] but before 1969 such reorganization proposals elicited mostly discussion, with very little action. While the results were slow to materialize, however, the postwar period's renewed interest in reform contributed greatly to Unigov's successful creation. The discussions projected the idea of consolidation to prominence among public issues debated in the years preceding Unigov, and the numerous incremental reforms, which accompanied the larger debate, fully tested the public decisionmaking process with respect to government reform.

The League of Women Voters and the Chamber of Commerce

Leading the discussions as proponents of government consolidation were the League of Women Voters and the Chamber of Commerce. Both groups had many mutual interests in governmental reform and supported each other in public forums on a variety of local reform issues, but also each had its own primary interest that was central to its efforts. Thus, the league was most concerned about the effects of governmental structure on voter representation. It believed that citizens were confused by governmental complexities in Indianapolis and Marion County and consequently were discouraged from participating. The league's publication *Who's in Charge Here?*[7] reflected this concern.

The chamber's chief concern was the inefficiency they saw inherent in the overlapping, multiple government pattern. According to a 1964 chamber study,[8] an individual citizen-taxpayer in Marion County could be taxed by 10 to 16 taxing units (see Chart 2). The study argued that this not only meant added costs to the taxpayer but also contributed to budget complexities that confounded taxpayers and administrators alike.

Government Study Committees

Complementing the efforts of the League of Women Voters and the Chamber of Commerce were several government-sponsored study committees, formed locally as well as by the state General Assembly. Many of these were formed at the request of the chamber or the league, but the decisive impetus came from government officials frus-

---

6. E.g., see Metropolitan Area Study Commission of Marion County, *Report and Recommendations for the Eighty-Eighth Session of the General Assembly, State of Indiana* (Indianapolis, 1952); League of Women Voters of Indianapolis, *Who's in Charge Here?* (Indianapolis, 1960); and Indianapolis Chamber of Commerce, Governmental Research Department, *A Primer of Local Government in Marion County* (Indianapolis, 1964).

7. *Who's in Charge Here?*

8. *Primer of Local Government.*

trated at being unable to get things done. This frustration produced a third reform element that became prominent in the pre-Unigov discussions: the objective of these study commissions was to make government organizationally more efficient and to equate authority with responsibility. If this reform was accomplished, it would result in the identifiable leadership that the league wanted and produce the tax savings and budget controls sought by the chamber.

Perhaps the most important of numerous government-sponsored study groups appearing in the 1950s and 1960s was the Greater Indianapolis Progress Committee (GIPC), formed in 1965. GIPC was a bipartisan citizens' group representing a wide spectrum of the greater Indianapolis community, including a large number of civic leaders. One of its most active subcommittees was a task force on government that issued several papers favoring reform in the years immediately preceding Unigov. The progress committee was then and still is a widely respected citizens' group, being credited with numerous public accomplishments. Its support greatly enhanced the Unigov concept's prospects.

The media were also very responsive, providing substantial coverage throughout the period. This was especially true of the print media. In addition to their regular reporting, all three daily newspapers[9] published special features on the governmental problems and editorialized in favor of some form of consolidated countywide government. In fact, the *Indianapolis Star* concluded a 13-part series with just such an argument on the eve of the Unigov debate.[10]

These long-continued discussions, focusing public attention on reform issues, may have been especially influential in paving the way for passage of the Unigov legislation. This kind of public attention also represented a usually subtle but nearly constant reminder that many people saw Indianapolis as not having much to offer as a city. Community leaders were sensitive to the city's "corn pone" image, and when the newly elected government had the opportunity to do something dynamic in 1968, it had the added motivation of wanting to prove the critics wrong.

Politics

The spoils system governs the appointment and tenure of many, perhaps most, employees of the general governmental units, although the schools and many of the other special purpose units are at least

9. There are now two major Indianapolis newspapers; the *Indianapolis Times* ceased publication in 1965.

10. "Area Moves Slowly to Metropolitan Government," *Indianapolis Star*, March 10–22, 1968.

partly exempted from partisanship and the spoils system. Moreover, elements of professionalism and tenure are also found in some areas of general governmental employment.

In Indianapolis and Marion County, both major parties have strong and active organizations and present candidates for most elective positions. In recent decades, Democrats have been much more successful than Republicans in elections in the City of Indianapolis. In contrast, Marion County (including Indianapolis) has returned Republican majorities substantially more often than Democratic. Thus, in the 10 Indianapolis mayoral elections preceding the reorganization, the Democrats won seven times and the Republicans only three. Moreover, when they were successful, the Republicans tended to win by narrower margins than the Democrats.

There is no such single measuring rod of party success at the county level because the counties have so many elected officials. Nevertheless, in Marion County the Republicans clearly have controlled a majority of the county offices and the state legislative delegation most of the time since the New Deal days of the 1930s, although there were Democratic victories in 1948, 1958, and 1964. Republicans also generally win in most, though not all, of the suburban municipalities. Margins of victory are seldom very large in either city or county, however, the winners usually getting 50 to 60 percent and the losers 40 to 50 percent.

Party organization is important in both the city and the county, and there is strong, active staffing at the county, ward, and precinct levels. The county has probably been a more significant political party unit than the city, and the county chair usually directs city campaigns, as well as those in Marion County.

1964 and the Period of Democratic Ascendancy

The Democrats swept the Indiana elections in 1964 at the time of Lyndon Johnson's victory over Barry Goldwater. After that election the governor was a Democrat, both houses of the General Assembly were controlled by Democrats, and the Marion County state legislative delegation, which dominates legislative consideration of matters affecting Indianapolis, was also Democratic. The Indianapolis city government was also controlled by the Democrats, who had won the mayor's office and council elections in 1963.[11] Moreover, the Democratic county chair, James W. Beatty, a young attorney, was also corporation counsel for the City of Indianapolis.

Both Beatty and Indianapolis's democratic mayor, John J. Barton, felt frustrated by the inability of the city's chief executive to control

---

11. In Indiana, municipal elections are held every four years, one year preceding US presidential elections.

the activities of many semiautonomous agencies and boards that were in charge of a large number of local functions. Beatty prepared a series of 14 related bills whose purpose was to increase the elected officials' control—particularly that of the mayor—over the boards governing health, sanitation, parks, airports, welfare, and other functions. These bills generally did not propose changes in the agencies' basic structure or territorial jurisdictions. Instead, the primary aim was to alter the way board members were appointed and to make it clear that members could be removed by the appointing official.

A *"Power Grab."* The *Indianapolis Star* and the *Indianapolis News* gave the proposals considerable attention and opposed them vigorously. (These are now the only two daily papers in the city. Both are owned by the same organization and are generally conservative politically.) The *News* called the proposals a "power grab," a phrase that gained immediate currency in the community and the General Assembly. Perhaps the measures' strongest opposition came from the public officials who would be affected. Particularly affected were officials of the Citizens Gas and Coke Company and the County Health and Hospital Corporation. As might be expected, the Republican Party leadership also spoke out strongly against the bills. At one point the GOP county chair, H. Dale Brown, claimed that "nothing like this has been attempted in Indianapolis since the days of the Ku Klux Klan."[12]

Elements of the Democratic Party also had strong reservations. Some were reported to have urged Mayor Barton to force Beatty out and to take the Democratic county chair's job himself. The mayor, who was more conservative than his county chair, disassociated himself from the proposals to some degree, saying that "most of the bills . . . were being promoted by the Democratic organization, not the city administration."[13]

Because of the heavy opposition, Beatty's proposals were only moderately successful in the General Assembly. Some of the bills failed, and some were vetoed by Governor Roger D. Branigin. While the governor was a Democrat, he was also much more conservative than the Marion County Democratic leadership and had been favored for the office by the *Star*, which seldom supported Democrats. Five of the 14 bills did become law, substantially increasing the mayor's power over one city board and four countywide agencies.

Metropol. Undaunted by the difficulties attending the 1965 "power grab" proposals and the prospect of facing a Republican-

12. "Alarm, Pressure Modify Some 'Grab' Bills," *Indianapolis Star*, February 21, 1965, p. 1.
13. "Mayor Power Play Lashed," *Indianapolis Star*, February 6, 1965, p. 1.

controlled lower house, the city administration returned to the following session of the General Assembly, in 1967, with another major reorganizational proposal, calling for a metropolitan police department. This time, the authorship was attributed to the Greater Indianapolis Progress Committee (GIPC), the bipartisan civic group noted earlier, and chaired by Frank E. McKinney, Sr., chair of the board of one of the state's largest banks and former national chair of the Democratic Party. The GIPC focused much of its attention on capital improvement projects, but it also had committees that considered governmental reform. The proposal for a metropolitan police department in 1967 was stimulated by one of these committees.

Following the recommendations of the GIPC committee report, Representative John Mutz (Rep., Indianapolis) introduced a bill to give the city police department countywide jurisdiction. Metropol (the name commonly given the bill) would also have occasioned a major reorganization of the operation, powers, and duties of the police force. One section, for example, required that the police chief be appointed from outside the department. The county sheriff was to be retained, but with duties essentially limited to that of jailkeeper. Other provisions were similarly far-reaching, provoking strong opposition. At this point Mayor Barton then appeared at a General Assembly hearing against the recommendations, effectively ending further consideration of the bill.

The 1965–1967 reform efforts had effects that went beyond the governmental changes themselves and had a decided though indirect impact on the subsequent Unigov debate. One immediate effect was to establish the merger idea as a topical issue for discussion. This development was fairly well publicized by a local government study committee authorized by the 1965 General Assembly. Also important was the political impact generated when the Democrats pushed a reorganization plan. This did a number of things. It put Democrats on record as favoring reform; it alerted Republicans and thereby precipitated a response; it identified sources of opposition. Not least in importance was the lesson learned from the split in the Democratic Party. This tended to weaken their bills' chances considerably and made the party vulnerable to defeat.

Mayor Barton had increasingly noticeable differences with his party chair. A group of "young Turks" led by Beatty had recently wrested control of the party machine from an "old guard" centered around former mayors Phillip Bayt and Charles Boswell. With the support of this old guard, Barton attempted to oust Beatty from the party chairship in 1966 but failed. Beatty in turn challenged Barton in the 1967 mayoral primary. Barton, with the advantage of incumbency, prevailed over the party organization in a heated campaign that left many wounds.

The Republicans Return to Power

While efforts to extend the mayor's influence were being considered, important changes were occurring within the Republican Party in Marion County, changes that were crucially significant for the subsequent reorganization efforts.

The Republican Action Committee

Disappointed with the sweeping defeats in 1964, a group of Republican partisans calling themselves the Republican Action Committee began an intraparty struggle to unseat the regular Republican leadership. The Republican Action Committee presented a complete slate of candidates in the May primary of 1966, including candidates for the precinct committeemen, who in turn choose the county leadership. They won a decisive victory in the primary, every one of their candidates for public office being nominated, and they gained an overwhelming majority of the precinct committeemen. At the GOP county convention four days after the primary, the longtime county chair was replaced, and a member of the Republican Action Committee, L. Keith Bulen, a young attorney and former member of the General Assembly, was elected by acclamation in a brief 35-minute meeting.[14]

Many of the people who worked with the Republican Action Committee in the 1966 elections continued to be active in the city campaign of 1967, the general elections of 1968, and the Unigov effort in 1969. This new Republican leadership was generally young (although including some older persons), relatively prosperous, and well educated. Bulen rapidly became one of the state's most powerful Republican politicians. His Marion County forces were successful in the legislative races of 1966 and the mayoralty campaign of 1967 and provided the decisive margin in nominating the successful Republican candidate for governor in 1968. Bulen then became Republican national committeeman, and in a state that had no Republican US senator, he became the chief channel for national Republican patronage in Indiana.

Lugar's First Campaign for Mayor

In the 1967 mayoralty campaign, the Republican Party primary resembled the Democratic race between Barton and Beatty: both contests were in large measure between old and new leadership.

In the Republican Party, however, youth prevailed. Bulen and

---

14. "County Republicans Elect Bulen 'Party Chief,' " *Indianapolis Star,* May 8, 1966, p. 14.

most of the others who had been active in the 1966 Republican Action Committee campaign supported one of their own group, Richard G. Lugar. Six weeks before the primary, Lugar was designated as the candidate of the leadership by a special 20-member screening committee. In choosing Lugar, the screening committee turned down strong bids by two GOP stalwarts, Judge William T. Sharp and former mayor Alex M. Clark (1952–1956). Disenchanted with the committee's choice, Clark announced his own candidacy a week later (with Judge Sharp's endorsement). In spite of the decided edge the choice by the screening committee gave Lugar, Clark managed to revive antiorganization factions and mounted a formidable opposition.

Lugar's advantage, based in considerable measure on party organization support, became evident as the campaign progressed. He defeated Clark for the nomination by a decisive but not overwhelming margin—21,551 to 17,000. Thus, the recently captured regular party organization responded to the challenge with a victory and established Lugar as a vote getter.

Richard Lugar was then only 35 years old. A descendant of German immigrants who settled in central Indiana in the early part of the nineteenth century, Lugar achieved a distinguished record as an Indianapolis schoolboy; he made Eagle Scout at age 13 and graduated from Shortridge High School first in his class of 600 in 1950. He won Phi Beta Kappa honors at Denison University in Ohio, where he also graduated first in his class and went to Oxford as Denison's first Rhodes Scholar. He studied politics, philosophy, and economics at Pembroke College, Oxford, and served as president of the student body at Pembroke College and as president of the American Students' Association at Oxford University.

After college, Lugar served in the navy three years, then returned to Indianapolis to reestablish two family businesses. He also became active with civic, social, and educational groups. He was elected to the Indianapolis school board in 1964 and served as its vice-president from 1965 to 1967.

During the summer months preceding the 1967 general election for mayor, Lugar and Bulen successfully healed their differences with Clark and his supporters and conducted an active campaign. Much younger and more active than Barton, Lugar made nearly 400 speeches and drew strong support from a highly motivated and well-managed party organization under Bulen's direction. The result was a Republican victory by a margin of nearly 9,000 votes. In addition to Lugar's victory in the mayoralty campaign, the Republicans also won a majority of the City Council seats.

The last previous Republican victory in a mayor's race had been 16 years earlier, and this was only the third such victory in 40 years. Lugar's winning campaign received substantial contributions in influence, money, and manpower from suburban as well as city Republicans. In soliciting contributions in the suburbs, one Republican fundraiser emphasized the metropolitan interrelationships, saying that "the mayor controls by his appointment boards and agencies which operate countywide and affect residents outside city limits even though they don't vote for the mayor."[15]

The Planning Stage: Developing a Draft Proposal

On January 1, 1968, Richard G. Lugar took office as the Republican mayor of Indianapolis. In his 1967 campaign Lugar had said nothing specific about governmental reorganization, although he had set up a task force on government reorganization. He was certainly aware of past changes in authority and responsibility and of the proposals emanating from the Greater Indianapolis Progress Committee and the general community debate over reorganization. Committed to dynamic, active leadership, he was even more frustrated than his Democratic predecessor by the dispersion of responsibility and power among the various local government agencies.

In describing these frustrations, he frequently used as an example the Eagle Creek reservoir in northwestern Marion County, a major stream impoundment whose development required changes in roads, land use, health and sanitation facilities, and governmental services of many kinds. As chief executive of the central city, Mayor Lugar was necessarily interested in the Eagle Creek project but found responsibility for action on it divided among agencies over which he had limited influence. In some cases, they were actually extraterritorial activities of the city government; in other instances, the agencies were run by boards over which he had only partial appointing authority; some were county agencies over which he had no control; in still other instances, state and federal offices were involved and could be persuaded to do certain things only if the local community spoke to them through clear and direct channels. Lugar summed up the reasons for his exasperation: "Why are eight different authorities responsible for drainage, five for transportation, and so many for the development of 4,000 acre Eagle Creek Park that the whole lake is becoming a quagmire of frustration and not a park?"[16]

Lugar was not the only official interested in the possibility of reorganization. The president of the Marion County Council, Beurt

15. "Money Shortage Worries Lugar H.Q.," *Indianapolis Star*, October 8, 1967, p. 8.

16. Richard G. Lugar, "The Need for County Leadership in County Modernization," speech to the Thirty-Fourth Annual Conference of the National Association of Counties, Portland, Oregon, July 28, 1969, p. 2.

SerVaas, a prominent businessman and civic leader, and Indianapolis City Council president Thomas C. Hasbrook, an executive in the Eli Lilly company, had both been active in the new Republican leadership, and soon after the 1967 Republican victories in the city elections they had begun conversations on possible increased city-county cooperation. John Walls, chief staff officer of the Greater Indianapolis Progress Committee, had been co-opted into Lugar's new administration as deputy mayor and was also very interested. Walls was less an active partisan than a professional public administrator, which he was by virtue of training and experience.

Policy Committee

Within a month or two of Lugar's becoming mayor, SerVaas called the first in a series of unofficial meetings of city and county government and party leaders to discuss ways to promote intergovernmental cooperation and to establish government priorities on a countywide basis. Senior among those attending was John Burkhart, president of the College Life Insurance Company, president of the Capital Improvement Board (one of the ad hoc agencies created to build new capital facilities for the area), a longtime active member and leader of the Chamber of Commerce and other civic groups, and one of the chief financial backers of the Republican Action Committee. Also in regular attendance at the early meetings were Mayor Lugar, county chair Keith Bulen, Hasbrook, Walls, Lawrence M. Borst, a veterinarian and chair of the Marion County legislative delegation, and Charles L. Whistler, an attorney and president of the Metropolitan Planning Commission. This group, later known as the policy committee, worked out the overall concept for Unigov.[17]

As discussions progressed, others were invited to meetings of the policy committee. One such was Carl R. Dortch, chief executive of the Indianapolis Chamber of Commerce, longtime government researcher, and member of the Governmental Research Association. Dortch had been chair of the school reorganization study several years earlier and was a veteran of most of the struggles to get various kinds of reform legislation through the General Assembly. Physician E. Henry "Ned" Lamkin, Jr., and John Mutz, active members of the Marion County legislative delegation, were also frequent participants.

From the first gathering, a series of informal Sunday cocktail-dinner meetings began, held monthly from February to October 1968 at John Burkhart's house. The flexible attendance and the cocktail-

---

17. The group was not officially attached to the Greater Indianapolis Progress Committee. The latter was a much larger body, including numerous Democrats as well as Republicans, and discussions in such a forum could not have been as frank or confidential as those in the policy committee.

dinner format suggest the informal atmosphere prevailing at these meetings, for which no chair was selected or secretary appointed. No agendas were prepared, nor were minutes kept. The group was confident that with their new leadership team in office they could do something dynamic for Indianapolis. The completion of Eagle Creek reservoir, an areawide road system, and the revitalization of the downtown mile-square were considered, among other priorities. Each time the group felt stymied by the governmental arrangement, discussion turned to how the organization of government could be improved to help them gain their priorities. Eventually they agreed to develop a whole new structure of government. Hasbrook described the evolution of the Unigov concept: "We considered several projects large and small. But each time we were frustrated by the limitations of authority that were placed on us by the legislature and the cumbersome structure we had to work with. Unigov was a kind of distillation of these frustrations."[18]

Mayor Lugar's participation and leadership were always recognized as central and indispensable. He was knowledgeable about efforts at local government reorganization elsewhere, having been impressed by the reorganizations in Nashville and Jacksonville, and was confident that Indianapolis could do as much or more.

These 1968 discussions, as well as the political campaigns of that year, were characterized by a considerable degree of enthusiasm, optimism, and camaraderie. Undoubtedly the discussions were conducted in an atmosphere of partisan as well as civic interest, but it would be a great oversimplification to view the activities as a clandestine political plot. The participants were actively interested in governmental reform to further what they considered to be the general public interest. Nevertheless, as members of one political party they also undoubtedly felt that one good way to further the public interest was to promote the goals and effectiveness of their own party.

Two things helped keep the Unigov discussions out of public view during this period. First, public attention was focused on the new mayor's immediate tasks of assembling an administrative staff and responding to the economic and racial problems of 1968. Second, it was a part of the overall strategy to keep Unigov under wraps until the concept was well developed. This strategy would prevent the opposition from marshaling its forces early and perhaps, more important, keep some of its proponents from killing it with interminable debate and delay.

Early Business Ties

Mayor Lugar tried to solidify his support in the business community by involving businessmen in his programs and activities. Con-

18. Thomas C. Hasbrook, interview with James Owen, Indianapolis, May 23, 1972.

fronted by both unemployment and the threat of racial strife, the mayor sought to combat both with a single program. If he could find jobs for inner-city blacks, he reasoned, the employment picture would brighten and thereby reduce the likelihood of rioting. To implement this plan, Lugar turned to the Chamber of Commerce's Voluntary Adviser Corps (VAC) and the Greater Indianapolis Progress Committee.

The VAC committee, staffed largely by personnel directors from local businesses, was intended to provide direct assistance to the unemployed in helping them find jobs. The volunteers were each given the name of a person seeking a job. They would then work with that person on a one-to-one basis until the individual found a job and was secure in it. Mayor Lugar gave his personal endorsement to this committee and worked with the business executives to plan its activities. He also went on television to describe the committee's program and to urge 2,000 volunteers to join it.

VAC's success obviously depended on the volunteers' effectiveness in helping the unemployed find jobs. To augment the volunteers' efforts, the mayor organized a GIPC task force on employment to try to secure more job openings in business and industry. This group of volunteer business executives was directed by Juan C. Solomon, an Eli Lilly company employee on full-time executive loan to the task force.

In another move to tap the business community, Mayor Lugar appointed Donald L. Robinson—director of governmental affairs of the Indianapolis Chamber of Commerce—to the city post of deputy controller. Robinson received a salary of one dollar a year from the city while retaining his regular income from the chamber. As will be seen later, these close working relationships between the business community and Mayor Lugar's administration were to continue throughout his term, providing him with a major source of support for his Unigov proposal.

Lawyers' Work Group

The discussion and planning respecting organizational reform were not limited to general policy and strategy. The participants, particularly the mayor, realized that a great deal of detailed technical work would be essential to the reorganization effort. In the late spring of 1968, when the discussions of the policy committee had got off to a good start, Mayor Lugar asked Lewis C. Bose, an Indianapolis attorney with considerable legislative drafting experience, to prepare a memorandum on the possibilities and problems of metropolitan government reform in Indianapolis. After the policy committee had considered Bose's memorandum, Lugar again met with Bose, asking him to serve as the coordinator of a legal research team to prepare legislative drafts to implement the ideas that might emerge from the deliberations then taking place.

This was still in the late spring and early summer of 1968, long before the Republican victories of November 1968 made it clear that there would be Republican majorities in the county and state governments and before any discussion in the press or other public forums of specific governmental reform proposals. Bose, after a long discussion convinced him of the mayor's commitment and the enterprise's potential, agreed to undertake the drafting task with such assistants as he could recruit.

Being the state capital, Indianapolis has many lawyers experienced in legislative drafting. The larger business firms often facilitate and encourage such work by some of their staff members. Moreover, some of the local government units—most of them dominated by persons who had been participating in these discussions—had good attorneys. In any event Bose was able to secure talent that he considered of high quality, and some eight to ten lawyers spent a great many hours considering and refining alternative drafts. Bose also received some assurance of remuneration, which, while undoubtedly inadequate compensation for lawyers of the quality he secured, nevertheless kept their work from being entirely a "labor of love."

During the months in the planning stage, Bose and his lawyers' work group met each week, primarily to determine the present structure of the various governments, what their functions were, and their statutory or constitutional origins. With this groundwork laid by late summer 1968, a rough draft proposal was prepared and presented to the policy committee for consideration. Mayor Lugar, recognizing the technical aspects of their work, left the lawyers' work group pretty much on their own, while continuing to direct the campaign to marshal support for the idea. Communication between the policy committee and the lawyers' work group was maintained throughout by Charles Whistler, who was a member of both, and by John Walls, who sat in with the lawyers from time to time.

Through this network compromises were negotiated and incorporated in the draft bill, attempting to strike a balance between what was needed for local government reform and the political practicalities of what would be likely to pass the legislature. The emerging consensus had four major components: (1) Indianapolis would be converted into a countywide metropolitan government. (2) The Unigov principals decided on a single countywide executive of the strong-mayor type. (3) Considerations of political expediency convinced them to omit the school districts from the plan and (4) to exclude the municipalities of Beech Grove, Lawrence, and Speedway from the jurisdiction of the extended metropolitan government. With these four principles established, the remainder of the Unigov debate became a process of negotiation and compromise over specifics.

Securing Political Support

With the policy committee for Unigov as their primary goal for the 1969 legislative session and the lawyers' work group effort in progress, the next order of business for the mayor and the policy committee centered on marshaling political and legislative support for Unigov. To ensure legislative passage, one primary objective was Republican control of the General Assembly and the state executive offices.

Many reasons are given for the successful passage of Unigov in 1969, but the most frequently cited is the fact that the Republican Party was then in control of both the executive and legislative branches of government on the city, county, and state levels.[19] Mayor Lugar concurred with this assessment: "I cannot conceive of Unigov coming under other circumstances than very powerful political unity within the Marion County legislative delegation, within the structure of Ward Chairman and Precinct Committeemen in Indianapolis and Marion County, without overt support from Indiana GOP District Chairmen and GOP legislators from these districts, without the camaraderie of the 1968 campaign and especial interest manifested in our situation by President Nixon and Vice President Agnew."[20] The partisan strategy that took Unigov from an idea to an accomplished fact was succinctly outlined by John Walls in a speech a year after Unigov's passage:

> Now I am not pushing the Republicans in this sense, but I am suggesting another reality in terms of the politics of reorganization. If you are going to get it done, you will have to recognize that it is the political process that does it. We can scurry around with citizen committees and with all kinds of studies and research, but when it comes to the final analysis you must have 26 votes in the Indiana Senate, and 51 votes in the House of Representatives or you're dead. And you have to have a governor who will sign the bill when it's passed. We were fortunate . . . , in terms of strategy, in having Dick Lugar at the helm in Indianapolis. An indication of his leadership is the solidarity with which we were able to go to the General Assembly in 1969 and achieve this result.[21]

19. See D. M. Lawrence and H. R. Turnbull, III, "Unigov: City-County Consolidation in Indianapolis," *Popular Government* 36(25) (November 1969); Robert V. Kirch, "Unigov: Metropolitan Reform or Partisan Politics?" *Proceedings of the Indiana Academy of Social Sciences*, n.s. 4(4):153 (1969); and "Self-Help and the Cities," *Nation's Business* 59(7):24 (June 1971).

20. Richard G. Lugar, speech to Robert A. Taft Institute of Government, New York, May 21, 1970.

21. John W. Walls, "Local Government in Indiana," in *Modernizing Our State Government* (Notre Dame, Ind.: Center for Continuing Education, University of Notre Dame, 1970), p. 52.

The first official opportunity to work for legislative support occurred in the May primaries of 1968 when the Republican Party electors chose Marion County's legislative candidates for the November election. Though there had still been little or no public discussion of reorganization, Mayor Lugar, Keith Bulen, Beurt SerVaas, and John Burkhart (chair of the Republican slating committee) played a decisive role on behalf of legislative candidates known to favor the idea of governmental reorganization and who were in harmony with many of the mayor's programs. Most of them had also been active in the Republican Action Committee's successes the previous two years. The efforts of the slating committee culminated in primary victories for Marion County's entire organization-backed Republican slate.

A major opportunity for Marion County Republicans to expand their power base statewide came when the state GOP convention opened with Mayor Lugar as the keynote speaker. Under Bulen's direction, the Marion County forces combined to secure the gubernatorial nomination for Secretary of State Edgar D. Whitcomb, and their choices for the entire slate of state candidates were selected. The convention closed with Bulen named as Republican national committeeman from Indiana. The *Star's* comment on these maneuverings was that "such a display of power with finesse may never be seen again at a state GOP convention."[22]

Shortly thereafter, Mayor Lugar attended the national GOP convention as a delegate and platform committee member. His efforts on behalf of Richard Nixon not only established Lugar's credentials as a supporter of the national GOP ticket but also increased the back-home demand for him as a speaker. From this base, Lugar mounted an exhaustive statewide campaign continuing through the November election, speaking in support of GOP candidates while also stockpiling political debts for later collection. Afterward, Lugar commented that much of his 1968 Unigov strategy involved campaigning throughout Indiana not only on behalf of state candidates but also more particularly for state senators and representatives.[23]

A Restructured Committee and a New Place of Work

In October, as events multiplied and the prospects for electoral success appeared bright, the policy committee decided they could not keep abreast of developments using their previous mode of operation. Accordingly, the committee was restructured and a new work plan established. Hasbrook explained the transition as follows: "After the

22. Editorial, *Indianapolis Star*, June 23, 1968, p. 8.
23. Patrick Healy and Raymond L. Bancroft, "Three Mayors Review Their Governments," *Nation's Cities* 7(11):28 (November 1969).

bare bones plans were laid at John Burkhart's, several of us met every Sunday for a couple of months in the Mayor's conference room with the assignment to pull the specifics together."[24]

While nearly the same people were involved as before, the mayor's conference room had advantages of location and access to needed materials, making it a more effective place "to pull the specifics together." William A. Brennan, Jr., a Democratic realtor, and William H. Hardy, a black member of a public relations firm, were added to the group to give some balance to the previously all-white Republican committee, and they proceeded to work with the attorneys to complete the first draft of the bill and then to form a task force for a public airing of the proposal.

24. Hasbrook interview.

5

Public Discussion Stage

The overwhelming Republican victory in the general election of November 5, 1968, caused a dramatic change in the Unigov discussions. Mayor Lugar underscored the election's importance on the debate's outcome when asked whether the Unigov effort would have been dropped had the Democrats won in 1968. His immediate response was yes, but then he added: "I shouldn't say that so quickly. I don't know . . . but I suspect we would have had to move in a different way entirely. As it was, we did use, very forcefully . . . the fact that the Republicans had won these offices."[1] While the question was academic, the answer strongly suggests the partisan nature of the proposal, which in turn made everything hinge on the election's outcome. A Democratic win would have entailed a major change of strategy, probably meaning the end of any plans for a countywide form of government.

With the Republicans now in control at every step of the legal decisionmaking process—from mayor and council to governor—Unigov's proponents were assured at least favorable hearings by the legal decisionmakers. To take advantage of their position, however, it was imperative that they seek broader public support. Accordingly, the earlier tactic of quietly marshaling the support of key influentials changed to an all-out appeal for public support, giving the debate an entirely new dimension. Timing and quick action were also essential because the newly elected state officeholders would assume their duties in January 1969, a short two months away. The General Assembly would then have only a fast 61-day regular session before another election, and the plans for Unigov legislation had to be completed in a very short time.[2]

Some Early Disclosures

As noted earlier, part of the policy committee's previous strategy had been to keep its Unigov plans under wraps until a propitious time

1. Richard G. Lugar, interview with James Owen, Indianapolis, February 2, 1972.
2. The General Assembly did not have regular annual sessions until passage of a state constitutional amendment in 1970.

for an announcement. In order to limit the length of the public debate and to keep it out of the November election campaign, the release was planned for after November 5, 1968. But this major release was preceded by three earlier kinds of public disclosure in October. While these disclosures did not open the public debate prematurely, they had other important effects on the Unigov debate that needed to be considered.

At least one important state Senate candidate included the Unigov concept in his speeches, although Unigov was not an issue in the fall campaign. "In the fall, at all the meetings, I talked about this. I didn't call it Unigov. I called it combined government or something like that. I was probably the only one that really did it."[3] This kind of low-key statement was important in that it refuted the contention that none of the assemblymen had run on the merger idea. It was also significant that Senator Borst had assumed this responsibility. As head of the Marion County delegation to the General Assembly and sponsor of the Unigov bill in the Senate, Borst was a most visible exponent of Unigov, and people could recall his early statements on it.

The metropolitan government plan also got fleeting preelection attention in the press when a reporter for the *Indianapolis News* uncovered the story. On October 15, Hugh Rutledge wrote an article that outlined Mayor Lugar's plans to present a metro bill to the 1969 General Assembly.[4] This was the first news story on Unigov, but it failed to arouse enough public interest to stimulate follow-up articles, and Unigov was allowed to remain a virtually unnoticed issue for three more weeks. Instead of hurting Unigov's chances by upsetting its timetable, Rutledge's early disclosure actually helped its proponents. Unigov's most important boost came from the *News* publisher, who included a boxed-in statement with the October 15 article, affirming the newspaper's support for the concept of metropolitan government.

THE NEWS PROPOSES
METROPOLITAN GOVERNMENT FOR ALL OF
MARION COUNTY, HEADED BY AN ELECTED
COUNTYWIDE LEGISLATIVE BODY. ABOLISH
THE BOARD OF COUNTY COMMISSIONERS AND
HIRE A COUNTY MANAGER.[5]

This supporting statement became an important point of discussion later when the *News* began to editorialize *against* Unigov and the mayor sought its support.

3. Lawrence M. Borst, interview with James Owen, Indianapolis, May 30, 1972.
4. "City, County Metro Plan Prepared for Assembly," *Indianapolis News*, October 15, 1968, p. 1.
5. Ibid.

The Rutledge article also referred to a statement by Mayor Lugar to the effect that "if such a measure fails in the next General Assembly . . . his administration will push an 'aggressive annexation campaign.' "[6] This lightly veiled threat, which may be related to Nashville's successful consolidation referendum after an aggressive annexation campaign in 1962,[7] was repeated throughout the Unigov debate and may have prompted some people to support Unigov. Because Unigov passed and the annexation threat was never tested, it is hard to tell if it had a strong influence.

The third early disclosure of the metro plan was even more restricted in scope than the first two and also failed to stimulate a public debate, but it played an important part in later developments. In October the Indianapolis Chamber of Commerce conducted a letter poll of its 4,800 members to determine what issues the membership would be most concerned about in the 1969 legislature. Seventy-six percent of the approximately 500 returns expressed strong support for the metro concept, and another 13 percent indicated casual support for the idea, totaling an overwhelming 89 percent (see Table 4).[8]

This was a major point in the chamber's activities in supporting Unigov. Up to this point, Carl Dortch's support for Unigov had to be guarded, as it was based on his personal views and on earlier chamber statements on similar proposals. With evidence of strong membership support, however, the chamber's support could be stated more emphatically as expressing the wishes of the chamber membership. It thus could have a greater bearing on the outcome.

The Mayor's Task Force

The first move to a public debate of Unigov began on schedule, three days after the Republican Party's victory in the general election of 1968, when Mayor Lugar announced that Thomas Hasbrook and Beurt SerVaas would cochair a yet-to-be-named task force to study governmental organization. The Mayor's Task Force on Improved Governmental Structure for Indianapolis and Marion County first met on November 27, its composition emphasizing Mayor Lugar's heavy reliance on the business community for support of his proposal.

The task force consisted of 42 members, appointed in two groups.

6. Ibid.

7. David A. Booth, *Metropolitics: The Nashville Consolidation* (Lansing: Institute for Community Development and Services, Michigan State University, 1963), pp. 85–87.

8. *Indianapolis Chamber of Commerce Issue Survey, 1969 Indiana General Assembly*, from the files of Donald L. Robinson, former director, Governmental Affairs Division, Indianapolis Chamber of Commerce.

Table 4– *Chamber Poll on Legislative Issues (percentages)*

Governmental Reorganization	Strong Support	Casual Support	Opposed to Issue	No Interest
Metropolitan government for Indianapolis–Marion County (excluding schools)	76	13	9	2
Convention for new state constitution	36	31	20	13
Removal of issuance of auto license plates and drivers' licenses from political control and patronage system	89	7	3	1

Source: *Indianapolis Chamber of Commerce Issue Survey, 1969 Indiana General Assembly,* from the files of Donald L. Robinson, former director, Governmental Affairs Division, Indianapolis Chamber of Commerce.

The first group of 29 appointees was a blue-ribbon assemblage of influential business and civic leaders, comprising the main body of the task force (see Appendix 1). The second group—inactive at this stage—consisted of the 23 members of the all-Republican Marion County delegation to the General Assembly, who served as ex officio members.

The first group of 29 appointees reflected Mayor Lugar's concern with business-community support, largely to the exclusion of other groups. Twenty-three of the appointees came directly from the business sector, representing the area's largest manufacturers, banks, news media, law firms, utilities, and real estate agencies. These have customarily been sources of support for metropolitan government reform efforts in other cities.[9] Three of the remaining seven appointees also had business ties. The three government officeholders on the task force—Hasbrook, SerVaas, and William G. Schneider (county commissioner)—were part-time government employees with full-time business interests. The newspaper and broadcast media, numbering eight of the 29 original appointees, comprised the largest single group represented.

Although business-community involvement was the primary objective of the task force appointments, the scope of the membership was broadened a little by the addition of the three nonbusiness appointees. These included a Presbyterian minister—who later was Lugar's successor as mayor—a labor representative from a carpenters' apprenticeship program, and the only female appointee, from the League of Women Voters. The scope of the membership had also been broadened by including three black businessmen among the business appointees. Geo-

9. Thomas R. Dye, *Politics in States and Communities* (Englewood Cliffs, N.J.: Prentice-Hall, 1968), pp. 252–254.

graphical representation was evenly balanced between the city and the suburbs. While nearly all of the appointees had Indianapolis business addresses, half of them resided outside the city limits.

Mayor Lugar's reliance on business-community support for Unigov went beyond the obvious consideration that the Indianapolis business community generally supported metropolitan government plans. It was with the business community that he had his greatest influence. He was a businessman himself and had involved the business community in many of his projects. Moreover, as a Republican, the mayor could expect a large measure of political support from this group—an essential factor in view of the partisan nature of the proposal. In fact, few known Democrats were appointed to the task force. Those who were, for example, realtor William Brennan, had other known interests that prompted them to favor Unigov. With this alignment of potential supporters Mayor Lugar could be assured of a friendly reception for Unigov and expeditious task force consideration and action on the proposal.

Role of the Progress Committee

Although largely absent from task force membership, some Democrats did have a further voice in the Unigov debate through their membership on the Greater Indianapolis Progress Committee. The preceding chapter noted that the progress committee had been largely bypassed in the initial planning for Unigov. Once those plans had been formulated, however, and the public debate opened, the progress committee was involved in significant ways—though it did not predominate. Its volunteer members represented the community's highest level of business and civic leadership. Moreover, the progress committee had sponsored a series of successful community projects, capped by a multimillion dollar convention center, making it an accepted and respected vehicle for community improvement. It was also significant that the progress committee had been founded by Mayor Barton, Mayor Lugar's Democratic predecessor, and the successor to Frank McKinney as its chair was Jack E. Reich, a Democrat and prominent businessman. This helped balance the Republican management of Unigov's early development. Thus, when Mayor Lugar took office, he was able to convince the progress committee of Unigov's merits, and he brought a certain additional level of prestige and legitimacy to his proposal, which in the absence of a referendum proved of great importance.

Task Force Meetings

The mayor's task force held its initial November 27 meeting in Mayor Lugar's conference room. Hasbrook and SerVaas, chairs of the City Council and the County Council, respectively, served as cochairs.

The mayor and the two cochairs made opening statements, followed by a wide-ranging discussion of governmental problems and possible actions.[10] Most of those present—perhaps all—knew that the mayor and others had been discussing the possible reorganization for some time and that several attorneys had been working on its technical aspects.

The spirit of the discussion indicated that the time seemed ripe for a substantial governmental reorganization, although the possibility of reservations and objections from some quarters was recognized. A few spokesmen from the suburbs suggested that some of their areas might be reluctant. A black journalist, Marcus Stewart, Jr., of the *Recorder* indicated the need to carefully consider adequate representation for the black minority, and Mayor Lugar and his associates agreed that this was an important consideration.

Some argued that school district consolidation should be included in the program, while others, who had witnessed the school consolidation movement in the 1960s and participated in earlier Unigov discussions, counseled strongly for caution and restraint in dealing with the schools. Some sentiment was expressed favoring a city manager. The mayor indicated his willingness to consider this but also noted that he personally preferred a strong political executive with a professional administrator—he mentioned Walls as an example—serving as a managerial subordinate. In short, while several reservations were expressed and debated, clearly there was substantial sentiment for drastic change. The first meeting closed with general agreement on the desirability for quick action in view of the pending legislative session and the need for good technical work, which the mayor and the cochairs indicated was already underway. After this first meeting the task force met again (on December 13 and December 19) for more substantive discussion, and its report was issued after the meeting of December 19.

In his letter inviting prospective members to join his task force, Mayor Lugar charged them with three specific assignments (see Appendix 2):

1. To direct the preparation of legislation for presentation to the 1969 Indiana General Assembly by a committee of lawyers who will prepare the actual bill.
2. To work with the members of the General Assembly and the public in promoting this legislative program.
3. To give guidance to the Mayor and other public officials in establishing the governmental structure following a successful legislative effort.[11]

10. This meeting's discussion was recorded and transcribed and is on file in the mayor's office.

11. Richard G. Lugar, mayor, letter to task force members, November 6, 1968, from the files of the Greater Indianapolis Progress Committee.

Despite this broad charge, several factors—including the short time available for action—narrowed the range of task force activities and limited it largely to assignments 1 and 2. Assignment 3—guidance in setting up Unigov—was not carried out because the task force stopped meeting long before the Unigov bill was passed. The establishment of the newly formed government was thus left to Mayor Lugar and other public officials.

The task force's role in assignment 1—preparing the legislation— was its most important function. Although the major work of directing the preparation of a legislative bill was assumed by others, the task force made important contributions. Its review and approval of the Unigov concept provided the drafters with important guidelines within which to work, thus achieving a more or less public resolution of some vital issues that would otherwise have been left to the select drafting group. For example, the task force approved a single county-wide executive and council and the exclusion of courts, schools, and three municipalities from the merger. In addition, the task force made several specific suggestions that were incorporated in the bill. After its longest debate, the task force voted to enlarge the membership of the proposed council from 15 to 25. It also rejected a referendum proposal with only one dissenting vote.

Judge Niblack's County Task Force

Two other suggestions the task force presented to the attorneys did not originate with it but came from a task force of uneasy county officeholders led by Marion County circuit court judge John L. Niblack. Judge Niblack's county task force was not entirely against Unigov, having been formed to obtain a voice in Unigov's preparation rather than to defeat it. Nevertheless, Niblack's group disturbed the mayor's task force's proceedings and temporarily stymied Lugar's effort to marshal public support for Unigov. This county task force comprised a group of 13 Republican county officeholders, most of whom had not been consulted in the drafting of Unigov and who were thus afraid that their interests would not be considered in the new plan (see Appendix 3). As Judge Niblack said at the time: "The county group was formed because we felt like orphans."[12] In addition to the officeholders' fears, there was also something of an intraparty struggle between the GOP's old guard, led by Judge Niblack, who had been county judge for nearly 20 years, and the group of Republican new-comers, especially Mayor Lugar and party chair Bulen, who were making all the plans.

After private consultations with Mayor Lugar and Beurt Ser-

12. "Judge Niblack Heads County Task Forces," *Indianapolis Star,* December 5, 1968, p. 41.

Vaas,[13] the county group's main fears were allayed, whereupon their suggested changes focused on two points. These were noted in a six-page memorandum that largely favored Unigov, prepared by Judge Niblack and presented to the mayor's task force at its final meeting. One request was that the election of the new mayor and council not be held in 1970 but be delayed until a later date. This would permit a longer transition period and did not disturb the term of incumbent officeholders until new elections could be held. This request was approved by the task force, and the election was slated for 1971.[14]

The other request related to Unigov's administrative organization. Originally it was contemplated that the administration would be a hierarchical arrangement with straight lines of authority from the mayor to the department heads. But Judge Niblack held out for council-appointed "watchdog" review boards to oversee each department. This request was also approved and incorporated in the draft proposal, but the review boards were not given substantial powers. To sum up, both changes were significant but not basic. In any event the results were announced on December 19, the same day the mayor's task force announced its final approval of the Unigov concept and disbanded, leaving the actual bill drafting to others.

Task Force Accomplishments

The mayor's task force made important contributions when it approved the Unigov concept and allayed the fears of Judge Niblack and county officials. Moreover, the sense of commitment task force members gained by their having been involved gave them credibility and effectiveness in performing assignment 2, to promote Unigov legislation among the General Assembly and the public. Undoubtedly, developing public support was the task force's major achievement, as well as the primary reason it was formed.

The idea that developing public support should be the primary function of the mayor's task force originated with the policy committee several months earlier. At that time the committee delegated areas of responsibility among its members, Senator Borst being asked to sponsor the project in the General Assembly. One of his conditions for accepting the assignment was that the metropolitan government proposal come from a citizens' group. Borst, an experienced legislator, was doubtless mindful of the unfavorable reception the public and the General Assembly gave the privately prepared "power grab" bills in 1965. To avoid this fate, the public initiative for Unigov should not

13. As a member of the Marion County Council, SerVaas was also a member of the county task force.

14. "Plan Ties 'Watchdogs' to Metro Government," *Indianapolis Star*, December 20, 1968, p. 1.

come from the policy committee, whose restricted, partisan member-ship made it vulnerable to the "power grab" label. The initiative must at least appear to come from a more broadly based group, that is, the task force and the community leadership it represented.

One task force member, Eldon Campbell, general manager of tele-vision station WFBM, expressed this responsibility quite accurately: "I think the single solitary purpose was to get the visible leadership of this community absolutely accurately informed, so that no one in a leadership position was wandering around the streets making state-ments which were inaccurate."[15] Although the task force did not ex-plicitly and officially organize a public campaign to promote Unigov, the fact of their support was given broad currency throughout the campaign and was especially effective in the General Assembly. Fur-thermore, several task force members added prestige to the debate when they spoke to public groups as members of the speakers' bureau, formed later.

Perhaps the task force members were most effective in promoting Unigov simply because of who they were. Their blue-ribbon status meant that all were active with other civic committees, as well as professional and social groups in which many of them held offices. This no doubt afforded them many opportunities to answer questions or defend Unigov in a variety of public forums, and they were very influential in the public discussion that preceded legislative action.

Mayor Lugar's original task force instructions omitted any sug-gestion that it had the option of turning down the whole plan. Instead, its principal contribution was to promote the program with the public and the General Assembly. This was Lugar's and the policy commit-tee's primary objective, reflected in the way the task force's member-ship and organization were geared. The overriding effect was that the Unigov principals successfully got the approval of an important seg-ment of the community while retaining effective control over the Uni-gov effort.

The Detailed Drafting

Most of the background research and the general outlines and format of the Unigov proposal had been done by the Unigov princi-pals in the summer and fall of 1968, but the actual drafting of the complex and lengthy bill took place in a 33-day period between De-cember 19, when the mayor's task force completed its work, and Janu-ary 21, 1969, when the bill was introduced to the General Assembly. During this period the lawyers' work was most intense.

15. Eldon Campbell, interview with James Owen, Indianapolis, June 8, 1972.

When given the go-ahead to draft the Unigov bill, attorney Lewis Bose faced a very demanding schedule. Senator Borst had originally asked that drafting be completed on January 10 so that the bill could be introduced very early in the session. Although this target date was missed, the drafters worked very hard. At least one of the lawyers worked every day except three of the 33 days, which included the Christmas—New Year holidays.

The lawyers were able to complete the long bill in a month, in part because Mayor Lugar had included them in the early stages of the planning, and they had already done constitutional and statutory research on the subject as far back as the previous spring. After this preliminary legal work was completed in late summer 1968, Bose and Charles Whistler continued to meet with the Unigov planners, especially during the task force stage. Thus, when they and the other lawyers met again in mid-December, they could proceed quickly with the necessary bill writing.

The lawyers' work group essentially had the technical drafting job of preparing Senate Bill 199 (SB 199), the Unigov bill, whose major policy features, including many practical compromises, had been decided during the preceding 12 months. Accordingly, the lawyers' primary concern was to express these features in an organized fashion and embody them in a legal format. This task was neither easy nor unimportant: proposals for governmental change can flounder for lack of adequate draftsmanship.

As chair of the lawyers' work group, Bose took the major responsibility for drafting the bill. "The lawyers all suggested that, in as far as my strength would hold out, I should write it, and assign parts to them."[16] This procedure was followed, with Bose preparing an outline of the bill and then concentrating his efforts on the first five sections, which dealt with definitions, powers, organization, and procedures of the projected new administration.

Bose and Whistler kept the group task-oriented, allocating assignments to those specialists who had the most knowledge and interest in each subject area, thus capitalizing on the members' special expertise. This procedure was particularly effective when sections on the individual departments were written. For example, the section on the Department of Transportation was written by Robert Davies, who had worked on the countywide thoroughfare bill in previous sessions of the General Assembly. Wayne Ponader, who in the previous session had worked on a metropolitan police bill, wrote the section on the Department of Public Safety. Another lawyer, Mark Murphy, a member of the Board of Park Commissioners, wrote the section on parks and recreation. Attorney Robert Elrod, recently chair of a local govern-

16. Lewis C. Bose, interview with James Owen, Indianapolis, June 14, 1972.

ment study commission in Marion County, helped in a variety of areas.

Although Bose was in direct charge of the research and drafting, Whistler, who had also been a member of the policy committee, was a chief participant in crucial portions of the drafting process. He was particularly effective in negotiating prelegislative compromises that were included in SB 199, making the lawyers' task something more than a purely technical exercise. Most of these compromises were made necessary by a small but influential conservative element in the community and were also influenced by the Unigov proposal's reception by the press.

The Media: Placating the *News* and the *Star*

The media generally supported Unigov, giving it good news coverage and in many cases editorializing for it. The television stations came out most strongly in support of Unigov, giving it broad news coverage and offering special telecasts of debates and panel discussions. One station, WTTV (Channel 4), prepared a half-hour videotape for statewide distribution. The other three television stations, WISH, WFBM, and WLWI, supported Unigov with editorials (see Appendix 4). All the radio stations also gave favorable coverage, with the exception of one, WTLE-AM, whose broadcasts are directed to the black community.

No major opposition to Unigov came from the suburban newspapers, which were divided on the matter, or from the *Recorder* and the *Herald*, two black community newspapers. Instead, the principal press opposition came from the *Indianapolis News* and the *Indianapolis Star*. Both of these dailies were owned by Eugene C. Pulliam, shared the same conservative editorial policy, were Marion County's only daily papers, had a large state circulation, and were generally known to influence many elected officials, including members of the General Assembly.

During the first month of the public debate on Unigov, when the task force was deliberating, these papers did not give extensive coverage and took no editorial position. One reason for the light coverage was the fact that previous task forces had not produced substantial results, and there was no assurance that the current one would be any more newsworthy. In fact, the *Star* did not even report the second meeting of the task force, on December 13.

Both papers had traditionally supported the metropolitan government concept, and their opposition to Unigov focused on specific issues—especially the proposed increase in the mayor's executive powers. The criticism appeared largely in the editorial pages of the

News, the afternoon paper.[17] The News attack was directed by its editor, M. Stanton Evans, who opened the fray on December 23 by likening Unigov to the 1965 "power grab": "When the Democrats came up with their own variant of the 'strong mayor' approach in 1965, the News opposed it as a 'power grab.' We see no reason to favor this approach now that a different version of it is being advanced by Republicans. Rationalizing City-County relations and extending proper services to make government more fully responsible is one thing. Eliminating checks and balances and putting all power in a supermayor is quite the opposite."[18]

On December 31, specific charges against Unigov appeared in another News editorial attack entitled "It's a Grab." This article made it clear that the mayor's proposed control of various appointments raised the ire of the News: "To take a specific example, consider the changes which would occur in one of the most vital agencies of local government—the Metropolitan Plan Commission. This powerful agency at present has nine voting members, four chosen by the mayor, two by the county council, two by the county commissioners, and one by the city council. Under the Lugar plan this agency would be superseded by a Metropolitan Development Commission—all nine members of which would be appointed by the mayor."[19]

Soon after the "It's a Grab" editorial appeared, Mayor Lugar arranged a meeting with representatives of the News and Star to discuss their antagonism toward Unigov. Representing both papers were the publisher's son, Eugene S. Pulliam, assistant publisher of the Star, and M. Stanton Evans. Accompanying the mayor were Carl Dortch, Beurt SerVaas, John Walls, and Charles Whistler. The mayor pointed out that Unigov was something that over a period of time the News and Star had supported in concept, and thus he was concerned over the present opposition. The newspapermen responded that the proposed appointive powers of the mayor would make him too powerful, which was what Mayor Lugar had expected. The outcome of the meeting was an agreement that the powers of the new mayor would be limited in crucial areas and that the newspapers would support Unigov during the coming legislative session.

The results of this meeting were immediately reported to the lawyers' work group, whereupon two important sections were added to SB 199, greatly curtailing the mayor's powers. Section 304 was added, restricting the mayor's appointment of directors, deputy mayors, and administrators to one-year terms and requiring approval by a

17. During the prelegislative debate the Star neither attacked Unigov editorially nor supported it. But it did publish several readers' letters to the editor opposing Unigov.

18. "Too Much Power," Indianapolis News, December 23, 1968, p. 6.

19. "It's a Grab," Indianapolis News, December 31, 1968, p. 6.

majority vote of the City-County Council. Section 808 narrowed the mayor's control over the proposed Metropolitan Development Commission by dividing the appointments to its nine-member board three ways: four to be made by the mayor, three by the City Council, and two by the county commissioners.

The newspapers responded to these changes with support for Unigov and favorable editorials. The *News* published an editorial headed "In the Balance" almost immediately after the changes: "The recent move by Mayor Lugar's task force on metropolitan government to get more balance into the plan for countywide voting here is an encouraging one. The task force has taken a step in the right direction and we trust that other such intiatives will be forthcoming."[20] The *Star* waited until the bill had been introduced to print its editorial, "Consolidation Will Come": "There is little doubt consolidation will take place. In time even its now most zealous enemies are likely to demand it to rationalize the government of what in many ways is now a single community split only by outdated boundary lines whose irrelevance is plain to anyone who travels along them."[21]

A Speakers' Bureau

In addition to Unigov's public airing through the task force and the media, there was a further attempt to reach the citizenry through a speakers' bureau. This was not a highly mobilized and intense public relations effort but rather a loosely organized, low-key attempt to explain Unigov to the people. Robert Beckmann, Mayor Lugar's public information director at the time, described its formation: "The speakers' bureau was not a highly institutionalized thing. We didn't sit down and determine that we needed a speakers' bureau and then drum up business for it. We didn't need to, because the speakers' bureau was the result of a large number of phone calls into the mayor's office."[22]

The speakers' bureau began functioning shortly after Thanksgiving when approximately 25 volunteers were briefed on Unigov's progress to date. These speakers were chosen from various groups, such as a toastmaster's club, the League of Women Voters, and the Jaycees, where there was already a level of civic mindedness and a willingness and ability to address public gatherings. It was also important that volunteers already have a fundamental knowledge of the processes of state and local government because with the bill's being amended

20. "In the Balance," *Indianapolis News*, January 14, 1969, p. 4.

21. "Consolidation Will Come," *Indianapolis Star*, January 23, 1969, p. 6.

22. Robert D. Beckmann, Jr., interview with James Owen, Indianapolis, June 8, 1972.

frequently, it would have been an exhaustive job to keep them informed of the changes.

In any event, the 25 volunteers were usually given assignments expected to be the least controversial, the more difficult ones being handled by selected city officials who were in a position to know of bill changes immediately as they occurred. The more important speaking engagements were reserved for some of Unigov's principals, such as Lawrence Borst, Lewis Bose, John Walls, Charles Whistler, and Mayor Lugar. It was advantageous to have these men out on the hustings, as they were in the best position to dispel misinformation and allay fears that could otherwise prove damaging. The reverse flow of information received was also valuable in helping them understand the political pressures on the legislators, and it gave them useful guidance for negotiating further compromises as necessary.

Arranging the speaking engagements was the responsibility of John Walls and Robert Beckmann. Calls coming into the mayor's office requesting speakers were channeled to Walls, who decided who could best fill each assignment, and then he asked Beckmann to follow up with the necessary arrangements. This was no mean feat, as the mayor's office was regularly receiving about 200 requests for speakers each month, and the Unigov debate raised the figure substantially. It was estimated that the speakers reached approximately 75,000 people in many kinds of meetings, including church groups, professional organizations, civic clubs, PTAs, and social clubs. Several thousand pamphlets and a smaller number of "I Love Unigov" bumper stickers were also available for public distribution.

In spite of the effort to publicize Unigov through the task force, the media, and the speakers' bureau, there was still some feeling that more needed to be done. Certainly, a greater effort to reach the public could have been made. Advertising space could have been purchased in the media, instead of relying on public service time and editorials. A series of neighborhood meetings could have been held, and door-to-door campaigns waged. Much more money could have been spent on printing and mailings. These things were not done largely because of time and budgetary limitations. Avoiding public debate until after the November election was a political decision, but after the election, time and money were the chief constraints on the campaign for Unigov.

The Legislative Delegation

During November and December 1968, between the election and the opening of the General Assembly, the Marion County delegation (see Appendix 5) met several times to discuss important issues in

I L♥VE UNIGOV

A bumper sticker used to promote Unigov during the legislative debate.

prospect for the coming session. At least two of these meetings were held in Mayor Lugar's conference room, Unigov being the central topic. The meetings were unstructured, had no agenda, and no one presided, even though Senator Lawrence Borst and Representative "Ned" Lamkin, delegation leaders in the Senate and House, were present.[23]

The discussions were open. Senator Borst opened the first meeting by outlining the need for governmental reorganization in Marion County, emphasizing the importance of a unified front among Marion County legislators when Unigov was presented to the General Assembly. This was the theme throughout the meetings. Portions of the draft bill were discussed at length, but only a few minor amendments made. The discussions also gave the delegation useful briefings on the most recent developments in the drafting and prepared them to answer queries from their legislative colleagues.

The only strong objection to the Unigov plan expressed in the meetings came from Senator Joan Gubbins, who wanted the bill submitted to a voters' referendum for approval. Senator Gubbins's appeal was countered by several others, whose main argument was that the change in local government proposed in the Unigov bill was not revolutionary and clearly fell within the General Assembly's jurisdiction. Moreover, it was noted that a referendum would be expensive and time-consuming. Senator Daniel Burton, an early opponent of Unigov who had swung around in favor, seemed to express the opinion of many by commenting that the people elect their representatives to do the legislative work, and if they are dissatisfied, they can vote the representative out.[24]

Several of the legislators present spoke in favor of Unigov, as did nonlegislators Thomas Hasbrook, Richard Lugar, Beurt SerVaas, and Charles Whistler. Keith Bulen, Republican Party county chair, did not attend, but the presence and position of the other Republican Party mainstays left no doubt that Unigov had the party organization's support.

23. Minutes of meetings with the Marion County legislators, December 27, 1968, and January 2, 1969, from the files of the Greater Indianapolis Progress Committee.
24. Ibid.

In spite of a low attendance—only 12 of the Marion County delegation's 23 members turned out for the first meeting—the session, along with the other political preparation, proved successful in helping get a solid majority of the delegation to favor Unigov. When the General Assembly convened, only 3 members of the county's entire delegation were considered doubtful supporters.

Drafting Decisions

The main elements of the Unigov proposed reorganization were:

1. Consolidation of the executive and legislative functions of the city and county.
2. Election of a single, strong chief executive (though not quite as strong as was originally planned).
3. Election of a single strong council.
4. A substantial degree of administrative integration, with related functions grouped into major departments.
5. Provision of different taxing and service districts for particular functions or groups of functions.
6. Exemption of the school districts.
7. Preservation of the suburban municipalities.

Despite the imagery of the term *Unigov*, the proposal fell far short of complete unitary consolidation. In part, this was due to doubts about the desirability of thorough consolidation, but also many of the exceptions represented concessions made pragmatically, and somewhat reluctantly, to real or anticipated opponents of more sweeping change. Other exceptions were made to avoid changes that would have required a constitutional amendment.[25]

The measure's most important departures from full city-county consolidation deserve further comment:

1. While some key organs of the county and city were consolidated, Marion County and the City of Indianapolis continued as separate legal entites. This was constitutionally necessary, as the state constitution has many provisions dealing with counties—and a few with cities—making it difficult to avoid constitutional difficulties if a complete consolidation had been attempted using only statute law.
2. Although many Unigov proponents probably favored school

25. Amending the Indiana constitution is difficult and time-consuming: an amendment must be approved by two successive legislatures, in exactly the same form, and then approved by the voters in a statewide referendum. The proponents of this measure did not want to embark upon such an effort.

district consolidation in principle, the policy committee decided very early that any attempt to change the school system would endanger the proposal. Consequently, the 11 independent school systems were untouched.

While the reorganization measure was being considered (and subsequently), the central-city school system was involved in heated controversy and litigation over racial segregation practices. This had a major impact on Unigov's implementation, a point that will be considered more thoroughly in Chapter 8.

3. The elective county offices were hardly touched. Under Unigov, eight elective offices were continued: the sheriff, prosecutor, auditor, treasurer, recorder, coroner, surveyor (all prescribed in the constitution), and the assessor (provided by statute law). Their duties remained essentially the same, and they were affected only to the extent that budgetary control and general legislative control (subject, of course, to the general state statute) are now vested in the City-County Council. By retaining these county offices, the bill avoided constitutional entanglements and in considerable degree escaped the opposition that the elected officials and their adherents would probably have mounted.

The posts of the three county commissioners—who constituted the closest approach to a general county executive and legislative organ—were handled in an ingenious fashion. While the positions were not abolished, they are no longer separately elective. Instead, the county auditor, treasurer, and assessor serve as county commissioners, exercising certain minor residual functions not transferred to the mayor or City-County Council. Two of the three incumbent county commissioners at the time opposed the bill, but they lacked sufficient influence to block it.

4. The nine townships were untouched, thus avoiding or at least muting opposition from the elective township trustees. The chief functions of Indiana townships are what the law calls "poor relief," that is, general assistance (as distinguished from the categorical assistance administered by the County Department of Public Welfare), and tax assessment under the supervision of the county tax assessor but operating on appropriations by the City-County Council.

5. As originally drafted, the Unigov bill provided for a department of local government coordination, under the mayor, presumably to have substantial supervisory authority over all of the county officials and agencies. Since the officials who would have been affected were greatly disturbed at

this—including Circuit Judge Niblack—the provision was dropped.

6. The largest suburban municipalities were excluded from the territorial jurisdiction and tax base of the consolidated city-county, although as part of the county they are subject to the controls and taxes enacted by the City-County Council when acting in its capacity as governing body for the entire county. Since the mayor and City-County Council act as the executive and legislature for the whole county, citizens of the excluded municipalities are permitted to vote for them, as well as for their own mayors and city councilors or town board members.

The bill excluded all cities except Indianapolis, as well as towns of over 5,000 population. When Unigov was being drafted, it was believed the exclusions would affect only the cities of Beech Grove and Lawrence and the town of Speedway, each with about 15,000 population and each having a good deal of civic pride in its autonomy and municipal service levels. Between Unigov's enactment and the effective date of its statute, the town of Southport (previously with only about 1,000 people) annexed some additional territory and population, changing its status to that of a city and making it one of the excluded municipalities.

In any event, officials in most of the small cities and towns opposed Unigov, regardless of whether or not they were to be excluded. But it was believed that excluding the larger ones would help mollify the potentially most effective suburban opposition.

7. Most of the functional agencies that already had a degree of independence and autonomy were allowed to retain some of their independence. The Airport Authority, the Health and Hospital Corporation, the County Board of Public Welfare, the County Home, the City-County Building Authority, and the Capital Improvement Board were preserved. Although one of Beatty's 1965 proposals would have given the mayor some power over the County Welfare Board, this was not seriously considered in the Unigov effort. The health program was originally to have become one of the consolidated city's major departments, but the authors of Unigov backed off from this proposal when they detected substantial opposition. The Unigov statute provided that the budget of the Health and Hospital Corporation is to be approved by the City-County Council. The same is true of the Airport Authority, over which the mayor had substantial appointing power under existing law. To sum up, all of the agencies are some-

what more independent than the regular executive departments of the city-county government, although only public
welfare retains its complete separation and autonomy.

8. Existing territorial arrangements respecting individual local
governmental services were changed very little by Unigov.
As noted earlier, many functions had already been extended on a countywide basis. Others—for example, sanitation, trash collection, libraries, and public housing—were
available to an area larger than the city but smaller than the
entire county. The bill provided for special taxing and service districts to support individual functions but made no
significant changes in preexisting boundaries.

   Fire and police services, the only major services still
confined within the limits of the city, were to be administered and supported in special service districts. Under the
new act, enlargement of the police service district was
made somewhat easier than had been annexation to the old
city. Extension of the fire service district boundaries, on the
other hand, was made significantly more difficult under the
new act than annexation had been in the past. Thus, annexation to the fire service district now requires the request
of the majority of the owners of real property or the owners
of real property amounting to 75 percent of the assessed
valuation in the area affected. Politically, this meant that
the bill's sponsors feared the potential opposition of volunteer fire departments—which serve the suburban areas—
more than they did the potential opposition of the sheriff,
who provided police service to the unincorporated area.

9. No changes were attempted in the judicial system.

10. Apparently no real thought was given to extending any local government functions beyond Marion County even
though the official standard metropolitan statistical area includes seven other counties, and arrangements for mutual
consultation on some matters already existed. In fact, the
Unigov framers, knowing that Indiana law permits cities to
annex adjacent land in another county, expressly protected
adjacent counties against annexation by the newly consolidated city-county by making annexation impossible. This
was done to allay the fears of the adjacent counties.

These general provisions were incorporated in the original draft
bill, but the process of negotiation and compromise continued throughout the legislative session, with a decided effect on certain articles.
These changes are considered in the following chapter, along with
discussion of the legislative process.

6

The Legislative Stage

Legislative consideration of Unigov began when the ninety-sixth session of the Indiana General Assembly opened on January 9, 1969, although the Unigov bill was not actually introduced until January 21. The legislative phase ended on March 13, 1969, when Governor Edgar D. Whitcomb signed the Unigov bill into law. Once the General Assembly convened, all the reorganization effort focused on the legislative process. For example, Mayor Lugar continued his exhaustive schedule as the chief spokesman for Unigov, but with important changes. Moving the Unigov debate into the legislature shifted much of the leadership initiative away from the mayor and to the bill's legislative sponsors. The mayor's efforts to organize support in Marion County were now extended to a statewide campaign to persuade General Assembly members to support Unigov. While the mayor and his associates continued to play an important part in the Unigov debate, they recognized the autonomous nature of the General Assembly and left day-to-day management of the bill to the legislators.

Leadership, Organization, and Strategy

Senator Lawrence Borst and Representative "Ned" Lamkin, delegation leaders in the Senate and House, respectively, provided the legislative leadership for the proposal. They had been a part of the Unigov discussion from the beginning and were personally committed to the idea. The practice of keeping the entire Marion County legislative delegation informed as developments occurred also facilitated passage of the leadership reins to the legislators.

The Unigov bill was introduced 12 days after the General Assembly convened. In the interim, the Marion County delegation assisted by organizing the legislative leadership and informing legislators from other parts of the state about their plans for a metropolitan form of government. In the 1969 General Assembly the Republican Party had a 73 to 27 edge in the House and a 35 to 15 advantage in the Senate, giving it a large working majority. The 15 house members and 8 senators from Marion County were all Republicans. Physician Otis R.

Bowen (Bremen), who had been a candidate for the Republican Party's nomination for governor in 1968 and was to be the nominee in 1972, was reelected speaker of the House. Allen E. Bloom (Fort Wayne) was elected president pro tem of the Senate, sharing that body's leadership with Lieutenant Governor Richard E. Folz (Evansville), who served as president of the Senate. In the House, Speaker Bowen named Representative Lamkin as chair of a 15-member Affairs of Marion County Committee, comprising 11 Republicans and 4 Democrats, with seven members from Marion County. In the Senate, Lieutenant Governor Folz appointed Senator Borst chair of its Committee on Affairs of Marion County, along with the 7 other members of the Marion County delegation. Senator Albert J. LaMere (Munster) was the lone Democratic member.

During the early stages, the Marion County delegation made a concerted effort to establish contacts with their fellow legislators to apprise them of the Unigov proposal and what they thought about it. This was done primarily through the informal exchanges of getting acquainted and reacquainted that accompany each new session. But delegation members were also asked to maintain ties with specified legislators to ensure that no one was missed. The plan was not to solicit votes in the early stages but merely to keep channels of communication open. They asked for votes later.

According to Senator Borst, the decision as to which chamber should be the house of origin was important in Unigov's case: "Politically speaking, we felt the Senate would be far-and-away the hardest chamber to get it [Unigov] through because the conservative membership is stronger there. And we knew if we could get it through the Senate we could get it through the House."[1] Thus, the principals and sponsors of Unigov, hoping that the Senate's strong leadership and favorable committee would compensate for the heavier opposition expected in the upper house, chose to introduce their bill in the Senate.

Senate Committee Consideration

After a weekend drafting session, the attorneys completed the final version of Senate Bill 199 (SB 199), and Senator Borst introduced it on January 21, 1969. SB 199 was received and read that day and submitted to the Committee on Affairs of Marion County.

Because of opposition in the Senate, the major Unigov compromises were made in that body. After the bill was approved by the Senate, it passed the House with a large majority with no major amendments of the Senate-approved version. Accordingly, this dis-

1. Lawrence M. Borst, interview with James Owen, Indianapolis, May 30, 1972.

cussion of the legislative procedure concentrates on the Senate and on the committee and second-reading stages.

By the end of its first week's deliberations the Senate committee had identified a number of technical errors in SB 199, as well as several controversial sections that, unless amended, would probably impede the bill's progress or prevent its passage altogether. Accordingly, Senator Borst met with attorneys Bose and Whistler to make the necessary revisions. The attorneys' actions at this stage illustrate their insight into the workings of the General Assembly and reflect the professionalism that went into the bill's preparation. Instead of making the necessary changes and resubmitting a modified SB 199 to the committee, the attorneys chose to draft and submit a completely new bill. The new draft was completed early in February and was introduced on February 4 as Senate Bill 543 (SB 543). The original bill was left to die in committee and thus never reached the floor. By this procedure, a "clean" bill was presented to the General Assembly, devoid of all the deletions and additions that otherwise would have shown up in an amended version of SB 199.[2] Furthermore, the process of SB 543 was expedited when Bose got his law partner, William H. Evans, attorney for the Republican majority in the Senate, personally to present the bill for printing, thus enabling the bill to be submitted directly to the committee without the usual printing delay, the time thus saved being important in a short session.

Major Compromises

Except for the modifications noted, SB 543 was an article-by-article duplication of SB 199. On the other hand, the changes were extensive and substantial. There were five major changes in all, three of them amendments and two outright deletions. These changes make it clear that the Unigov legislation did not move uneventfully through the General Assembly on a straight partisan vote despite the large Republican majority. On the contrary, the most effective arguments against Unigov came from within Republican Party ranks.

The first two amendments were in Article III, which provided for the officers of the consolidated city and county. Under the original provisions, the first mayor and council of the merged governments were to be elected in 1970. This was amended to postpone elections until 1971. The preferences of elected officers (mostly Republican) whose terms would be shortened by the earlier election prompted this change, which had been agreed to in discussions between Mayor Lugar and county officials.

A possible legal entanglement was the dominant reason for the

2. Amended sections of a bill must appear in canceled ("strike-out") type, followed by the substituted new material, which appears in italics.

second amendment to Article III, dropping the proposed 5 at-large councilmembers from section 306 and instead having all 25 council-members elected from single-member districts. But the change also had significant political considerations. Thus, the Republicans expected to gain an electoral advantage with the extension of council elections on a countywide basis, so including 5 at-large seats had obvious partisan overtones and advantages for the Republicans. But it was believed that the one man, one vote provisions of recent US Supreme Court decisions would probably apply to Unigov elections, and this temporarily overcame partisan considerations, resulting in dropping the at-large seats. Later in the session, however, thinking on the one man, one vote matter shifted once more, and 4 at-large seats were added to the 25-member council.

Amendments and deletions affecting articles VI, XI, and XIV comprised the most far-reaching changes affecting the Unigov bill. Under the original provisions of Article VI, setting up the departments, the mayor would have gotten extensive powers to revise or create departments under his administration. Thus, under section 604 of the original bill the mayor needed only to submit his reorganization plan to the council, whereupon the plan would automatically become effective unless the council mustered a majority against it within 60 days. Requiring a council majority to vote against a mayor's plan in order to stop it, instead of requiring a majority vote for its approval, would give the mayor a decided edge.

But the new provision, section 604 of SB 543, reversed this procedure, requiring a mayor's plan to receive an affirmative vote of two-thirds of the council's members to pass. Apprehensions of a strong executive on the part of the Indiana legislators prompted the change.[3]

SB 199's Article XI would create a Department of Public Health, including the Health and Hospital Corporation (a special district government established in 1951). Officials of the Health and Hospital Corporation protested, fearing loss of the corporation's bonding power along with its autonomy. Mindful of the successful campaign of some of the same officials against a similar provision in the 1965 "power grab" bills, the attorneys deleted the entire article from SB 543. Thus, the original eight-department administration was reduced to seven.

The administration was further reduced to six departments when SB 199's Article XIV was left out of the new bill, dropping the proposed Department of Local Government Coordination, which would have given the mayor vast influence over the agencies and governments included under Unigov: "The Department of Local Government

---

3. Phillip S. Wilder, Jr., "State Government Reorganization in Indiana: Pressures and Resistance," *Indiana Academy of Social Sciences, Proceedings*, n.s. 10:13 (1965).

Coordination shall provide for liaison, coordination, and cooperation among county agencies, local government, independent agencies and the unified city to the end that duplication of services is avoided, conflicts among officials are resolved, cooperation promoted, and more efficient governmental operation achieved."[4]

Although the jurisdiction of the Department of Local Government Coordination would not have included townships, cities and towns, or independent agencies, the department might have had extensive authority over elected county officials, judges of the county and municipal courts, and all other countywide agencies that were not separate municipal corporations. Unfortunately for those who favored the arrangement, the officials potentially most affected were the same ones who had formed the county task force of Republican officeholders in December 1968. Out of respect for the political power of this group, especially Judge Niblack, the entire article was dropped.

Senate Floor Debate

A week after being submitted as SB 543, the new Unigov bill had been amended and reported from committee with a "do pass" recommendation. With two significant exceptions, the committee's amendments were technical in nature. The first significant change was the amendment of Article III to put back in a number of at-large councilmembers, reversing the earlier change (noted above) and increasing the council from 25 to 29 members, the 4 additional members to be elected countywide. Some of the political motives for this were noted earlier, but also it was considered a structurally sound idea to establish at-large seats to help give the mayor (regardless of party) a working majority in the council. Thus, it was presumed that the party winning a countywide vote for mayor in a given election would also take the at-large seats. It was further assumed that the at-large seats would help assure a ruling majority on a council whose posts were expected to be both highly contested in most elections and rather evenly split between the parties.

Another significant change was addition of a new section to Article XV, providing for transfer of territory between the consolidated city and the excluded cities. This was a reciprocal process, that is, the consolidated city and the excluded cities were each given the power to annex real estate within the other municipalities' territorial limits. But the implementation formula—requiring approval of both annexing and disannexing cities and leaving final arbitration to the circuit court—was so complex as to signify an annexation stalemate for the foreseeable future. This was, nevertheless, acceptable to the Unigov principals, as it appeased its suburbanite proponents and would also limit

4. Indiana Senate Bill 199, 1969, Art. XIV, sec. 1402, p. 153.

infringements on the consolidated city's territory. Presidents of the excluded cities also saw the amendment as safeguarding their territorial integrity against depredations by the consolidated city-county.

Second Reading

With SB 543 thus amended and reported favorably out of committee, after the required two-day waiting period Senator Borst "called down" the bill for a second reading on February 14. Action at the second reading centered on amendments from the Senate floor. This was critical as successful amendments at this stage could have drastically changed the bill, delayed it, or defeated it entirely. Five amendments were proposed and defeated in nearly straight party-line votes. Three of these motions are discussed here to illustrate the difficulty of Unigov's passage, highlighting the opposition and some of its motivation.

In many respects, the bill's greatest hazard was posed by the proposal of Senator Joan Gubbins—the only Marion County senator to vote against Unigov later when it came up for final passage. She moved to strike everything after the bill's enacting clause, substituting a study commission charged with preparing an entirely new plan for metropolitan government. The Marion County delegation thus confronted a maverick in its midst.

An unwritten rule made this most awkward. The Indiana General Assembly is like other state legislatures in having adopted certain informal "rules of the game" by custom and tradition. One such rule has been stated in general terms by Thomas Dye: "Another informal rule is the practice in many states of passing bills that would affect only one area of the state without debate or opposition when the delegation in that area unanimously supports that bill."[5] This rule was closely adhered to by the Indiana General Assembly and had special significance for the Unigov effort of the Indianapolis–Marion County delegation. As the only first-class city in the state and the largest delegation in the legislature, Indianapolis–Marion County was traditionally (though sometimes grudgingly) accorded a considerable amount of autonomy by the other delegations. Marion County also sends the largest and most highly organized delegation to the state Republican convention, giving it added power when Republicans control the legislature, as they did in 1969. Because of these considerations, SB 543 had been written to apply only to counties with cities of the first class, that is, only to Marion County, and an extensive effort was made to have a united delegation behind it. Thus, when one of their own members broke ranks to speak against Unigov, this threat-

5. Thomas R. Dye, *Politics in States and Communities* (Englewood Cliffs, N.J.: Prentice-Hall, 1968), p. 129.

ened the credibility of Unigov's sponsors among their fellow legislators. Moreover, Senator Gubbins's possible use of her conservative image to persuade other conservative senators to go against Unigov on a close vote was an obvious threat.

Senator Gubbins's motion was voted down 14 to 34 on a nearly straight party-line vote. Opposing the motion were one Democrat, Senator Robert E. Mahowald (South Bend), and 33 Republicans. In favoring the amendment, Senator Gubbins was joined by one other Republican, Senator Leo Sullivan (Peru), and 12 Democrats. One senator from each party abstained.

Though the opposition from within their delegation was irritating and potentially dangerous to Unigov, a still more serious threat came in the Democratic motion to submit SB 543 to a referendum. The referendum question had been an important issue throughout the debate and had been raised at all the earlier public meetings.

The bill's proponents defended their opposition to a referendum in several ways. They argued that referendums were not required by general law, and since the legislature clearly had the power to enact or not to enact the bill, a referendum could only be advisory. In support, they cited a recent Indiana Supreme Court decision:[6] "Subordinate divisions of the government are but parts of the state government as a whole. The state, by its legislature, may abolish, consolidate, combine, eliminate, or create new governmental corporations, or authorize such alterations to govern those who live in a given area. There is no constitutional guarantee for the continued existence of a governmental subdivision of the state. They are all creatures of the legislature."[7]

While the referendum is considered to be an important part of the democratic process in dealing with major legislative measures in many other states, this was not the case in Indiana, which was not regarded as a reform state. The initiative, the nonpartisan ballot, and the recall vote, popular at the turn of the century, had not been adopted as part of the Indiana political process, and the referendum was seldom employed. Although Hoosiers observed their neighboring states voting regularly on school tax levies and other issues, they had not employed the referendum themselves. Thus, the Unigov proponents were not bound legally or by custom to seek a referendum vote.

Unigov advocates also opposed the delay and expense a referendum would require. Obviously, they also wanted to avoid the difficulties, controversy, cost, and effort of a referendum campaign. Later, Mayor Lugar said: "To have gone the route of referendum risked polarization of the worst sort along racial or sociological lines. Secondly,

6. Richard G. Lugar (mayor), Thomas C. Hasbrook (City Council president), and Beurt SerVaas (County Council president), letter to members of Marion County legislative delegation, January 23, 1969.

7. *Woerner* v. *City of Indianapolis*, 171 NE 2nd, 34(1960).

to throw an issue which has tested the wisdom of the best constitutional lawyers in the state to persons who have not the slightest idea of what government was before or after is not wise."[8] Probably most important was their belief that they had the political muscle needed to pass the bill without a referendum provision and their willingness to use it.

In any event, the closest vote during the second reading was on the motion for a referendum, defeated by 18 in favor and 28 against. Once again party allegiances prevailed in a highly partisan vote, despite substantial Republican defections. All 28 votes against the motion were cast by Republicans. Three of the seven defecting Republicans voted with the Democrats, and four abstained.

A nearly complete party-line vote also defeated a third amendment submitted by Democrat Senator Robert J. Fair (Princeton): "No person elected Mayor under this act shall be eligible for election for any other public office, local, county, state or federal during the four-year term for which the Mayor has been elected, whether or not he continues in his office as Mayor."[9] This obvious attempt to curtail Mayor Lugar's political ambitions for the near future underscored the partisan nature of the bill's support and opposition. Every Democrat voted yes on Senator Fair's motion, along with Republican Senators Gubbins and Frank J. Biddinger (Marion), but otherwise the Republican majority held firm to beat down the motion 17 to 13.

Third Reading and Final Vote

Motions for amendment on the third reading require the approval of two-thirds of the Senate, so normally at that stage a bill is presented directly for passage without amendment. This was also SB 543's course when, after being "called down" by Senator Borst the next day, it came before the Senate for a vote. The debate was restricted to the question of whether the bill should pass and was ended by Senator Borst after one hour, whereupon the vote was taken.

The principal debators on a third reading, Senators Borst and Gubbins, had already presented their views at the second reading, so the debate did not attract much attention on the floor, where at times fewer than half of the members were present. But the vote itself attracted a great deal of attention because of its closeness. In Indiana, passage of a bill requires a majority of the full Senate membership, so 26 yes votes were necessary. The bill passed by a vote of 28 to 16, with 6 abstentions (see Appendix 6).

8. "City-County Consolidations, Separations, and Federations," *American County* 35(11):17 (November 1970).

9. *Journal of the Indiana State Senate, Ninety-Sixth Session of the General Assembly* (Indianapolis: C. E. Pauley & Co., 1969), p. 1234.

Republicans cast 25 of the 28 votes for passage, one short of the required constitutional majority. Two senators from Saint Joseph County cast 2 of the 3 Democratic votes, a part of the sponsors' strategy. Senators Robert Mahowald and John J. Frick (South Bend) supported the Unigov plans primarily because they were currently involved in the formulative stage of reorganizing the governments in Saint Joseph County. Although no outright vote trading was involved, it was no coincidence that when their plan was ready for the next legislative session, Senator Borst introduced it in the Senate. The third Democratic vote, cast by Senator Wilfred J. Ullrich (Aurora), was unanticipated and went unexplained.

The Republican vote shows several interesting anomalies. As expected, of course, Senator Gubbins voted against the bill. The Marion County delegation's solidarity was also broken by the abstention of Senator Charles E. Bosma (Beech Grove). Senator Bosma's abstention had been anticipated and was more easily tolerated than Senator Gubbins's action, as Bosma did not speak against the bill or try to persuade others to vote against it. His decision was essentially political: although his Senate constituency was Marion County where he ran at-large, his home and base of political support was in Beech Grove, one of the suburban cities where sentiment was strongly against Unigov. Accordingly, he kept the principals apprised of his situation, and in turn his abstention received their begrudging approval.

Political and geographic considerations also prompted 3 of the 6 senators from counties immediately adjacent to Marion to cast negative votes. They were concerned that Unigov might eventually be extended to their counties. The bill's sponsors attempted to allay such opposition by including a clause forbidding annexation of territory outside Marion County, a limitation not normally imposed on Indiana cities. Nevertheless, Senators Paul W. Swisher (Mooresville) and James B. Young (Franklin) were not convinced and voted against the bill, whereas Senator Keith C. McCormick (Lebanon) abstained. In all, 6 of the Senate's 35 Republicans voted against the bill, and 4 abstained (under Indiana's legislative procedure abstention is equivalent to a negative vote).

In summary, the Republican majority was obviously essential to SB 543's passage, but clearly it did not sweep through the Senate entirely on the basis of Republican dominance. In fact, its most effective opposition came from Republicans, both inside and outside the Senate, who forced several committee amendments greatly reducing the scope of the original Unigov bill. Moreover, the fact that some Republicans, mostly conservatives, withheld support made Unigov's passage depend on a few essential crossover votes by Democrats.

In any event, with the bill through the Senate, Mayor Lugar and several of his colleagues, who had spent the Saturday afternoon of the final Senate debate and vote in considerable anxiety, could now breathe a bit easier. A major hurdle had been surmounted.

House Action

Four days elapsed between February 15, when SB 543 passed the Senate, and February 19, when Speaker Otis Bowen handed it down for the first reading in the House of Representatives and assigned it to the Affairs of Marion County Committee for consideration. The leadership of the Unigov debate then passed from Senator Borst to Representative Lamkin. Lamkin had been a member of the policy group that had worked through the previous year, had joined in the decision to propose a metropolitan form of government, and had participated at each level of the public Unigov debates. As the bill moved through the Senate, he had kept abreast of its progress, maintaining a step-by-step liaison with Senator Borst and the other members of the Marion County delegation.

Senate action had amended or deleted many of the bill's more controversial provisions, leaving few if any items on which compromise was necessary in the House. Accordingly, SB 543 went through committee and a second reading in good time and with little opposition. Thus, five days after being referred to committee it was reported out with a recommendation of "do pass" as amended. The committee amendments, while numerous, were all technical, and the House quickly concurred in the committee report when the bill was handed down for a second reading on February 27, three days later.

At the second reading, the Democrats repeated several of the motions that had been made at the same stage in the Senate, submitting five amendments designed to weaken or defeat the Unigov bill. If passed, the Democratic amendments would have required a referendum, barred the excluded cities from voting in the countywide mayoral election, removed the four at-large council seats, prevented the new mayor from running for another political office for the duration of his term, and provided for a merit employment system for Unigov. Each proposed amendment was, however, quickly defeated by a solid majority in a highly partisan vote. The entire bill passed 57 to 34, with every Democrat voting no. In addition to the 57 Republicans voting yes, 9 Republicans abstained, and 7 voted no.

Trouble with the Speaker

At this point, party lines appeared to be holding well, and prospects were encouraging for final passage when the bill was handed down for its third reading. But Speaker Bowen delayed handing down the bill, and events took an unexpected turn that almost dealt the proposal a fatal setback.

The speaker was in a position to control the agenda during the final days of the short session. Unless he "handed down" the bill, it could not come up for final passage. According to House rules, the earliest SB 543 could be handed down for the third reading was Friday, February 28.

When the calendar was released that morning and SB 543 was not listed among the scheduled events, Mayor Lugar was disturbed and apprehensive. At a press conference held that evening, the mayor charged that the speaker was holding up the final vote on Unigov. He gave out the speaker's unlisted phone number, urging citizens to flood his office with phone calls supporting the bill. The speaker took immediate umbrage at the mayor's action. "Bowen, visibly angered at Lugar's charges, said he would not hand down the bill until he was convinced it has the support of the majority of Marion County residents."[10] The mayor's apparent blunder in alienating the most powerful individual in the General Assembly was compounded by the telephone response to his appeal. The speaker's secretary announced the results as only 102 calls favoring Unigov of the 1,188 calls she received.

Mayor Lugar realized that a dispute with Speaker Bowen so near the end of the session would surely kill the bill and had his chauffeur deliver a personal letter to Bowen on Saturday, apologizing for his action and stating that he was "misinformed" about the mechanics of handing down a House bill.[11] Lugar's lack of legislative experience was certainly a contributing factor, but his rash decision to intercede was more likely the result of a long, exhausting, and nearly conclusive campaign for Unigov. As a Democratic legislator put it: "The boy wonder really lost his cool."[12]

Speaker Bowen had been a candidate for the Republican gubernatorial nomination at the convention the previous summer and had been defeated in large measure through the efforts of Marion County chair Bulen and his associates. Nevertheless, the speaker's action was probably not a vindictive response to the actions of the Marion County delegation, as Bowen still had political ambitions. He ran for and was elected governor in 1972 and would not want to antagonize a powerful contingent of his party. But he was deeply interested in significant statewide legislation concerning taxation—matters which were more important to him than the government of Marion County, and he probably wanted as much leverage as possible with the Marion

10. "Lugar Charges House Speaker with Sitting on Bill," *Indianapolis Star*, March 1, 1969, p. 1.

11. "Lugar Apology Sent in Uni-gov Outbursts," *Indianapolis Star*, March 2, 1969, p. 1.

12. "Lugar Charges House Speaker . . . ," *Indianapolis Star*, March 1, 1969, p. 1.

County delegation in connection with the tax controversies. In any event, leaders of the delegation apparently did all they could to make peace with the speaker. He finally handed down the bill for its third reading on Wednesday afternoon, March 5, the last possible day a Senate bill could be considered for final passage in the House.

Action at the Third Reading

Action at the third reading in the House went much as the bill's sponsors expected. The short debate centered on a moving speech, delivered by Representative Lamkin (see Appendix 7), later designated "best speech of the session" by the city staff of the *Indianapolis Star* (who also voted Mayor Lugar's run-in with Speaker Bowen as the "top goof" of the session).[13] After two Democratic motions to delay passage were voted down by the Republican majority, the final roll call vote went 66 to 29 in favor of passage (see Appendix 8).

Unigov had become more strongly a party issue in the House than it had been in the Senate, and Republican dominance assured its passage. The two Democrats who bolted and voted for the bill were representatives Joe Barber and Burnett C. Bauer, both representing St. Joseph County (including South Bend), which as noted earlier had its own plans for reorganization. Of the five Republicans who voted no on Unigov, only one, Representative Roger L. Jessup (Blackford, Grant), represented an area outside of the Indianapolis standard metropolitan statistical area (SMSA). The remaining four were Otis M. Yarnell from Marion County and Robert H. Bales, H. Jack Mullendore, and Jack N. Smitherman, the three representatives of Hendricks, Johnson, and Morgan and Shelby counties, four counties bordering Marion County on the east and the south.

After the final vote in the House, SB 543 was returned to the Senate for concurrence in the House amendments. As these amendments were minor, there was no need for the time-consuming process of a conference committee, and the Senate concurred in the amendments that same evening. The bill was sent to the printer to be enrolled in its final legislative form and was subsequently signed by the speaker of the House and the president of the Senate on March 10, the final day of the session, and presented to Governor Whitcomb for his signature. He signed the bill into law on March 13.

Legislative Tactics

The crucial role of the Marion County legislative delegation had been recognized long before by Unigov sponsors. Its leaders were

13. "Behind Closed Doors," *Indianapolis Star*, March 9, 1969, p. 3.

members of the mayor's policy group, and the delegation had been thoroughly briefed. In addition, partly responsible for the bill's passage was the very effective program to organize support both inside and outside the General Assembly. The very high level of support from the Marion County delegation in both houses was essential. Speaker Bowen had said that "it would be helpful if most but not necessarily all of the Marion County delegation supported the bill."[14] The proponents lost two members of the eight in Marion County's Senate delegation and only one of the fifteen-member House delegation. As noted, the Senate's dissenters were Joan Gubbins, identified with a very conservative portion of the Republican constituency, and Charles Bosma, whose personal and political base was in Beech Grove, a suburban community strongly opposed to Unigov. The House dissenter was Otis Yarnell, a member of the Brotherhood of Railroad Trainmen.

Party Caucuses

In a further attempt to solidify delegate support for Unigov, Keith Bulen, Republican Party county chair, arranged a series of working dinner meetings. Marion County assemblymen caucused each Monday night during the ninety-sixth session to set legislative priorities and strategy. Despite his considerable power as party chair in a county where legislative candidates were slated by a special screening committee and elected at-large, Bulen used the dinner meetings for political arm-twisting to get votes for Unigov. In the Unigov discussions he apparently did not discourage criticism and debate, and he recognized that a few delegates might have special problems in constituencies such as Beech Grove or in the labor unions. For the most part these meetings allowed the delegates to apply their own self-discipline with respect to their Unigov votes. Of course, they realized that the mayor and party chair solidly favored the proposal and sensed the potential risks of not going along.

Representative Yarnell, the only House member who went counter to the position of the delegation, acknowledged the consequences when he said he did not fear failure because he did not plan to seek reelection.[15] Nevertheless, he did not buck the organization vigorously, did not campaign against the bill, and like Senator Bosma, kept the party informed of his stand. Also like Senator Bosma, Yarnell attributed his position to the Unigov opposition in his home constituency.

Educating themselves to keep their colleagues informed of the

14. "Lugar Remains Hopeful of Approval of Uni-gov Plan by General Assembly," *Indianapolis Star*, January 20, 1969, p. 21.

15. "Uni-gov Bill Sent on Way to Governor," *Indianapolis Star*, March 6, 1969, p. 1.

many changes in the bill took a good deal of the delegates' time, but the effort undoubtedly had the desired effect. Members of the House from other areas generally deferred to the Marion County delegation with regard to Unigov.

Keeping Legislators Informed

To complement Keith Bulen's caucus dinner meetings, Mayor Lugar hosted a series of luncheons with small groups of legislators, during which he explained the Unigov bill: "The process continued after the election in terms of 'courting,' in groups of five or six, legislators from outside Marion County. I explained the law to them personally. We saw 91 of 127 of them in this way, and made a fairly accurate headcount."[16] These carefully planned luncheons, attended by both Democrats and Republicans, included Deputy Mayor John Walls, Representative Lamkin and Senator Borst, plus other Unigov principals who could be present. The mayor was briefed on each legislator's previous and present stand on metropolitan government bills and was prepared to respond to inquiries and doubts.

These were low-key meetings emphasizing information on the bill and answering of questions. A second purpose was to make it clear that Unigov was the Marion County delegation's primary goal for the ninety-sixth session and to demonstrate that the bill was supported by the task force and the mayor's administration.

This special effort was necessary in part because of legislative jealousies between Marion County's delegation and the other legislators due to the favorable position Marion County sometimes seemed to enjoy in the General Assembly. Because of this, it had become a legislative custom to allow only one major Marion County bill to pass at any given session. Thus, it was imperative to let the General Assembly know that Unigov ought to be that bill in 1969.

In keeping with the mayor's intent of maintaining a low-key mood at the luncheons, party leader Bulen was not present at any of them. As the luncheons were bipartisan, Bulen's open participation would work against getting some hoped-for Democratic support. Even if the luncheons had been limited to Republicans, anti–Marion County jealousies in the General Assembly might have come to the fore, stirred up by parallel jealousies within the state party organization.

Mindful of the tenuous relationships between Marion County and the rest of the state and respecting a legislative taboo against mayors or other nonlegislators soliciting votes, Mayor Lugar did not

16. Richard G. Lugar, "Three Mayors Review Their Governments," *Nation's Cities*, November 1969, p. 29.

approach legislators directly to solicit Unigov votes, except for those whom he knew personally.[17]

Despite the playing down of overt and partisan political activity at this stage, the bill was clearly political. Moreover, Mayor Lugar was not above pushing for a partisan vote when the occasion presented itself. As he said later: "I'll be candid. I know this is good for Republicans. That's how I sold it to the state legislature."[18] But the luncheons were not the proper occasion for partisan pleading, and the mayor had to go elsewhere to do his politicking.

Lincoln Day Dinners

Although custom prevented Mayor Lugar from seeking votes from most legislators directly, he could appeal for votes indirectly through their constituents. He did this in a number of statewide appearances during the General Assembly session. This time custom was on his side, most of his appearances being at traditional Lincoln Day dinners that Indiana Republicans hold to celebrate the February birthday of the party's first president.

The fortuitous timing of the dinners in the middle of the General Assembly's consideration of SB 543 afforded the mayor excellent opportunities to state his case for Unigov. As *Star* reporter Robert P. Mooney anticipated, Mayor Lugar's sales pitch was a soft-sell approach, aimed at persuasion rather than the extraction of political favors.

> Hizzoner won't be brash enough to make his own legislative program the main theme of talks honoring the 16th President of the United States. But Lugar is clever enough to slip in a loud and clear message.
>
> The message probably will move his Republican-dominated audiences to urge their own legislators to support his proposals.
>
> Lugar's battle cry will stress that it takes a Republican administration, few and far between in the state's largest city, to unstick the gears of an archaic, expensive and overlapping Model-T form of government.[19]

While he did not overtly trade on the political capital he had accumulated in the previous year's successful Republican campaign, Mayor Lugar's message was indeed loud and clear. His mere presence in

---

17. Mayors and other officials are generally welcome to appear before the General Assembly in giving testimony and explaining bills, but regardless of their party or the nature of the legislation, they are expected not to solicit votes outright.

18. Phyllis Myers, "Jurisdictions: Why Did Indianapolis, of All Places, Take a Step Toward Metropolitanism?" *City* 3(3):39 (June 1969).

19. "Lugar Intends to Lobby for Uni-gov," *Indianapolis Star*, January 5, 1969, p. 12.

support of Unigov was enough to remind Republicans what it was he sought.

Demonstrating Public Support

Although the General Assembly had been assured there was no legal precedent for a referendum, some legislators continued to voice concern about the extent of active public support for Unigov. The principals then sought to substantiate their claim of broad public support. Up to this point, support had been generated largely through the leadership of the business, civic, and Republican Party organizations. Thus, while Keith Bulen, the Marion County delegates, and the mayor were engaged in a program to educate the General Assembly on the merits of Unigov, another campaign attempted to show that the public was included in the debate and generally supported the concept. This campaign included (1) solicitation of letters supporting Unigov, (2) a petition and a poll, and (3) a series of public hearings held by the legislative delegation.

Unigov Mail

In spite of Mayor Lugar's appeal to out-of-state Republicans to express their support for Unigov by writing to their legislators, only a light response came in for or against it. Only a few letters were sent by individuals, and the pros and cons were about evenly divided. As to quality, the opposition letters may have given a slight edge to the Unigov proponents because they merely repeated the expected conservative, suburban arguments that had been heard throughout the debate.

Letters from individuals were thus not very important, but several letters from local organizations were useful to the proponents. Groups such as the Christian Inner-City Association, the Indianapolis Civic Progress Committee, the Jaycees, the Indianapolis Real Estate Board, and the Greater Indianapolis Progress Committee sent letters to their legislators, including board resolutions supporting the Unigov concept. In each case, care was taken to note that the resolution supported the *idea* of Unigov but not necessarily all of the bill's specifics. A letter from the president of the Real Estate Board made this quite plain: "We do not wish to be drawn into the debate over the intimate details of the make-up of the bill. We fully expect that there will be many changes before the bill is ready for adoption in its final form. We do wish to cast our support for the basic principle."[20]

20. Letter from W. A. Brennan, Jr., president, Indianapolis Real Estate Board, to Lawrence M. Borst, senator, January 28, 1969.

Seeking support for the *concept* of metropolitan government while avoiding arguments on the fine points of the bill was a persistent theme of this campaign and a practical way of marshaling backers for the Unigov idea. In any event, the principals made good use of these letters, duplicating them and compiling them into a folder, along with other supportive materials, for media use and for distribution to the legislators.

There was no direct mailing to legislators by organizations opposed to Unigov, but the Association of Indiana Counties, Inc., did attempt to reach legislators indirectly through several "Legislative Flash" mailings to their membership and a statewide media release. Consequently, the only organizational mail legislators received on the issue supported SB 543. If this mail had any effect at all, it was undoubtedly favorable. Unopposed in this way, Mayor Lugar gained some ground in his bid to demonstrate public support for Unigov. Nevertheless, his gains were not extensive because his support was still seen as coming from organizations already known to support the concept. In short, the mayor had to turn elsewhere in trying to demonstrate support among the general population.

Two Petitions

Meanwhile, recognizing the apparent vulnerability of the mayor's claim of public support for Unigov, some members of the opposition distributed an anti-Unigov petition. Soon afterward the mayor drafted a petition of his own and went even further by arranging for a telephone survey.

The drive to secure signatures on the anti-Unigov petition was headed by two Republican officeholders, county recorder Marcia B. Hawthorne and county commissioner William G. Schneider. Petition forms were made available for distribution from their offices, as well as those of county prosecutor Noble R. Pearcy and circuit judge John Niblack.[21] This petition effort did not represent outright opposition to Unigov as such but asked that the bill not be passed immediately and called for a two-year delay and study period.

Readers will recall that county commissioner William Schneider had been a member of the mayor's task force that had endorsed the Unigov concept, and Judge Niblack had presented specific requests to the task force, which had been accepted. Thus, to repeat, the petition was not a head-on attack, but essentially a conservative, delaying strategy by incumbent officeholders and politicians who were worried about the prospect of quick and drastic change. Apparently, it did not get a very strong response. Senator Gubbins announced that she would

21. "GOP Petitions Seek Uni-gov Plan Delay," *Indianapolis Star,* January 21, 1969, p. 10.

deliver the signed petitions to the Senate Committee on Affairs of Marion County, but her promise was never fulfilled.

The day after this opposing petition was announced, Mayor Lugar announced his appointment of city market master Frank J. Murray to head a drive for signatures on petitions supporting Unigov.[22] When the mayor persuaded Murray to join his administration in January 1968, he removed a potential block to his Unigov plans in the 1969 General Assembly. As former head of the Indianapolis Taxpayers' Association, Murray had established the reputation as a legislative gadfly, who was able to obstruct the passage of most bills not to his liking. The mayor's announcement, following the opponents' announcement by one day, had the evident purpose of countering the county officials' effort. When the opponents' drive faltered, the mayor also allowed his own to die.

A Telephone Survey

About the time Murray's pro-Unigov petition drive was losing momentum, the Indianapolis Jáycees, who had previously gone on record supporting Unigov, volunteered to conduct a phone survey of the public's attitude toward Unigov. The mayor accepted their offer, and 40 callers from the Jaycees and their counterpart, Jayncees, conducted a day-long survey on February 14, 1969, supervised by project director Thomas E. Lyons, director of qualitative analysis for Herron Associates, an Indianapolis market research firm.[23]

The callers dialed 2,800 numbers selected at random from the Indianapolis telephone book and contacted 1,500 respondents. Three criteria were used in screening respondents: "To qualify to register their opinion, citizens must be 21 years of age, must live in the household that was called, and must have said that they were familiar with the Unigov proposal now before the General Assembly."[24] These criteria eliminated about four-fifths of the respondents, leaving 281 respondents (19 percent of those called) whose votes were counted. The big falloff was due principally to the large proportion of respondents who could not claim familiarity with the Unigov proposal, even though it was then before the state legislature.

In any event, the survey found 69 percent of the *qualified* respondents favoring Unigov. Although Unigov received favorable majorities from respondents both inside and outside the city, the pro-

22. "Lugar Plans Petitions on Uni-gov," *Indianapolis Star*, January 22, 1969, p. 1.

23. "Uni-gov Passes Poll," *Indianapolis Star*, February 15, 1969, p. 4.

24. Thomas E. Lyons and Donald Foster (president, Indianapolis Jaycees, 1969), undated news release from the files of the Greater Indianapolis Progress Committee (see Appendix 9).

Unigov vote was much larger in the city than in suburban areas. Inside the city the favorable vote was 78 percent (138 for and 33 against);[25] outside Indianapolis only 52 percent favored Unigov (57 for and 53 against).

As indicated by the campaign soliciting pro-Unigov letters, as well as the mayor's petition and the Jaycee poll, the effort to build public support was not of the highly organized variety usually seen in referendum-based mergers. As Mayor Lugar subsequently commented: "The tactics employed have often been improvised on short notice."[26] Nowhere was this more evident than in his efforts to demonstrate public support for Unigov. Nevertheless, his and Bulen's attempts to unify their delegation and educate the legislature were highly effective. The fact that he could succeed while failing to demonstrate unqualified public support for Unigov is largely attributable to his operating from a powerful and prestigious governmental and political base that he helped to create. A related contributing factor was the disorganization of the opposition and its comparative lack of access to the political forums. This does not mean the opposition was wholly ineffective in its bid for votes against Unigov. But the mayor did have the upper hand in trying to demonstrate public support through the mailings, the petitions, the telephone survey, and the party infrastructure. The opposition, although still poorly organized, became more visible during the final attempt to open the debate to the public—the legislative public hearings.

Public Hearings

The legislative hearings comprised another phase in the public debate on Unigov. Three legislative public hearings were held in February when SB 543 was at a crucial stage. Public participation was somewhat less than expected, the small turnout numbering mainly the same participants who had been active in the debate since the previous November. Thus, the hearings probably did little more than reinforce the stance that the legislators had already taken. Nevertheless, we can learn something about the character of the opposition and the proponents from the public hearings, which brought the opposition into sharper relief and forced the proponents to try harder to maintain their predominant position.

Two public hearings were sponsored by the Committee on Affairs of Marion County in the Senate and its sister committee in the

25. Ibid.
26. Richard G. Lugar, speech to Robert A. Taft Institute of Government, New York, May 21, 1970.

House, but all were actually joint hearings in that members from both committees participated. The hearings were also similar in format and so are considered together.

The *Christian Science Monitor* was quite accurate though perhaps simplistic in stating that the most active opponents were black militants, ultraconservatives, and the Democratic Party: "By arguing its merits he [Mayor Lugar] drew the dual wrath of black militants and the John Birch Society; both testified against it in public hearings. Some legislators, Democrats in particular, viewed the idea suspiciously as an attempted power grab by the Mayor."[27]

Black Spokesmen

Leaders of black communities in Indianapolis generally opposed the measure. Before the Unigov consolidation, blacks accounted for only about one-fourth of Indianapolis's population, and there was no early likelihood of a black majority in the city. Nevertheless, some black leaders argued that their position in the Democratic Party was rapidly becoming dominant, and since the Democrats usually won the city elections, they were approaching the point where they could at least control the party that controlled the city government. In their view, consolidation with the overwhelmingly white population of the suburbs would clearly dilute that political power.

Of the four people who testified against Unigov from the black community, only one, Charles "Snookey" Hendricks, spoke directly from the streets as a black militant. The others, Democratic attorney John Preston Ward, NAACP representative Andrew Ramsey, and the Reverend Father Boniface Hardin, repeated the commonly held argument that "they had mixed reactions about the legislation but unanimously opposed it on the ground that it would dilute the black vote."[28]

But Hendricks, who later described himself as an "ex-convict, ex-dope fiend, ex-everything who became a radical or militant when I was released from the penitentiary,"[29] was most violent in his attack, and in doing so, he exposed a major weakness in the Unigov opposition. This weakness was the sharp cleavage between the blacks and the suburbanites, neither being willing to join with the other against Unigov. When told of Mayor Lugar's comment that the greatest danger to the proposal was an unlikely coalition between inner-city blacks and suburban whites,[30] Hendricks replied: "There never was a coali-

27. "Young Indianapolis Mayor Relishes Urban Challenges," *Christian Science Monitor*, March 31, 1969, p. 10.

28. "Suburbanites Among Objectors to Uni-gov," *Indianapolis News*, February 8, 1969, p. 3.

29. Charles "Snookey" Hendricks, interview with James Owen, Indianapolis, July 19, 1972.

30. Lugar, "Three Mayors Review Their Governments," p. 33.

tion. We were fighting Unigov on different terms. They were fighting it on terms of integration. . . . We were fighting it more on a political basis. Like I told the whites . . . your only reason for fighting Unigov is that it opens up housing to blacks in your area."[31]

In addition to differences between inner-city blacks and suburban whites that polarized the opposition, differences within the black community prevented it from making a concerted effort against Unigov. William T. Ray, a black Republican realtor and Unigov supporter, gave two reasons why blacks had mixed reactions to the bill: "There was a large group of the black community—much the same as whites—who just weren't informed. Those who did know what was going on couldn't decide whether the plan would dilute their vote or extend their tax base."[32]

Frank P. Lloyd, a prominent black physician and respected figure in the Democratic Party, as well as in both the black and white communities, substantiated Ray's views with his own explanation of the black community's failure to unite against Unigov: "There was just no black leadership in this community. Blacks are just not organized at all. And, if you looked at blacks in the community, we were divided even on that. For example, I certainly am not against Unigov. But I would prefer that the schools be under Unigov. I was part of the Democratic try to get the police and fire metropolitanized for the very simple reason that I wanted to extend the tax base."[33]

Conservative Opposition

Though none of those who testified identified themselves as members of the John Birch Society, testimony from spokesmen of a conservative bent surely reflected the society's views. One, Claude Martin, who at a later meeting accused Mayor Lugar of attempting to set up a type of government that "is endorsed by a Communist front group,"[34] claimed that Lugar was endeavoring to establish a "local dictatorship."[35] Another speaker, Chet Webb, who served as the Marion County chair for the George Wallace presidential campaign in 1968, waved a copy of the *Communist Manifesto* in front of the crowd as he accused Mayor Lugar of attempting to establish a Marxist dictatorship.[36]

The rancor displayed in these two statements did not attract much following from the other opponents in the audience. In fact,

31. Hendricks interview.
32. William T. Ray, interview with James Owen, Indianapolis, June 16, 1972.
33. Frank P. Lloyd, interview with James Owen, Indianapolis, June 15, 1972.
34. "150 Hear Unigov Pros, Cons," *Indianapolis Star*, February 22, 1969, p. 9.
35. "Mayor Makes Plea at Stormy Meeting," *Indianapolis Star*, February 8, 1969, p. 14.
36. Ibid.

Marion County Democratic chair James Beatty, who followed Martin and Webb to speak against Unigov, rose and said: "Some of the attacks on this bill have been so outrageous my sense of justice almost forced me to come up and speak for it."[37]

The Democrats Divided

The opposition was also divided by the Democrats' move to disassociate themselves from the conservatives and their inability or unwillingness to join with Republican officeholders who opposed Unigov. Moreover, the Democrats were divided among themselves. Although they agreed that Unigov was a tool to bring Republican voters into the city, they disagreed on the bill's overall merits. This was brought out early in the legislative session by a newspaper article entitled "Demos Divided in Legislature on Unigov Bill." In it, Senate minority leader David Rogers (Dem., Bloomington) was cited as commenting, "Democrats are divided on the issue," while adding that he personally approved of it.[38]

Although Beatty did not speak in favor of the bill, neither did he oppose it with the vigor of a county chair who was about to give up "85,000 votes" to the other party. Beatty opposed the bill, but more for what it did *not* include: "I would be willing to take the political disadvantages that would come from supporting this legislation if we were really going to get something," he said, "but we are not."[39]

Past history almost forced Beatty to take this course. In his own push for governmental reform in 1965, he had gone firmly on record favoring the major precepts of the Unigov proposal. This helped explain his approach of attempting to discredit the bill for what it did not include while by innuendo trying to convince conservatives that the more inclusive approach was what Unigov ultimately intended to take. While Beatty's attack was well designed, it failed to provide a common ground from which the diverse elements of the opposition (including those within his own party) could jointly campaign against Unigov. Partially for this reason Beatty did not use his party's financial and organizational resources to wage a precinct-by-precinct campaign to generate a show of public disapproval for Unigov. There was too great a risk that such a campaign would expose the opposition's differences and thus actually help the Republican proponents.

37. "Suburbanites Among Objectors to Unigov," *Indianapolis News*, February 8, 1969, p. 3.

38. Robert P. Mooney, "Marion County Round-Up," *Indianapolis Star*, January 22, 1969, p. 5.

39. "Suburbanites Among Objectors to Unigov," *Indianapolis News*, February 8, 1969, p. 3.

The Voice of Labor

Two labor spokesmen also testified against Unigov. Max E. Brydenthal, president of the Marion County AFL-CIO, stated labor's case against Unigov when he said that it "leaves out countywide police, fire and schools, plus Beech Grove, Lawrence and Speedway."[40] But this frequent argument was interpreted as much in favor of Unigov as against it. Moreover, when the labor leaders failed to support their testimony with a more concrete demonstration of their membership's feelings, they also failed to present a viable opposition to Unigov.

Dissident Republicans

Although Judge Niblack did not appear at the hearings, several Republican officeholders from outside the city, who were still unsatisfied, did appear, along with Senator Gubbins, to give opposing testimony. However, because their positions as elected officials and the tone of their statements suggested a party-at-interest motive, they were not persuasive. Having lost Judge Niblack's leadership, they were too weak to be effective against the Marion County Republican organization. Nevertheless, they were not entirely impotent, for they helped persuade the state organization of county officials to oppose the proposal, which may account for the loss of some rural Republican legislators' support.

A Coordinated Effort

While the opponents were beset with intergroup and intragroup differences and appeared before the legislators with uncoordinated and sometimes conflicting statements, the more organized proponents presented consistent and mutually supportive testimony. Most of the arrangements coordinating the proponents' preparations were directed through the mayor's office.

As expected, many leading business and civic organizations that had previously endorsed Unigov sent representatives to the hearings. Carl Dortch appeared for the Chamber of Commerce, Jack Reich for the Greater Indianapolis Progress Committee, and Mrs. Edward Leary for the League of Women Voters; all read statements endorsing Unigov. These three and others were joined by Mayor Lugar, Thomas Hasbrook, and Beurt SerVaas to represent the view of elected officials. Speaking on behalf of some black citizens were William Hardy, Arthur Pratt, and the Reverend William Dennis. Rev. Dennis said:

40. "150 Hear Unigov Pros, Cons; House Unit to Consider Bill," *Indianapolis News*, February 22, 1969, p. 9.

"The single-member council districts will ensure that the black community will have indigenous, authentic leadership."[41] This argument was based on the expectation that among new council districts would be several central-city districts with black majorities and was the heart of Unigov's effort to secure black support. Rev. Dennis's statement, directed at a single issue of representation, was intended to dispel an underlying fear in the black community that Unigov would dilute their political power.

The proponents repeated this kind of approach throughout the hearings, each spokesman taking up a different issue and attempting to offset a specific claim against Unigov. Such an approach is most effective when coordinated to avoid duplication, while ensuring that every point of debate is covered. This strategy was implemented by Mayor Lugar's office.

Two Government Agencies Appeased

In addition to Rev. Dennis's remarks on black representation, three others stood out as particularly effective in helping to reduce fears about Unigov. Bernard Landman's statement that his board "unanimously approved" the bill was crucial;[42] as president of the board of the Health and Hospital Corporation, he thus allayed the fears and suspicions of the other special district governing boards whose budgets would also come under the new government's review. This achievement was particularly satisfying for Mayor Lugar, who recalled the strong, successful battle the Health and Hospital Corporation board had waged in 1965 against the "power grab" bills.

Also satisfying was the testimony of two former school board presidents, Sol Blickman and Mark Gray. In spite of their obvious school connections, neither made a direct comment on the exclusion or inclusion of schools under Unigov but simply made statements that generally supported the bill. There was good reason for this approach. As the Reverend Landrum Shields, black president of another Indianapolis school board, pointed out later, the relationship of the schools to the Unigov plan was a volatile issue that needed to be handled cautiously: "To have included schools in Unigov would have raised the spectre of racial integration—a desegregation suit brought by the National Association for the Advancement of Colored People, joined by the Justice Department, already is pending in court here—and would have meant instant death for the plan. We cooperated with the Mayor by not killing Unigov. . . . I don't think Mayor Lugar is planning to attempt to include the school board in Unigov any time soon."[43]

41. Ibid.
42. Ibid.
43. "Indianapolis' Mayor," *Wall Street Journal*, March 19, 1971, p. 8.

Although the school officials were in fact deliberately cooperating with the mayor in order to keep the schools out of Unigov, a public statement would have unnecessarily raised the ire of those who preferred to have the schools included. At the same time, those who were opposed to the schools' inclusion were tacitly reminded that the schools would not be affected by Unigov. The Unigov principals thus succeeded in securing the support, or at least passive adherence, of a crucial part of the community, while not giving the opposition a rallying point for unified action against Unigov.

Too Much Organization?

The principals' ability to plan and coordinate their moves enabled them to present testimony that effectively countered the opponents. Nevertheless, their penchant for organization was not always to their advantage, causing some embarrassment on at least two occasions.

The first incident stemmed from their decision to hold the public hearings in the auditorium of the City-County Building instead of a chamber of the General Assembly. Republican county recorder Marcia Hawthorne spoke for many opponents when she objected to this as a planned stratagem to favor the bill's proponents. She contended that "other legislators would be impressed by the number of protestors against the bill" if the hearings were held in the statehouse.[44] Senator Borst explained that adequate space for such a large gathering was not available in the statehouse at the time when the hearings were scheduled, but his explanation was not entirely satisfactory. And when House speaker Bowen later requested a public hearing by the House committee "in order to be fair to all concerned," he further stipulated "that the hearing should be held in the House chamber at a convenient time for all interested persons."[45]

In complying with Speaker Bowen's request, the principals outdid themselves by overzealous management. When the third hearing was held on the floor of the House, the Unigov principals packed the audience with crews from the Metropolitan Park Department. Many of these turned out in their work uniforms, a dead giveaway to reporters covering the hearing, who exposed the stratagem before the meeting started. Many of the workers thereupon went home early, and the hearing proceeded without any measurable input from this group. The park workers' appearance did little more than embarrass the principals at the hearing, but the incident almost caused a bigger uproar when a front-page story alleged that the workers had been promised compensatory time off for their efforts. Further embarrassment was

44. "125 at Uni-gov Parley See Officials Outburst," *Indianapolis Star*, February 5, 1969, p. 12.

45. *North East Topics* (Indianapolis), February 20, 1969, p. 1.

averted when the mayor said he "didn't know anything about it," and primary responsibility was assumed by the parks director, Kenneth Simpson.[46]

In any event, at the hearings the Unigov principals had considerable success in unifying supporters and demonstrating support in the General Assembly. While the various opposing groups could have been collectively formidable, their attempts to block Unigov were stymied by several long-standing differences among them, for example, between the blacks and suburbanites. Unable to overcome their differences, they did not put up an effective opposition. But an even more important cause of opposition weakness was the indecision within each group over the merits of the Unigov bill.

Conclusion: The Elements of Success

An obvious contributor to the success of the reorganization proposal was the experience accumulated through the gradual extension of municipal-type services to larger geographical areas, with special emphasis on the county. The "municipalization" of the county had been proceeding for more than two decades on a piecemeal, function-by-function basis, without any structural reform of the county government.

The City-County Building is probably worth a special note because of its symbolic impact. From 1962, when it was first occupied, until the reorganization, it was the tallest and most imposing single building in Indianapolis, indeed in the whole state. It had been constructed in one of Indianapolis's typical ad hoc arrangements, via a City-County Building Authority. City and county offices were distinct, and there was relatively little interaction. Existence of this combined headquarters structure helped prepare officials and leading citizens psychologically for some form of consolidation.

Consolidation as a Topical Issue

The Unigov proposals were also aided by the general popularity of the consolidation idea. This showed up in four ways. First, the recruitment of volunteers, especially the attorneys who did the research and drafting, was enhanced by their familiarity with the subject. Second, much public support for the Unigov concept came from business and civic groups that were already in harmony with the reform idea. Third, Unigov did not strike the legislators as a completely new issue, as many of them had served or were serving on

46. "Park Crew Ordered to Unigov Hearing," *Indianapolis Star*, February 22, 1969, p. 1.

legislative or citizens committees to study local government problems and were sympathetic to reform proposals; for example, two crucial Senate votes came from Democrats who were preparing similar legislation for another county.

The fourth way the reorganization effort was aided came about a bit paradoxically. The frequent earlier floating of governmental reorganization plans and their failure to move in the legislature left much of the potential opposition unimpressed with the initial Unigov announcement in October 1968. Furthermore, when Unigov did emerge as a realistic proposal in December 1968, some of those who were opposed were handicapped by their having previously gone on record favoring the consolidation idea.

Also contributing to pro-consolidation sentiment was the political leadership's growing frustration with the functional specialization and autonomy of the territorial extensions of individual functional services. This was clearly evident in the Barton administration's effort to extend the control of the city's elected chief executive.

A Measure of Political Partisanship

The extent and intensity of Indiana's political partisanship facilitated the Unigov reorganization. The Republicans promoted it, as is evident in Marion County Republican Chair Bulen's statement that Unigov was his "greatest coup of all time."[47] Mayor Lugar, a bit more subtly, said: "The genius of American political systems is well illustrated in our successful battle for united government in Indianapolis or 'Unigov' as the press promptly dubbed our efforts."[48]

The political setting that ultimately made Unigov's passage possible developed in two stages. First, the power of the Republican Party in Marion County was substantially enhanced by the Republican Action Committee's 1966 party reorganization campaign. This brought a whole company of ambitious and far-sighted newcomers into the party and got many of them elected to city, county, and state offices in the succeeding two years. Mayor Lugar was among them.

The second stage was set when a single party got control of all the key instruments of government at both state and local levels in 1968. This was due in large measure to the efforts of the Marion County team and promoted a high degree of party government and responsibility. The party leadership seized the opportunity to extend and consolidate its prospects for power.

While the political setting helped Unigov at each stage of its development, perhaps the most obvious illustration of the partisan

47. "Indianapolis' Mayor," *Wall Street Journal*, March 19, 1971, p. 8.

48. Richard G. Lugar, speech to Robert A. Taft Institute of Government, New York, May 21, 1970.

impact on the debate was in the General Assembly. The wholly Republican Marion County delegation was nearly unanimous in support, and the large statewide Republican majority assured passage of the Unigov bill. The importance of a partisan vote in the legislature is summed up in Mayor Lugar's assessment: "In terms of the votes cast in 1969, many of them I am certain were influenced by the fact that I had helped them with their election campaign in the fall of 1968. There was a strong Republican loyalty and tie which held up on the votes which were cast on amendments as well as the decisive votes which passed in both the House and the Senate. The party lines held with few exceptions statewide."[49] And as a final note, a Republican governor signed the bill into law.

The Role of State Government

Indiana is not a home-rule state. In accordance with Dillon's rule, the state government controls local government affairs, and there is no legal precedent for establishing, dissolving, or restructuring local governmental entities by exclusively local action. The Indiana General Assembly must pass all reorganization proposals—a strongly established practice of direct legislative control that unquestionably was important to Unigov's passage.

Legislative arrangements applying uniquely to Indianapolis and Marion County are common, and their frequency made special action on governmental problems easier. For some years the legislature had had standing committees in each house, chaired and dominated by members of the Marion County delegation, to which all bills concerning Indianapolis and Marion County were referred. In effect, the county's delegation also comprised a sort of recurring constitutional convention for the county. This represented a form of home rule—but not one based on voters' referendums—since the General Assembly generally deferred to the wishes of the delegation on items applying only to Marion County. Moreover, at that time all members of the Marion County delegation in each house were elected from the county at-large. The delegation thus tended to be a fairly cohesive group, accustomed to working together.

Outstanding Leadership

The emergence of dynamic leadership in the personalities of the Unigov principals was a contributing factor that is intangible and impossible to measure but difficult to overemphasize. Leadership was essential in view of the many diverse political elements and personalities that had to work together if the Unigov bill was to succeed.

49. Richard G. Lugar, interview with James Owen, Indianapolis, February 2, 1972.

Mayor Richard G. Lugar.
Reprinted by permission of *Indianapolis Magazine,* copyright 1972.

    The policy committee's organization was informal, nonstructured, and highly personal. The early meetings when the principals were deciding to go for Unigov were mostly dinner sessions with no agenda, no minutes, and no one presiding. The only organization agreed upon was that certain qualified people would concentrate on certain tasks. For example, attorneys Bose and Whistler were given primary responsibility for legal research and bill drafting.

The policy committee was not only nonstructured but also wholly unofficial. It did not have the status of funding of a locally or state-approved charter consolidation committee, such as those that make most consolidation studies. Instead, its funding was on a catch-as-catch-can basis, and most of the labor was volunteer.

The one person who can conceivably be described as the executive director of the policy committee was Deputy Mayor John Walls, who on behalf of Mayor Lugar and the others did much of the legwork, arranging, and coordinating. But this was an unofficial service, mostly done in addition to his regular duties. In performing these services, Walls showed himself an excellent administrator, as well as totally committed to the Unigov project.

Most of the principals were high-status individuals in the community, each with a political following whose loss was risked by public advocacy of Unigov. Thomas Hasbrook was an exponent of Unigov in the city's governmental and political circles. Keith Bulen, John Burkhart, and Beurt SerVaas worked at the county and state levels. Senator Borst and Representative Lamkin steered the bill through the legislature. This kind of individual leadership by the principals was essential to Unigov's success.

With so many strong personalities making key contributions, it might appear that the Unigov leadership was wholly collective—that there was no *leader*. But in fact Mayor Lugar was the unquestioned leader.

Astute Draftmanship

The principals also were fortunate in securing excellent attorneys to draft the bill. The work on the original bill, SB 199, as well as its substitute, SB 543, was based on something more than just the authors' professional drafting skills. Thus, the principals had sought the most competent Indianapolis attorneys available, who, through their considerable statehouse experience, were able to recognize and deal with the bills' political and administrative ramifications, as well as the legal aspects. Thus, the authors could draft bills that skirted many politically dangerous pitfalls.

Willingness to Compromise

A further leadership attribute deserving special attention—which was probably crucial—was the proponents' willingness to accept realistic goals, settle for less than they might have wished, compromise, and anticipate and nullify the most important potential sources of opposition. Many outside "reformers" and critics of the reorganization point to the many things that were not done or even tried. The proponents concluded, probably accurately, that to have attempted more would have meant failure for the whole effort.

The importance of compromise was clearly stated by one of the chief negotiators: "This sort of effort can never succeed if one is intransigent in saying what its framework must be or what its specifics must be. It is possible to effect compromise—even compromise on large issues—in order to get a structure and a framework established. I think the mayor had a lot of very good judgment in shunting aside, avoiding, compromising out what would have been some head-on conflicts."[50] This kind of maneuvering enabled the principals, on learning that certain sections of the Unigov bill were offensive to influential county officials or special-district board members, to make modifications in return for the erstwhile opponents' active support or *inactive* nonsupport. Such negotiation also enabled the principals to check the opposition of a politically powerful county judge and to reverse the anti-Unigov attitudes of the editors of the *News* and *Star*.

Organizing Public Support

The weakness and disorganization of the potential opposition probably contributed almost as much to the bill's success as did the proponents' effective leadership. The county officials most significantly affected—the commissioners—were not very powerful politically; there were no large, strong suburban municipalities or any very vocal suburban leaders; the Democratic Party was ideologically divided, as well as rather ambivalent toward the proposal; the black population was neither militant nor politically well organized compared with black communities in most northern and eastern cities.

Despite the opposition's apparent weaknesses, the principals still had to demonstrate public support for Unigov. Promoting a governmental reorganization of such magnitude without some evidence of public support would have been a serious mistake. Also, as there was to be no referendum on Unigov, a number of legislators, including the speaker of the House, were curious as to the extent of public support. To satisfy this concern, the Marion County delegates conducted a vigorous program to educate their fellows daily on the progress of the Unigov debate. In support of this program, the principals conducted an extensive extralegislative campaign before and during the session. This effort was so far superior to anything attempted by the opposition that it moved one out-of-county legislator to remark: "Unigov . . . was . . . the type of issue where . . . no one [was] presenting the other side. Actually, their education program was so good I volunteered to speak in favor of it on the floor of the House."[51]

Two basic features of the campaign for public support made it effective. First, in each case where public support was sought, ap-

50. Charles Whistler, interview with James Owen, Indianapolis, June 14, 1972.
51. John R. Sinks, interview with James Owen, Fort Wayne, October 25, 1972.

proval was asked only of the Unigov *concept*, with specific reorganization issues skirted wherever possible. This was a particularly effective way of bringing in supporters, many of whom in a referendum might have voted against Unigov because they disapproved of specific provisions.

Second, timing was also a crucial factor. Introducing Unigov when the political setting was most propitious was the most obvious stroke of timeliness. The principals' intentionally keeping Unigov under wraps until after the November 5 election not only gave them a chance to size up "the lay of the land" before continuing; it also gave the opposition only a scant two months to organize before the opening of the General Assembly. Moreover, as Unigov's specifics were not announced until after the task force met the last time on December 19, the opposition had nothing of substance to respond to until the Christmas–New Year holidays.

When in session, the Indiana General Assembly's business is conducted at a hectic, rapid pace that sometimes overwhelms even experienced legislators. Accordingly, when the General Assembly convened shortly after the holidays, little chance remained for the scattered opposition, uninformed and inexperienced, to organize effectively and to "catch up" with the Unigov proponents. A suburban newspaper summed up the situation: "As so often happens, however, the ungreased wheels of public opinion may have moved too slowly to exert any influence—one way or another—on the well oiled gears of the Unigov machine."[52]

Major structural reorganization does not come easily in US metropolitan areas. Perhaps it would not have occurred in Indianapolis if any of the predisposing factors discussed had been missing. While every one of them might not have been absolutely essential, these factors appear to account for the success of the Indianapolis reorganization effort.

52. *North East Topics*, February 13, 1969.

7

Reorganization: Promise and Performance

The terms most frequently used in referring to the Indianapolis organization—*Unigov* and *city-county consolidation*—are both useful shorthand references but if taken at face value are substantially misleading. Governments in the Indianapolis region are far from unified. Despite the *Unigov* name, a complex variety of governmental units and agencies persists under a highly pluralistic arrangement. Moreover, the term *city-county consolidation* suggests much greater changes in the geographic base of services and taxation than actually occurred. In short, the Indianapolis reorganization is an interesting compromise between unity and plurality, between integration and continued autonomy of the components.

The Indianapolis reorganization can probably best be viewed from three different perspectives: (1) by looking at the areas used for service and taxation, (2) by considering administrative organization and control, and (3) by examining the political community. The reorganization made only minor changes with regard to areas for service and taxation, the existing geographic bases being continued with relatively minor modification. The most obvious changes made by Unigov were in administrative organization and control, with many (but not all) of the previously separate and autonomous city and county agencies grouped into a limited number of strong executive departments, each subject to a much higher degree of control by the chief executive and the council. The establishment of Unigov, in fact, was much less an act of geographic centralization than of administrative integration.

But perhaps the most important impact has been the effect on the political community, as the act made one major shift in political constituency, and the county became the important political unit. Political leadership and responsibility are now clearly and unquestionably held by the elected mayor, and the City-County Council is, at least potentially, a deliberating, appropriating, and policy-determining body of preeminent significance. In short, while the name *Unigov* may be an almost absurdly inexact description of the new *legal* entity, it is a meaningful and useful characterization of *political* realities, even if somewhat overstated.

This chapter will be devoted to a discussion of service and taxation areas. Subsequent chapters will deal with administrative organization and control and then the political community.

Service Areas

As noted earlier, a great many attempts had been made in the Indianapolis area to reconcile function with area. Many services had their bases extended beyond the existing city limits. While in some areas attempted adjustments had admittedly been unsuccessful, the limits of political acceptability had at least been tested. Recognizing those limits, the reorganized government retains a complex pattern of jurisdictional and functional relationships. The urban area's service districts can be thought of as a set of concentric circles, each associated with a function or a group of functions. These are now discussed, starting in the middle.

Center Township

Center Township comprises the innermost area (see Map 4), which is smaller than the old city limits, with about 270,000 people (40 percent black) and a 1977 assessed valuation of $683 million (about 30 percent of the county's entire valuation). Center Township remains as a separate unit of government, with an elected township trustee, a township assessor, and a three-member advisory board. (Although providing "poor relief" is Center Township's only significant function, this is not true of the eight surrounding suburban townships where fire protection is a significant budget item.)

Indianapolis School District

The next larger "circle" is the Indianapolis school district, a separate governmental unit with more than half of the county's population, less than half of its assessed valuation, and the largest budget of any local governmental agency or unit in the metropolitan area. As shown in Map 5, the Indianapolis district is surrounded by the county's 10 other independent school districts (listed below).

Marion County School Districts
Indianapolis City Schools
School City of Beech Grove
School Town of Speedway
Franklin Township Community School Corporation
Metropolitan School District of Wayne Township
Metropolitan School District of Perry Township

Metropolitan School District of Lawrence Township
Metropolitan School District of Pike Township
Metropolitan School District of Warren Township
Metropolitan School District of Washington Township
Metropolitan School District of Decatur Township

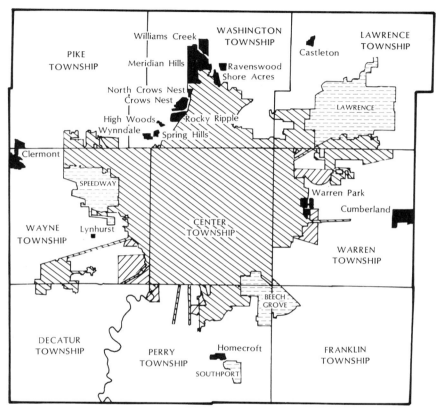

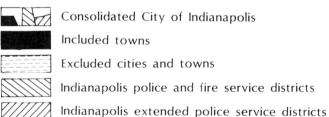

Consolidated City of Indianapolis

Included towns

Excluded cities and towns

Indianapolis police and fire service districts

Indianapolis extended police service districts

Map 4.

Units of Government After Unigov, Indianapolis–Marion County

Source: Consolidated Cities and Counties Act, *Indiana Acts of 1969*, Chapter 173. Prepared by Department of Metropolitan Development, Division of Planning and Zoning, Indianapolis–Marion County, December 1972.

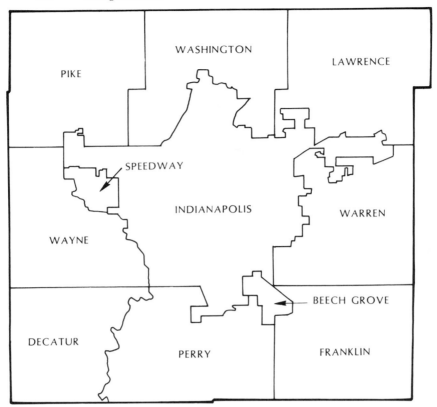

Map 5.

School Districts in Marion County

Source: Indianapolis Chamber of Commerce, March 1970.

The names of the districts are legal titles that signify whether the school corporation is that of a city, town, or township and denote the clear legal and financial separation made in Indianapolis between a civil unit of government and a school unit. The term *metropolitan*, as applied to the township school corporations, is rather misleading since it only indicates that the school district's administration was restructured under the Indiana 1959 school reorganization law. The metropolitan township districts retain their pre-1959 jurisdictional boundaries but are now administered by five-member, nonpartisan, elected school boards. Only Franklin Township continues to operate under the old township trustee system.

Like the townships, each school district establishes its own property tax levy, within strict state limits. The school's levy is not reviewed by the mayor or the City-County Council: after school board approval, school budgets go directly to the county tax adjustment board for review and approval.

Fire Service District

The consolidated city's fire service district is slightly larger than the Indianapolis school district, and fire district services are administered by Unigov's new Department of Public Safety. Jurisdictional limits are equivalent to those of the old City of Indianapolis and can be enlarged only on petition of a majority of real property owners or owners of property amounting to 75 percent in assessed valuation of the area to be added, a procedure significantly more difficult than annexation to the old city, which itself was hard enough.

Outside the fire service district, fire protection is provided by 16 "volunteer" departments in townships, towns, and the excluded cities. Since Unigov's formation many of these have developed a professional character, especially with the advent of general revenue sharing. New buildings, equipment, and rolling stock have been purchased, and many departments now have at least one full-time driver on duty for each shift. These volunteer fire departments are deemed locally to be quite effective and are politically influential as well.

Police Service District

Next larger in size is the consolidated police service district—the second major function of Unigov's Department of Public Safety. The police service district was initially coterminous with the fire service district. But expansion of the police service is easier than expansion of the fire service district, and Unigov's interim City-County Council (comprising nine members from the old City Council and five members from the old County Council) passed a series of annexation ordinances in 1970 extending the police service district.

The areas included were neither affluent nor populous but do contain some of the county's chief industries, so the annexation was significant in terms of assessed property valuation and tax base. The expansion was worked out in an accommodation with the industries. The city needed the larger tax base to avoid a tax rate increase soon after the reorganization. Initially it proposed a substantially larger expansion but settled for the one that was effected in 1970.

Outside the police service district, the sheriff's department provides police services. While the whole county shares in the financial support of the sheriff's department, services are actually supplied almost exclusively outside the Indianapolis police service district. Town marshals and city police forces in the small municipalities also provide local police services.

Sanitation Division/Board of Works

Liquid- and solid-waste services (sewerage and trash collection and disposal) are provided to an area substantially larger than the police service district. Under legislation enacted before Unigov this service area had for some time been expanding beyond the corporate limits of the old City of Indianapolis. Once a separate and rather autonomous department of the city, headed by a three-member, bipartisan board of sanitary commissioners, the sanitary division (sometimes called sanitary district) is now administratively part of Unigov's Department of Public Works.

The division has its own earmarked property tax sources for operations and bond retirement and also relies on sewer use charges and contract fees (e.g., it provides sewage treatment for Beech Grove). Annexation to the sanitary district is relatively easy: the Board of Works simply extends the appropriate taxing district to correspond to the extension of services. A recent legislative amendment divided the liquid- and solid-waste functions into separate taxing districts to permit one activity and its accompanying tax levy to be extended separately from the other. Both districts are still administered as sections of the Public Works Department's sanitary division.

Housing Authority

Under the Unigov law, the Housing Authority is authorized to operate five miles beyond the old city limits, as it did before Unigov. But in fact neither before or since Unigov has any public housing been built outside the old city boundaries. The Housing Authority's failure to extend its activities beyond the old city's boundaries is an issue in a school desegregation suit now in the federal courts. (This issue will be considered below at greater length.) The authority also does not participate in the rental subsidy program now favored by national policy.

Although it is a division of the Department of Metropolitan Development, the Housing Authority retains a limited degree of autonomy under its five-member board of commissioners appointed directly by the mayor rather than by the head of the department. While the mayor's power of appointment and removal limits the commission's independence, on matters of personnel and policy the commissioners sometimes serve as a buffer between the authority's staff and the department director. Most of the authority's funds come from the federal government and from rental fees on its buildings.

Consolidated City-County

Unigov itself, the consolidated city-county, is the next-larger unit in size, including all of the territory in Marion County except for the four small excluded cities noted earlier. Although the attention of the city's general government is now presumably focused primarily on this area, in fact it is the geographic base for very few services, and although Unigov is authorized to levy property taxes for city purposes on this countywide base, none has yet been levied. (The urban renewal district, whose boundaries are coterminous with Unigov's, has levied a tax.)

Library District

The Indianapolis–Marion County library district is slightly larger than the consolidated city-county, including all but two of the smaller municipalities. Its governing board, appointed by a variety of governmental officials, retains its pre-Unigov status as a quasi-independent entity.

Marion County

The county is the territorial and financial base for a substantial number of services—health and hospitals, parks and recreation, sewage treatment, planning and zoning, and airports, among others, along with the traditional county functions. Some of these are administered by departments of Unigov and some by the old county offices. Some are administered by agencies having different degrees of autonomy—although the power of the mayor to appoint and remove agency board members and of the council to control appropriations is a significant influence on most of these otherwise rather autonomous functions. An important financial decision was made by the Unigov council in 1977 and 1978 to use the whole county's tax base to pay the local share of the capital costs of the huge new sewage treatment plant rather than only the area currently served.

Unigov Taxes, Revenue, and Expenditures

The Unigov law made few budgetary and taxing changes in Indianapolis and Marion County. Various governments' fears of losing taxing and bonding powers was one of the chief concerns expressed about Unigov during the legislative debate. In accommodating these concerns, the governmental units were continued, including 11 school corporations, 9 townships, 5 independent municipal corporations, and the 4 excluded municipalities. Moreover, some agencies that were included in the consolidation retained all or part of their bonding or taxing powers. In short, under the Unigov umbrella is an array of 50 separate governmental units with 95 separate taxing units, subject to varying degrees of budget coordination or review by the mayor and City-County Council.

Property-Tax Rates

While governmental agencies sought to maintain their fiscal autonomy, citizens' groups argued that Unigov would cause property taxes to go up. In fact, although the level of services seems to have increased, there has been a definite attempt on the part of the Unigov mayors to hold property taxes down. In 1970, the first year under Unigov, the property-tax rate for the consolidated City of Indianapolis's municipal services was $3.95 per $100 assessed valuation—according to the best estimate of such a rate, using data on all the taxing districts and earmarked receipts in the rather confusing financial situation that prevailed during that transition period. By 1979 the rate had risen gradually to $4.25, before dropping precipitously to $3.50 in 1980 following a 1979 property reassessment (see Table 5).

Previously, the Indianapolis municipal corporation tax rate had been $4.15 in 1967, the last year of the Barton administration, and $3.95 in 1969, the last pre-Unigov year.[1] Total property-tax revenues raised increased from $43 million in the 1969 pre-Unigov district to $74 million in 1980 in the consolidated City of Indianapolis. Much of the increase under the consolidated government can be attributed to growth in the assessed value of real property (see Table 6). New housing developments were largely responsible for the incremental growth of $50 million each year from 1971 to 1979. A general reassessment in 1979 accounted for a major increase in the tax base from $1.5 billion to $2.5 billion.

Tax rates were held down in part because the Unigov mayors were committed to governmental economy. Perhaps more significant, however, was the 1973 state property-tax relief law holding property-tax rates of most public corporations to the 1973 level, except in very special circumstances. With rates thus effectively frozen, increased assessments and alternate revenue sources have provided funds needed to meet inflationary cost increases or to add some new activities. Despite the 1973 rate freeze, total property-tax receipts have in-

---

1. Comparisons between the old Indianapolis corporate budget and the consolidated City of Indianapolis budget can be made with a fair degree of accuracy and reliability, but not with great precision. Since special taxing districts were created within the consolidated city to coincide with user benefit districts, households that receive the full range of municipal services under the consolidated city are in large measure the same households served under the former government. There have been very few extensions of the property tax base beyond the pre-Unigov corporate limits. Accordingly, the budget figures now given for the consolidated City of Indianapolis generally correspond to those of pre-Unigov Indianapolis.

creased substantially under the consolidated government as new assessments (plus the small rate increases) have permitted the addition of about $28 million to the total annual city levy from 1971–1980 (an increase of about 62 percent) (see Table 7). By comparison, the annual school-tax levy, a separate property-tax component over which Unigov authorities have no direct control, increased over $30 million in the same 10-year period. The taxpayers are thus paying higher total amounts in property taxes than before, partly because the assessed value of their property has risen but also because of the levies of units not under Unigov's jurisdiction.

Other Revenues

There are several alternate sources of revenues that are almost constantly changing. Federal funds, the largest outside revenue source, comprised 36 percent of the total consolidated city budget in 1979 (see Chart 4). Three federal block grant funds have provided a fairly constant revenue source in recent years: in 1979 general revenue sharing (GRS) provided approximately $13 million annually, the community development block grant (CDBG), about $14 million, and the Comprehensive Employment and Training Act (CETA), $11 million. Under the new federalism initiatives of the Reagan administration, however, these funds have been reduced: by 1983 the GRS allocation had dropped to $12 million annually, the CDBG allocation to $9 million annually, and CETA to $4.5 million. (In 1983 CETA was reorganized and renamed the Jobs Training Partnership Act [JTPA].) As explained below, Indianapolis was able to anticipate these reductions and thereby lessened their effect somewhat.

After the federal government, the state is the most important source of outside revenue. State-collected taxes on gasoline, cigarettes, alcoholic beverages, intangibles, and inheritances, allocated to the city by complicated formulas, approximated 16 percent of the total budget in 1979 (see Chart 4). An additional one-time allocation of nearly $1.5 million in state revenue sharing money raised the state's share to about 20 percent.

Several miscellaneous local revenue sources have increased since Unigov. Some fines and fees have been increased, and methods of collecting them (as well as other delinquent taxes) have improved. For example, because of revisions in the sewer user tax, the sanitary district now bases its charges on the content as well as the volume of industrial and commercial waste.

Indianapolis's continued reliance on nonlocal (particularly federal) funds to offset increasing government costs may present serious problems in the near future. A very large portion of the consolidated city government's operating expenditures is now funded with federal

Table 5– *City of Indianapolis, General Governmental Expenditures by Function, 1971–1980*

	Departmental and Modified Accrual Basis				
	1980	1979	1978	1977*	1976
Protection of people and property	$ 63,722,974	$ 56,176,224	$ 52,707,326	$ 49,381,249	$ 47,375,257
Community cultural and recreation	11,075,128	13,226,978	13,261,962	12,559,381	10,937,759
Community development and welfare	39,002,629	24,893,126	39,877,920	22,822,520	19,620,904
Transportation and related services	22,112,721	27,237,327	32,552,587	22,242,998	21,635,872
Environmental services	25,230,458	26,435,700	25,291,946	24,545,885	18,242,571
Executive/ Legislative affairs of government	1,112,337	932,011	899,695	859,901	678,531
Administrative services	4,723,345	6,283,080	5,444,017	3,489,740	2,853,897
General debt services	22,623,305	22,505,676	18,823,564	18,913,029	16,902,808
Capital outlay	103,698,581	84,334,198	27,704,877	26,637,314	35,332,740
Total	$293,301,478	$262,024,320	$216,563,891	$181,452,017	$173,580,339

Note: Expenditures include general, special revenue, debt service, capital projects, and expendable trust funds.

Source: City of Indianapolis, *Annual Report*, December 31, 1980.

dollars, specifically general revenue sharing. While this program seems reasonably well established, the future availability of community development and JTPA funds appears to be less secure or predictable. Although Indianapolis resembles other large American cities in its dependence on federal dollars, a state-imposed tax rate freeze makes its situation somewhat unusual. To meet expected inflationary costs without reducing service levels, Indianapolis will need new sources of revenue in addition to future property-tax expansions. As already noted, property-tax revenue increases have depended almost entirely on increased assessments. The General Assembly has, for the last two sessions, considered alternate local government tax options to the property tax without success. This was the priority issue once again in the 1983 legislature where Indianapolis, working with other Indiana cities through the Indiana Association of Cities and Towns, sponsored major legislation to revise the local government tax structure. This legislation, which failed by a narrow margin on the final

Table 5   *(cont.)*

	Cost Center and Cash Basis			
1975	1974	1973	1972	1971
$ 44,610,297	$ 39,635,407	$ 35,703,195	$ 33,713,746	$31,209,800
9,922,548	8,085,801	6,976,580	7,405,572	6,222,882
25,599,548	17,898,373	19,451,291	15,508,536	9,047,933
28,575,156	24,685,888	12,612,870	15,582,806	17,662,398
14,568,395	12,618,226	10,714,445	10,176,899	9,247,932
657,344	540,800	527,051	501,083	647,175
3,476,444	2,949,649	2,748,638	2,025,807	1,835,391
15,886,926	14,743,762	15,228,000	13,238,686	13,078,783
†	†	†	†	†
$143,296,658	$121,157,906	$103,962,070	$98,153,135	$88,952,294

*Includes reduction of $1,944,343 from change in accounting method for inventories.
†Capital outlay expenditure segregation similar to 1976 through 1980 not presented owing to different recordkeeping procedures as to the classification of such expenditures.

day of the session, was designed to allow for greater property-tax flexibility or a local income tax option. This kind of appeal to the state for home-rule determination on revenue matters is the thrust of Indianapolis's quest for an improved financial status.

Although the full impact of the Reagan administration's economic and new federalism programs have not yet been fully assessed in American cities, early indications in the consolidated City of Indianapolis are that although the reductions will adversely affect some specific departmental programs, the overall operation of government will not be critically affected. That is not to say that Indianapolis does not have revenue problems. Mayor William Hudnut alerted the City-County Council to this possibility in the letter of transmittal accompanying his 1980 budget report: "Of concern to the City of Indianapolis, as well as all sectors of the economy, is the continued depressed status of the economy. While, to date, the economic slow-down has caused only minor concerns, a prolonged con-

Table 6— City of Indianapolis, Assessed and Estimated Actual Value of Taxable Property, Countywide, 1971–1980

Year	Real Property		Personal Property		Total	
	Assessed Value	Estimated Actual Value	Assessed Value	Estimated Actual Value	Assessed Value	Estimated Actual Value
1980	$2,507,678,729	$7,523,036,187	$988,386,510	$2,965,159,530	$3,496,065,239	$10,488,195,717
1979	1,595,243,630	4,785,730,890	879,451,950	2,638,355,850	2,474,695,580	7,424,086,740
1978	1,575,653,590	4,726,960,770	818,872,220	2,456,616,660	2,394,525,810	7,183,577,430
1977	1,531,868,740	4,595,606,220	759,910,400	2,279,731,200	2,291,779,140	6,875,337,420
1976	1,490,927,740	4,472,783,220	728,721,380	2,186,164,140	2,219,649,120	6,658,947,360
1975	1,431,659,294	4,294,977,882	653,642,710	1,960,928,130	2,085,302,004	6,255,906,012
1974	1,367,100,310	4,101,300,930	588,280,320	1,764,840,960	1,955,380,630	5,866,141,890
1973	1,314,065,700	3,942,197,100	550,663,020	1,651,989,060	1,864,728,720	5,594,186,160
1972	1,279,223,230	3,837,669,690	510,177,700	1,530,533,100	1,789,400,930	5,368,202,790
1971	1,226,104,710	3,678,314,130	543,469,630	1,630,408,890	1,769,574,340	5,308,723,020

Source: City of Indianapolis, Annual Report, December 31, 1980.

Chart 4

City of Indianapolis General Revenue by Source, 1979

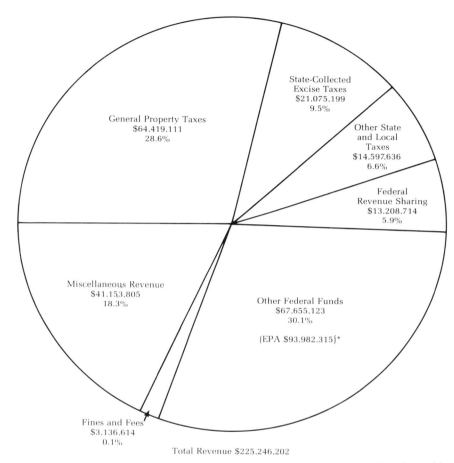

State-Collected
Excise Taxes
$21,075,199
9.5%

General Property Taxes
$64,419,111
28.6%

Other State
and Local
Taxes
$14,597,636
6.6%

Federal
Revenue Sharing
$13,208,714
5.9%

Miscellaneous Revenue
$41,153,805
18.3%

Other Federal Funds
$67,655,123
30.1%

(EPA $93,982,315)*

Fines and Fees
$3,136,614
0.1%

Total Revenue $225,246,202

Source: City of Indianapolis, *Annual Report,* December 31, 1979 (based on old Indianapolis corporate limits).

*A one-time EPA wastewater treatment facility construction grant of $93,982,315 has been deducted from federal funds and the total to better illustrate normal budget levels.

tinuation of this depressed state may cause a need to reexamine the City of Indianapolis' priority of services."[2] Cutbacks in federal revenues will certainly affect Indianapolis's budgeting strategies, but the state of the economy and state and local tax decisions may have an even greater effect.

2. William H. Hudnut, letter of transmittal, in City of Indianapolis, *Annual Report,* December 31, 1980, p. iv.

Table 7– City of Indianapolis, Property-Tax Rates and Tax Levies, All Overlapping Governments, 1971–1980

Year	City	County	Municipal Corporations	Total City-County Council Approved	School	State	Other	Total
				TAX RATES				
1980	3.5083	1.0924	0.9818	5.5825	3.8811	0.0100	0.5128	9.9864
1979	4.2584	1.3560	1.2040	6.8184	5.2343	0.0100	0.4972	12.5599
1978	4.2090	1.2910	1.1550	6.6550	5.1212	0.0100	0.3180	12.1042
1977	4.4390	1.2280	1.1720	6.8390	5.4548	0.0100	0.3110	12.6148
1976	4.0890	1.2380	1.1430	6.4700	5.5110	0.0100	0.2424	12.2334
1975	4.0960	1.1500	1.1130	6.3590	5.8148	0.0100	0.2875	12.4713
1974	4.1020	1.1680	1.0800	6.3500	6.0024	0.0100	0.1298	12.4922
1973	4.0590	1.1090	1.1820	6.3500	6.2206	0.0100	0.2036	12.7842
1972	3.9600	1.3720	1.0350	6.3670	6.1220	0.0100	0.2286	12.7276
1971	3.9520	1.3220	1.0010	6.2750	5.9538	0.0100	0.2773	12.5161

Year	City	County	Municipal Corporations	Total City-County Council Approved	School	State	Other	Total
				TAX LEVIES				
1980	$74,212,710	$38,191,016	$34,069,619	$146,473,353	$135,685,504	$349,606	$17,927,010	$300,435,473
1979	67,093,150	33,090,223	28,505,523	128,688,896	129,533,044	247,681	12,304,352	270,773,973
1978	63,312,315	30,913,328	27,889,042	122,114,685	122,628,456	239,453	7,614,592	252,597,186
1977	65,626,529	27,478,820	27,175,992	120,281,341	125,011,969	229,178	7,127,433	252,649,921
1976	56,846,231	27,405,965	25,338,965	109,591,161	122,324,214	222,100	5,411,954	237,549,429
1975	54,399,625	23,996,098	23,186,173	101,581,896	121,257,044	208,660	6,018,607	229,066,207
1974	48,882,404	22,852,505	21,104,722	92,839,631	117,368,956	195,655	2,550,716	212,954,958
1973	47,402,638	20,684,202	22,028,770	90,115,610	115,997,380	186,680	3,809,081	210,108,751
1972	44,758,868	24,569,932	18,531,888	87,860,688	109,547,754	179,081	4,079,278	201,666,801
1971	45,761,088	23,413,474	17,695,023	86,869,585	105,357,687	177,106	4,924,638	197,329,016

Note: Taxable property is assessed at 33⅓ percent of the estimated actual value.

Source: City of Indianapolis, Annual Report, December 31, 1980.

In anticipation of federal cutbacks in the late 1970s, Indianapolis set a policy requiring federal funds (except for general revenue sharing) to be used primarily for capital improvements. Thus, despite the reduction of block grant allocations during the Reagan administration, Indianapolis could be reasonably assured that its traditional public service programs would continue to operate at the same levels without added federal assistance. There is growing concern that most of the GRS allocation must go for the operation of the public safety departments, with a large amount of this budgeted for payment of the police and fire retirement plans. Thus, although the city feels that it is meeting present operational needs, it will not be able to meet new program demands or rising costs for current operations unless it can expand its revenue base.

In addition to Indianapolis's general preparation for federal funding cutbacks, Mayor Hudnut has attempted to direct and limit the cuts through his work with the National League of Cities and his influence on the Reagan administration. For example, while he accepted a 1982 decrease in the city's community development block grant from $11.5 million to $10 million, he promised to fight further cuts in the block grants and in general revenue sharing. As the outgoing president of the National League of Cities and a Republican mayor of a large city, Hudnut has been a regular and influential consultant to the Reagan administration on revenue matters. Moreover, his planners have worked successfully through Senator Lugar's office to obtain federal categorical grants for capital developments. These funds have helped to offset CDBG funds previously spent on downtown development.

In sum, while some of Indianapolis's programs have suffered revenue losses under the Reagan administration, the city's established budgeting strategies will probably permit continued operation without drastic curtailment until such time that other revenue sources can be established.

Fiscal Policy and Management

In addition to concern over future revenues, a more immediate problem is lack of flexibility in using funds. For example, most state allocations come from dedicated funds that must be spent on specific programs, and except for general revenue sharing most federal funds are also restricted in use. Another complication for Indianapolis is the fact that the tax-rate freeze applies *independently* to each taxing unit instead of cumulatively to the total budget. Accordingly, the mayor and council have limited flexibility to shift budget priorities from one taxing unit, such as the park district, to another, such as the police service district, but must operate with nearly the same interdepartmental priorities that were established in 1973. Federal general revenue sharing, permitting selective increments, has helped alleviate this problem.

It is very difficult to establish whether Unigov has resulted in any major changes in resource allocations by area, despite some shifts that suggest that the budgetary inflexibilities are not insurmountable. For example, transportation funds (largely from state-collected sources) are now pooled and used at the discretion of the administration, presumably where the needs are greatest. Sanitary district funds (based largely on user fees and federal revenue) are distributed on a near countywide basis, also according to need. Urban renewal, with only a small local tax levy, has now been changed to require suburban participation.

Nevertheless, the system's central feature—emphasized by its service and taxing districts and earmarked revenues—is the effort to relate the area that receives a service as closely as possible to the tax-base area that supplies most of the local funds to support the service. Consequently, Unigov does not yet represent any major thrust toward resource redistribution. Under the new governmental structure such shifts are now somewhat easier *legally*, but the realities of political power work against such redistribution.[3] Suburban political leverage has been significantly increased by the political reform, and the suburbs have little inclination to increase their financial contributions to help pay the service costs of the central city.

A number of Unigov departments are empowered to levy taxes throughout the entire consolidated city's jurisdiction, but do not. For example, it is legally possible for the consolidated government to levy a nearly countywide tax for the Department of Administration in order to cover its personnel, finance, and youth development divisions, as well as administrative costs for the mayor's office. But Unigov has not levied an areawide property tax for these services because they predominantly benefit city residents; instead, it has used a combination of federal funds, transfer funds, and miscellaneous local funds.

While under Unigov funding for the traditional functions—sewage, public safety, road building, parks, and general administration—has roughly doubled, new programs in community development and welfare have increased more than fourfold (from $9,047,933 in 1971 to $39,002,629 in 1980). Most of the latter provide funds for federally sponsored programs administered by the consolidated city's division

3. Admittedly, federal grants to the consolidated city increased greatly after Unigov's formation, and a large portion of these funds—especially community development, Title XX social services, and CETA funds—served central-city needs. While old Indianapolis benefited from increased federal dollars, so too did suburban areas formerly under the county's jurisdiction, which under Unigov became eligible for federally funded municipal services for the first time. While this constitutes a type of redistribution, it does not involve resources derived from local taxation.

of employment and training and the community services program. These expenditures, particularly those funded by the community development grants intended principally to revitalize depressed neighborhoods in the near downtown area, tend to counter criticism that Unigov's only successful programs are building projects, for example, highways and downtown developments benefiting the business community. As the reader will see below, the Unigov system and the new leadership that accompanied it made the consolidated City of Indianapolis much more competitive for categorical grant programs than had previously been the case.

Indianapolis does not have serious debt problems. State statutes set restrictive debt limits for local government units. Each important taxation district has its own bonding power, and most still have some margin of unused borrowing authority. Indianapolis's bonds are generally highly valued in the municipal bond market, having received a triple A rating by Moody's in 1972 and again in 1977. Only five of the nation's other 25 largest cities share a triple A rating with Indianapolis. This excellent record has been achieved only since Unigov. The high rating was conferred in large measure because the new structure's centralized financial management facilitates a much fuller disclosure of the city's public financial position than was possible under the former multiple units. Under the Unigov law the combined City-County Council has become the central budget clearing house for all the former city *and* county departments, as well as the quasi-independent municipal corporations. Thus, budget documentation and reporting are much more systematized than before, giving bonding houses a more comprehensive view of the debt status of the units involved.

Federal Programs

There has been a marked change in Indianapolis's attitude and posture toward the federal government, largely attributable to the policies and aggressiveness of the Lugar administration and its political connections in Washington during Republican national administrations. Nevertheless, governmental reorganization was also probably a major factor in bringing Indianapolis vastly increased federal support.

Indianapolis had never been a prominent participant in federal urban programs, nor had most other Indiana cities. Thus, Indianapolis was probably the nation's largest city that had refused to participate in federal public housing and urban renewal programs prior to the mid-1960s. The Barton administration began to participate, but still rather tentatively. In contrast, the Lugar administration, especially after Unigov, put Indianapolis in the front rank of all cities in practically every new or expanded federal grant program. Mayor Lugar was one of the most active proponents of federal revenue sharing in his roles as president-elect and president of the National League of Cities, as vice-chair of the Advisory Commission on Intergovernmental Relations, and as a member of the platform committee at two Republican National Conventions and in various other forums.

Increased Funding Under Unigov

There is little doubt that the change to Unigov was directly related to Indianapolis's success in obtaining demonstration and discretionary federal funds as a result of competitive bidding.[4] Michael Carroll, who as head of the Department of Metropolitan Development and later as deputy mayor was responsible for administering a very large proportion of the federal grants received, commented: "I do think that we were more competitive for federal funds, as a result of being a unique consolidated city-county government. The federal government wanted to experiment with consolidation situations. I'm positive, for example, that had we not been a consolidated city we would not have received $8.5 million in planned variations money."[5]

When the federal Department of Housing and Urban Development announced in 1971 that 20 cities would be given grants for "planned variations" as a supplement to their Model Cities program, Indianapolis was among them, receiving the largest single grant: $8.5 million. With these funds Indianapolis set up its community services program, which was consolidated with the Model Cities staff in January 1972. This combined agency, then in the mayor's office, was initially funded $15 million in federal money. These funds financed a general effort to improve governmental management and assisted a wide variety of community improvement programs, most but not all concentrated in enlarged Model Cities–type target areas.

Federal Program Directions

After Unigov's establishment, Indianapolis used the prestige of its new reorganization and Mayor Lugar's influence as one of the few Republican mayors of a large city to obtain from the federal government both increased funds and increased discretion in using them. It became one of the three cities first approved for unified planning programs, undertaking to combine land-use planning, transportation planning, and park and open space planning with the social planning activities related to manpower and Model Cities. In all, 17 separate planning agencies were combined. The unified planning program, administered

4. It would be difficult to determine whether as separate entities Indianapolis would have received more or less funds under the federal nondiscretionary formulas than as part of Unigov.

5. Michael A. Carroll, interview with James Owen, Indianapolis, December 19, 1977.

in the Division of Planning and Zoning, provided the basis for Indianapolis's being granted permission to submit integrated grant applications, using much of the same data and justification for various federal grant applications. Although complications at the federal level and the introduction of the community development block grant have now preempted this form of grant application, much of its effectiveness as a grant coordination mechanism remains in force in Indianapolis.

The federally assisted planning and community services programs had a significant impact on governmental structure. The unified planning program, and even more so the community services program, gave the mayor significant additional administrative controls over operating and budgeting procedures. Still more important, the chief executive's authority was greatly enhanced by the requirement for "chief executive review and comment," first implemented in the planned variations grant. This meant that all (or nearly all) local applications for federal grants had to be submitted to the local chief executive for review and comment before approval. Since few governmental agencies operate today without some occasions to seek and receive federal funds, this requirement has given the mayor's office much additional leverage and influence.

The community services program—now rather oddly located in the Department of Administration rather than in the mayor's office— as well as the manpower and related CETA/JTPA program activities and much of the community development grant activities have concentrated heavily on social services rather than physical development. Most of these social service activities have been provided in the older and decaying portions of the central city, although some are in previously unincorporated areas. (The planning division's position in establishing budget priorities was further strengthened by being given responsibility for preparing the Indianapolis capital improvement budget.)

Two low- and moderate-income communities, Mars Hill and Drexel Gardens, settled mostly by first- and second-generation immigrants from Appalachia, had virtually no urban services before Unigov: they were outside the city's jurisdiction, and the county provided no urban services. Mars Hill and Drexel Gardens are now designated target areas for federal funds, receiving combined funds from several federal, state, and local sources. These programs jointly give much more attention to the social needs of low-income segments of the population than under pre-Unigov city administrations. Admittedly, they are financed by federal funds rather than by direct contributions from the suburban areas. In considerable measure they might have been established under federal stimulus during the 1970s, even if Unigov had not been enacted. But the new structure certainly pushed programs like these quite vigorously and with better coordination of a variety of efforts than would otherwise have been likely.

Like his predecessor, Mayor Lugar, Mayor Hudnut continues to seek federal funds, but several factors have slowed the rate of federal allocations to Indianapolis. (1) When the Democratic Carter administration was in Washington, it seemed less receptive to applications from Indianapolis than the previous Republican administration.[6] (2) Much federal money is now allocated through general revenue sharing and community development formulas rather than through specific project proposals. (3) The consolidation may actually have hurt the city slightly, under distribution formulas that emphasize need and unemployment, because the formerly suburban areas with more wealth and less unemployment are now included in the city's statistics. (4) The present Republican administration's economic and new federalism programs have reduced federal grants to all cities.

In sum, it appears that the formation of Unigov and the vigorous search for federal funds complemented and reinforced each other. The governmental reorganization and the mayor's role as spokesman for the larger constituency helped attract federal funds. Moreover, the federal funds and the accompanying conditions—especially the requirement of review and comment—further enhanced the mayor's position.

Significant Changes in Services and Finance

The geographic pattern of public services and their finance is complex and pluralistic, and the governmental reorganization made no *fundamental* changes. Nevertheless, five changes are worth noting. (1) The police service district was enlarged somewhat. (2) The jurisdictional base for street and road building, maintenance, and traffic control was greatly extended. (3) The Department of Metropolitan Development's geographic jurisdiction is now larger. (4) The county is now the tax base for financing the local portion of capital costs of new sewage treatment facilities, replacing the smaller sanitary district. (5) A new public transit agency can now operate in a much larger area than it could have without the consolidation.

All five of these changes were enlargements of jurisdictional area. Only one (the transportation consolidation) was actually included directly within the Unigov statute; the other four have come about through ordinances passed by the Unigov council.

6. Former Indianapolis deputy mayor David O. Meeker, Jr., was assistant secretary for community planning and development in the US Department of Housing and Urban Development during the Republican administrations of Presidents Nixon and Ford.

Police Services

The appropriate area for police services is still being debated. Opposition to a countywide police force defeated a special legislative bill in 1967 (before Unigov), and in the spring of 1972, it stopped a city ordinance proposed for the same purpose, which was supported by the mayor and the president of the council. Mayor Lugar then stated that no further extensions of the police service district were in prospect, beyond those worked out with certain industries soon after Unigov's enactment.

Nevertheless, the issue surfaces almost annually. On August 31, 1972, council president Thomas Hasbrook, one of Unigov's architects and chief personalities, announced that the 1973 budget (which he was confident the council would adopt) proposed that taxes for the law enforcement services of the sheriff's department be levied only on county citizens living outside the police service district and the excluded cities. This would have shifted more than $1 million in annual tax levies from the central city to suburban taxpayers. Meeting opposition in the council, the proposal was postponed for "study" and has not reemerged. But small amounts of county tax revenue have supported the city police in subsequent budgets.

Recently, another attempt to merge the city and county police forces, led by State Representative John P. Flanagan (Dem., Marion County), produced a bill to establish a countywide public safety commission to manage the combined police departments. The proposed merger (which also called for a referendum) differed from earlier proposals to extend the city police jurisdiction. Some considered it a more realistic approach in view of the sheriff's status as a constitutional officer. Nevertheless, Flanagan's bill failed to get much popular support and died in committee. The sheriff, at the time also a Democrat, opposed the bill, alleging that the mayor's power to appoint the public safety commission (although with the sheriff's approval) would detract from the sheriff's constitutional role as a direct representative of the people.

No attempt has been made to merge the police departments of the contiguous municipalities of Beech Grove, Lawrence, and Speedway into the Indianapolis police service district. A survey made after Unigov's passage found most individuals in these communities believing they were getting better police services than they would under a larger consolidated force.[7] When residents in these three communities and three nearby Indianapolis neighborhoods were asked their opinions on the idea of merger, 80 percent from the outlying commu-

7. Elinor Ostrom et al., *Community Organization and the Provision of Police Services* (Beverly Hills, Ca.: Sage Publications, 1973).

nities opposed merger, and only 44 percent of those within Indianapolis favored merger.[8] With this strong opposition in the suburban communities and with only limited support in the consolidated city, merger of the city police departments is highly unlikely in the near future.

Streets and Roads

Before reorganization, the city government managed roads, streets, and traffic within its limits; the park district provided parkways and roadways within the parks; the county was the primary agent for roads and streets in the unincorporated areas; the small municipalities provided some service within their boundaries; and a new Mass Transportation Authority had been given substantial authority for major road arteries.

With the advent of Unigov, the road and street service and related activities of the city, county, park district, and the former transportation authority were all combined under the Department of Transportation (DOT). The small municipalities retain limited building and maintenance functions for local streets and roads. Although the act includes special taxing and bonding provisions—a 1971 amendment raised DOT's bonding indebtedness from 2 to 4 percent—funds to support DOT activities come almost entirely from state-collected revenues (primarily gasoline and cigarette excise taxes and federal funds). The formula for state excise tax distribution continues to allocate money to each of the former governmental recipients. The small municipalities, both excluded and included, continue to receive their pro-rated shares. These funds are allocated separately to each small municipality to be expended in each independent jurisdiction. On the other hand, funds allocated for the City of Indianapolis,[9] the county, the park district, and the former transportation authority are now completely combined and are spent by DOT without regard to jurisdictional limits.

Planning and Development

Many observers saw formation of Unigov's Department of Metropolitan Development as intended principally to centralize several municipal functions under the mayor. But it also represented appreciable extensions of territorial authority. Each of the department's divisions now has responsibilities for areas that go beyond the old city limits. The previously created city-county planning and zoning department

8. Ibid., p. 67.

9. The share formally allocated to the old City of Indianapolis under state statutes is now calculated on the basis of the population of the fire service district rather than on the population of the entire new city.

(the Metropolitan Planning Commission) was retained under Unigov. The Housing Authority's jurisdiction was extended by ordinance in 1970. The building permit and inspection authority of the city and county were combined by the Unigov Act, and code enforcement may now be exercised to the limits of the consolidated city. A major 1972 amendment enlarged the taxing base of the urban renewal district from the old city limits (or fire service district) to the area of the consolidated city (all of the county except the excluded cities). While the additional tax provided by the 1972 amendment is not large, this was a significant enlargement of the functional area.

Sewage Treatment Facilities

In a major departure from established practice, Unigov's City-County Council voted in February 1978 to extend the Indianapolis sanitary district's tax base to the county boundaries, with limited exceptions.[10] A proposed $300 million advanced waste-water treatment plant, ordered by the Environmental Protection Agency and 75 percent federally funded, prompted the decision. The major issue facing the Hudnut administration and council was who would pay to retire the bond issue needed to meet the local share of the project since user fees cover only operations and maintenance? The current residents of the Indianapolis sanitary district did not want to pay for capital outlays to permit the extension of sewer lines into the county areas. Suburban residents, on the other hand, argued that they would not be tied to the new system for a long time and therefore should not have to pay for service before receiving it.

In early 1977 Mayor Hudnut proposed a countywide sanitary district in an initial attempt to solve the problem. This was quickly withdrawn when it drew heavy criticism from suburban residents, who pointed to the promise by the Republicans who created Unigov that residents would not be taxed for services not received. Republican credibility was being tested in an area where Hudnut had acquired a great deal of his political support.

The following summer, when the bond issue was before the City-County Council, leader of the Democratic minority, Paul F. Cantwell, demanded that Hudnut agree to submit the sewer extension plan to the council for approval as a condition of Cantwell's support for the bond issue. Although normally sewer district extensions need only to be passed by the Board of Works, the Democrats' threat to block the bond issue forced the mayor to concede. The minority leader in the City-County Council is normally not in a strong bargaining position

10. Omitted from the area were the towns of Beech Grove, Lawrence, Speedway, and Cumberland; the Ben Davis Conservancy District; and several smaller areas served by private utilities.

either in the entire council or in his party. On this issue, however, where the council Democrats were in unanimous agreement, he could take the lead. Hudnut was willing to concede Cantwell and the council a larger voice in this issue as a practical way of getting the county-wide Indianapolis sanitary district—an arrangement Hudnut wanted but could not find Republican support for.

Accordingly, Hudnut had the Board of Works submit two plans to the council. Although he had earlier supported the countywide arrangement, he indicated a preference for a partial annexation that restricted the tax base for new works to areas within one-half mile of the extended sewer lines. The second plan, supported by City Controller Fred Armstrong, called for a countywide district (with minor exceptions) similar to Hudnut's proposal of the previous year. Mayor Hudnut then offered to sign whichever plan the council passed. In a close vote, the council favored the countywide district 16 to 13. All 10 Democrats, and 6 of 19 Republicans, voted for the measure. All of the 16 favorable votes to extend the district and tax base countywide came from councilmembers representing areas served by the older sanitary district.

Under the new arrangement, taxpayers are required to pay 27.9 cents per $100 assessed property valuation for bond retirement, a reduction of 6.4 cents per $100 from the rate established for the old sanitary district. The addition to the tax base of suburban areas *not yet served* permits a reduction in the taxes on the older, central county areas for sewerage capital outlay levied—even while major new treatment plants are being constructed. This represents a rather significant redistribution of resources.

Public Transportation

Perhaps the most obvious structural change after Unigov was establishment of the Indianapolis Public Transportation Corporation (Metro) in 1973. As in many other cities, the private bus transportation company could no longer operate with fare receipts only. The city, taking advantage of a general state statute passed several years earlier, set up the transit corporation to take over the bus system.[11] The general law was used, rather than a special enactment or modification of the Unigov statute, because of the delay and political controversy that might have been entailed by an attempt to get a special act passed.

11. Conditions leading to the formation of the public transportation corporation are described in Richard Hebert, *Highways to Nowhere: The Politics of City Transportation* (Indianapolis: Bobbs-Merrill, 1972), pp. 65–96. Hebert's report, published before the bus company became publicly owned, is critical of both the Unigov Department of Transportation for failing to adopt a favorable attitude toward public transportation and the private Indianapolis Transit Company management for its ultraconservative policies.

The law authorizes such a corporation to operate—and presumably collect tax levies—a considerable distance beyond the city limits; the statute says up to one mile for each 50,000 people in the city. Since Unigov now has nearly three-quarters of a million people, legally it could operate up to about 15 miles into all the surrounding counties. So far, however, its tax levy has been applied only to the consolidated city-county, its very limited transit activities outside the area being financed from the fare box or by contract with other governmental units.

To some extent the new transit authority violates Unigov's basic consolidationist and integrationist approach. Thus, although the transit board is appointed by the mayor and council and in practice has worked closely with Unigov's leadership, its finances are more completely independent than those of any comparable Unigov agency. It can levy its own property tax, and its proposed budget and tax rate need not be submitted to the mayor or the Unigov council but instead go directly to the county tax adjustment board for review. Recently, the need for transit subsidy has been so widely accepted that both the state legislature and the City-County Council have appropriated funds to help the transit corporation match available federal subsidies. A continuation or increase in council appropriations (their future being doubtful) would of course give the council a lever for stronger influence on the new agency, reducing its fiscal independence somewhat.

A Related Move to Redistribute Resources

A bill to change poor relief in Marion County, introduced in the 1978 General Assembly, was primarily intended to establish a county-wide property tax to pay the cost of local poor relief administered by the townships.[12] Since townships were excluded from Unigov, this move did not directly affect Unigov but was obviously an effort to redistribute resources.

The proposed tax would be levied equally throughout the county, and the proceeds used to relieve Center Township of the serious financial hardships in providing subsistence payments to the majority of Marion County's poor and unemployed. The proposal was essentially financial, although some administrative changes were included. Township jurisdictions were to remain the same, and they would retain their existing level of operations. Townships would continue to administer the payment of poor relief, and each township would levy its own separate tax for administrative and personnel costs. Thus, only the actual costs of the payments for the poor were to be shared.

---

12. In Indiana "poor relief" gives indigents short-term assistance for food and housing. Applicants receive no money for poor relief but are given orders for necessities by the township trustee.

Opposition to the bill came from surrounding townships and from other township officials statewide. Moreover, reform groups failed to support it perhaps because of substantial sentiment in Indiana to do away with the township poor-relief system altogether and to merge it with the county welfare offices. In any event, the bill did not pass. Another bill presented to the 1979 General Assembly providing state financing for poor relief generated little debate and died in committee. In short, there does not appear to be much support in Indiana for shifting the burden of poor relief to a larger territorial base. Nevertheless, these and other changes in jurisdiction and taxing district boundaries will continue to be debated and implemented from time to time. If they cannot be made directly by the reorganized government, they may be attempted through special acts of the state General Assembly, as before Unigov.

The Small Municipalities

The reorganization has had little direct effect on Marion County's small municipalities, whether excluded or included. They continue to receive essentially the same nonmunicipal services and pay the same kinds of taxes as before. Citizens in these communities vote for the mayor and councilmembers of the consolidated government and also for their own local municipal officials. While four *excluded* municipalities are technically not a part of the consolidated city, they *are* part of the county, receive all countywide services, pay all county taxes, and vote in Unigov mayor and council elections. They are included in or excluded from the service and taxation areas for particular functions, depending on the terms of the legislation or ordinances governing those functions.

There are 16 *included* municipalities under Unigov (see Map 6), each with a legal entitlement to establish town governments, to levy property taxes, and to provide local services under Indiana's town law.[13] Despite their legal status, most of the included towns do not function as active governments. Town board elections are irregular, and infrequent board meetings are quite informal. Most services are arranged by private subscription or provided by a larger governmental entity—fire by the township, police by the sheriff, sewer service by the sanitary district, water by a private utility, and most road services by the Indianapolis Department of Transportation. Few if any of the towns levy a property tax. They use general revenue sharing and state-distributed funds to contract for the few public services they provide.

13. There are currently only 13 recognized operating towns. The State Board of Accounts no longer lists High Woods, Shore Acres, and Spring Hills as active governments.

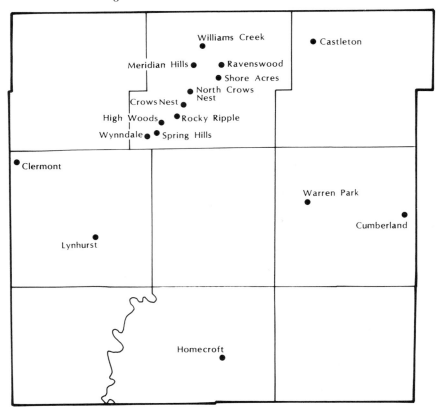

Assessed Valuation

Marion County	$3,496,065,239
Included towns	$47,155,849

Map 6.

Marion County and Included Towns

Source: City of Indianapolis, *Annual Report*, December 31, 1980.

Municipal Annexation Procedures

The transfer of territory by annexation is more difficult than before Unigov. Under the previous law a municipality could extend its jurisdiction by merely redefining its boundaries in regular council proceedings, whereupon the inhabitants of the annexed territory must seek a remonstrance in the courts to stop proceedings before the annexation went into effect. Cities could also annex across county lines.

Under the new law, an area wishing to be annexed must initiate action with a petition signed by 51 percent of the affected landowners and filed for the approval of both the annexing and disannexing governments. Should the disannexing government refuse to approve the petition, the petitioners must demonstrate in court the benefits of annexation. Although written to apply equally to the consolidated city and to the included and excluded cities and towns, these provisions clearly favor the latter.

Under Unigov there have been few jurisdictional shifts by annexation, and those that have occurred were small. The consolidated city itself has annexed no territory. Small but important areas were annexed to the police service district only. One included town, Claremont, annexed a small development on its north side but was turned down in a second annexation request for a larger development in 1977. Recently, there have been rumblings from a few other towns wishing to annex nearby areas to increase their population figures and thereby their entitlement to state and federal revenues, but no actual annexation attempts have been made. Moreover, as if to preempt possible future attempts, the 1980 General Assembly passed a law requiring all such annexation petitions to be reviewed by the combined City-County Council. Previously, jurisdiction on these petitions had rested in the Metropolitan Development Commission, a body thought to be somewhat more favorable to annexation proposals.

The Unigov law's provision that the initiative for annexation must be taken by the affected property owners was politically motivated to assuage the fears of surrounding counties that Unigov would extend its jurisdiction into their territory. Under the current law there is little chance that Unigov will soon annex any territory in counties adjacent to Marion County.

The strict provisions of the Unigov law also thwarted annexations by the four excluded towns, although they have expressed interest. Two of these communities, Southport and Lawrence, did manage successful changes under the old annexation provisions (before Unigov became fully effective), but further jurisdictional changes of this kind are no longer feasible.

Southport's expansion was probably the most notable, as the annexation brought in enough population to allow the community to incorporate as a city, thereby under the Unigov statute enabling it to be excluded from the consolidated city's jurisdiction. The city of Lawrence, by annexing more people and land, also extended its tax base. Lawrence's growth occurred in two relatively large annexations: Fort Benjamin Harrison (a 2,500-acre US Army post) was annexed in 1974, and the 5,871-acre Oaklandon area in 1976. The decisive factor in both cities' success was passage of the annexation ordinances by their City Councils before Unigov went into effect. The Oaklandon area ordinance, passed on December 29, 1969, beat the deadline by only three days. Although subsequent litigation dragged on for several years, the judges' confirming decisions rested on the law as it stood at the time the ordinances were passed.

In any event it is clear that significant jurisdictional changes among governmental units have been blocked by the Unigov statute's rigid requirement for joint approval by both the annexing and disannexing units and the law's lodging the annexation initiative with the area seeking annexation. Probably this status quo arrangement will persist until the General Assembly changes the law—a rather remote prospect.

8

Administrative Organization and Control

The reorganization act had an impressive effect on the structures for administrative control and coordination, far greater than its initial impact on the service areas or tax base areas of the various governmental functions. This is especially evident in the reorganization of numerous quasi-independent boards and agencies of the old city into a cabinetlike arrangement under Unigov and the establishment of a single executive and council elected countywide.

In attempting to consolidate administration and policymaking under the mayor, the Unigov Act created six major executive departments: administration, public safety, transportation, parks and recreation, public works, and metropolitan development (see Chart 5). Early versions of the Unigov bill also provided for a Department of Public Health and a Department of Coordination of Independent Boards and Authorities. The final version left the Health and Hospital Corporation as an independent unit but with redefined authority. The coordinating department was dropped entirely. If these two departments as they were initially proposed had been included in the Unigov bill, the consolidated city's authority would have included some jurisdiction over all of the civil functions of government within its area. While the existing arrangement is not so comprehensive, its departments do have considerable jurisdiction and authority.[1]

Executive Departments

Department of Administration

The Department of Administration, whose director is appointed by the mayor, is responsible for the general administrative functions

1. A detailed description of the structure and functions of the government units under Unigov has been prepared for the Greater Indianapolis Progress Committee. See *Unigov and You—A Guide to Local Government in Indianapolis and Marion County* (Indianapolis: Greater Indianapolis Progress Committee and School of Public and Environmental Affairs, Indiana University, 1977), p. 211.

Chart 5

Unigov Organization Chart, Consolidated Government for Indianapolis–Marion County

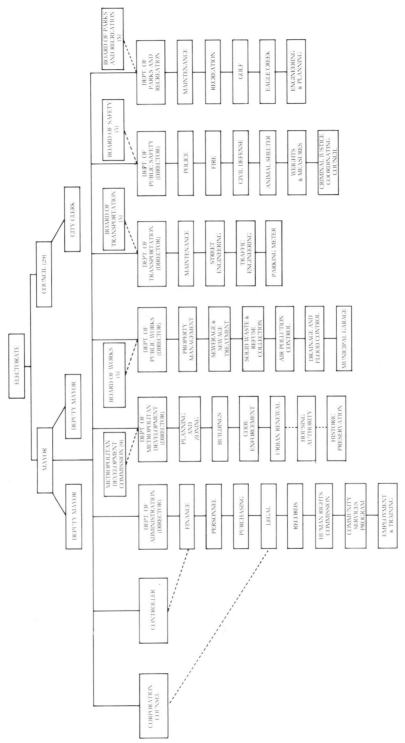

Source: City of Indianapolis, *Annual Report*, December 31, 1977, p. xiii.

of the consolidated city. These include functions previously performed by the city controller, city personnel office, city and county purchasing departments, city and county legal departments, and the city and county central data processing services.

While the county treasurer and county auditor continue to have their statutory functions, the Department of Administration does much of the financial planning through its finance and legal divisions. The joint budget and tax levy ordinance is prepared cooperatively by the elected auditor and the appointed controller for all county *and* city agencies, as well as for the courts. The City-County Council now receives a combined budget from a number of agencies, many of which previously submitted separate budgets to the City Council or County Council. The combined budgets now provide the council with a comprehensive view of spending, which was not available before Unigov. The controller and the legal department of the city-county (which actually drafts the budget ordinances) are both within the Department of Administration and are responsive to the mayor's direction.

Department of Public Safety

Consolidated into the Department of Public Safety are the fire and police forces, civil defense, weights and measures for both the city and county, and the municipal dog pound. The department is administered by the director of public safety (appointed by the mayor), assisted by a five-member safety board composed of the department director plus two members appointed by the mayor and two by council. The board's primary duty is to recommend matters of policy and management to the director. A large portion of the Unigov Act's language is occupied with regulations and reforms for the fire and police agencies, including provisions strengthening the merit and professional aspects of these services. Inclusion of these long-sought provisions in the act enabled Unigov's sponsors to secure fire and police support for the bill.

Department of Transportation

The director of the Department of Transportation (DOT) is appointed by the mayor, with council approval, and is directly accountable to the mayor. The department has countywide jurisdiction, including some authority in the excluded cities and town, having been given the road and street responsibilities previously exercised by the County Commission and the County Highway Department, the city street department, the Parks Board, and the Mass Transportation Agency. Transportation represents Unigov's most significant and thoroughgoing merger of city and county activities.

Parks and Public Works

A countywide Department of Parks and Recreation already existed before Unigov. The chief Unigov change was placing the department directly under the mayor, with a mayor-appointed director and a great reduction in the independence of the board. The previous five-member Board of Park Commissioners, three of whom were appointed by the mayor and two by the County Council, selected the director, made all personnel appointments, and submitted its budget directly to the City Council for approval. (There was some question as to the legality of the City Council's establishing a countywide tax rate. Accordingly, the park budget was also submitted to the County Council as a courtesy.) With the change, the mayor's appointee chairs the five-member board (the parks director, two mayoral appointees, and two council appointees), whose personnel appointments and budgets now come under the mayor's review.

The new Department of Public Works retains the former department's responsibility for the municipal garage, public buildings and grounds, some surface water drains, and general public improvements. Major responsibility of the former Department of Public Works over the streets—that is, their lighting, construction, and maintenance—was transferred to DOT under Unigov.

The new department also took over the activities of the Board of Sanitary Commissioners, which controlled the sanitation district, the county drainage board, the countywide Department of Flood Control,[2] and the air pollution control agency. Each of these formerly quasi-independent entities now operates under the director of the Department of Public Works and a five-member Board of Works. Thus, although the old department lost some significant responsibilities to DOT, it gained others, and the new Department of Public Works is a major unit.

Department of Metropolitan Development

The Department of Metropolitan Development is one of the strongest and most comprehensive agencies in the country. Establishment of this department was undoubtedly one of the more significant Unigov accomplishments. While the Department of Transportation may have represented a consolidation of greater magnitude, the Unigov principals could point to the Metropolitan Transportation Authority as a forerunner. The Department of Metropolitan Development was, however, a wholly new proposal and thus had to be sold politically.

It will be recalled that when the editor of the *Indianapolis News*

---

2. The drainage board and the Department of Flood Control are now consolidated as a single division of the department.

A view from the statehouse lawn of the Hyatt Regency Hotel complex, the centerpiece of the block-square Merchants Plaza. The plaza was a major achievement of the Department of Metropolitan Development in land acquisition and finance packaging.
From: Division of Planning and Zoning, Indianapolis–Marion County.

accused Mayor Lugar of seeking to be a "supermayor," it was the mayor's appointment power over the Metropolitan Development Commission that aroused the newsman's ire. To allay some of these concerns, the Metropolitan Development Commission was given greater policymaking powers than that given to the four other departmental boards. Moreover, the commission has nine members instead of the usual five, selected by three appointing authorities: four by the mayor, three by the City-County Council, and two by the county commissioners. (The departmental director was originally chosen by the commission, but a 1972 amendment made this a mayoral appointment.)

The department is organized in five divisions: planning and zoning, housing, urban renewal, buildings, and code enforcement. The division of planning and zoning took in the former Metropolitan Planning Commission, created by a 1955 consolidation of city and county planning and zoning functions, when the autonomous 11-member commission was superseded by the Metropolitan Development Commission.

The former Indianapolis Housing Authority became the Division of Housing, retaining much of its former identity although the mayor's powers of appointment and removal were strengthened, and most of the authority's actions must now be approved by the Metropolitan Development Commission. A major change brought the Indianapolis Redevelopment Commission completely under the department as its division of urban renewal, the powers of the former commission and board of trustees being assumed by the commission. Urban renewal's territorial jurisdiction has also been extended to the boundaries of the consolidated city. The division of code enforcement in effect extended the authority of the former city building commissioner to the territory of the consolidated city.

Executive Control

Unigov made the mayor the chief executive to a far greater degree than he was before. As the single elected executive for both the consolidated City of Indianapolis and Marion County, the mayor combines the political and governmental authority and jurisdiction that is central to Unigov's success. Administratively, the office of mayor has been restructured so that it closely resembles a cabinet arrangement. Lines of responsibility and accountability are much more clearly drawn, the mayor's office staff was enlarged, and budgetmaking was centralized.

Merged City and County Executive Offices

Extension of the mayor's authority countywide was not simply an expansion of the mayor's municipal powers to include the county. Instead, it merged the original mayoral powers with most of the executive powers formerly held by the county commissioners. Although there is no great distinction between cities' powers and counties' powers, Indiana cities do have more statutory authority than the counties, and administration can often be cumbersome if a new state statute must be enacted to authorize extension of an urban service to a rural jurisdiction. Creation of the Unigov City-County Council improved the situation somewhat because the council had clear authority to extend urban services into rural areas previously beyond the city's jurisdiction.

The transfer of power from the Board of County Commissioners to the mayor was ingeniously fashioned and far-reaching, but not total. The residual powers retained by the county commissioners' office are clearly limited: the commissioners still make some appointments (e.g., two to the Metropolitan Development Commission), sign county-backed bond issues, and administer the county nursing home. These duties are now performed on a part-time basis by the assessor, auditor, and treasurer, who serve ex officio as replacements for the three-member Board of County Commissioners, who were formerly elected in their own right. Their authority being thus reduced and their political base rendered ineffective, the county commissioners have conceded the dominant position to the mayor, who is fully recognized as the chief executive of both the county government and the consolidated city government.

The Mayor's Office

Before Unigov, more than 20 operational departments, commissions, or agencies reported directly to the mayor (Chart 1, p. 31). These old city departments are now administered by the six department heads, who are appointed by the mayor and serve at his pleasure and who also assist the mayor as members of a policymaking cabinet. Nothing in the Unigov law established a cabinet, but this kind of arrangement has been facilitated by the strong lines of responsibility and accountability between the mayor and the department heads.

The Unigov law did provide for one or more deputy mayors to assist the mayor in directing his staff and coordinating mayoral duties. The consolidated city now has two deputy mayors. One is generally assigned to the coordination of internal affairs, especially interdepartmental and mayor-council relations. The other deputy mayor principally provides liaison with federal agencies and other state and local governments.

Increased Budgetary Powers

The increased budgetary powers now centered in the mayor's office primarily affect the units of government organized under the consolidated city.[3] Within the consolidated city budget, the power of executive review is comprehensive and effective. Departmental budget requests are presented to the mayor, who reviews and consolidates them into a combined budget. This is given to the controller, who supplies additional detail, determines the required tax rates, and, along with the city attorney (both mayoral appointees), puts the budget into ordinance form for submission to the council. The power of executive review represents an increase of mayoral control over the old city units—as well as over some units with wider jurisdiction, that is, the Parks and Recreation Department and flood control district, which were merged under Unigov—but the mayor's veto power is

3. Budgets of more than 20 county civil and judicial units are still prepared by the individual departments (or courts), compiled by the auditor and submitted to the City-County Council without executive review. A recent League of Women Voters study stated that these combined budgets amounted to $29,439,000, or about 11 percent of all county budgets; see *Metro Budget Project* (Indianapolis: League of Women Voters, 1975), p. 47.

what gives him a conclusive voice in the budget process. Under Unigov he has item veto power over both substantive ordinances and appropriation ordinances—which also applies to the special taxing districts. As a two-thirds vote of the council is required to override a veto, the mayor's actions carry a great deal of authority.

As chief executive of both the consolidated City of Indianapolis and of Marion County, the mayor is the principal signatory and prime sponsor of federal grants, for example, general revenue sharing and community development. Administration of these funds gives the mayor an important role in determining county budget priorities, a major stride toward an integrated countywide budget. Despite the large sums of money involved, or perhaps because of them, federal dollars have been an important inducement to such budget integration. On the other hand, it should be acknowledged that the basic responsibility for enacting budgets under Unigov is still legislative, not executive, that is, the City-County Council is the body that ultimately decides on appropriations.

Legislative Integration

The reorganization of legislative functions had almost as significant an impact on the integration of local political control as it did in strengthening the mayor and the administrative agencies. The new City-County Council is now responsible for the legislative, deliberating, budgeting, and legitimizing functions formerly parceled out among the old City Council, the County Council, the County Commission, and (to a considerable degree) the boards and commissions previously responsible for health and hospitals, sanitation, public works, and transportation.

The council has 29 members, 25 elected from single-member districts and 4 at-large (see Map 7). It must establish a standing committee for each of the executive departments, and it may establish other committees. The council makes appropriations, levies taxes, passes ordinances, confirms many of the mayor's appointees, and makes some appointments in its own right.

To assist the council in its expanded budgetary duties, the Unigov law provided for an internal auditor's office, tied directly to the council through the clerk's office instead of being part of the controller's office. The clerk, appointed by council, keeps council records and arranges its meetings.

The City-County Council as a whole has legislative authority for the entire county on matters for which the county is the jurisdictional base. Under the Unigov Act the budgets of the special service districts and any ordinances relating exclusively to those areas must be approved by special service district councils, comprising councilmem-

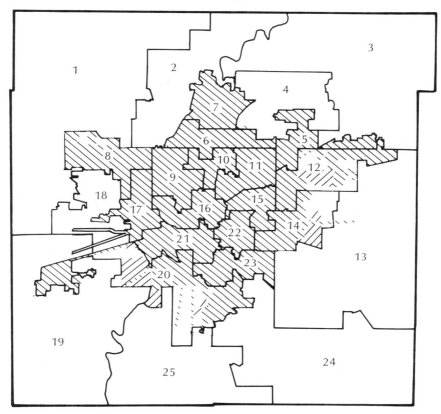

Indianapolis police and fire service districts

Indianapolis extended police service districts

Map 7.

Council Districts Under Unigov (1970), Indianapolis–Marion County

Source: 1970 census data. Prepared by Department of Metropolitan Development, Division of Planning and Zoning, Indianapolis–Marion County, April 1972.

bers whose electoral districts are wholly or largely in the affected service district.

The councils responsible for the fire and police service districts—approximately equivalent to the old city—presently consist of 16 members from the old city districts, plus the 4 members at-large. Without the at-large participation, providing for extra Republican members, these special service district councils would have been evenly divided between the two parties in 1971, as the Republicans and Democrats each elected 8 councilmembers from the special service area. The Democrats gained in 1975 when they captured 9 of the 16 district seats. Nevertheless, the Republicans' at-large spots still gave them an overall majority, 11 to 9. Until 1980, the Unigov statute authorized participation by at-large members in special district councils only if 60 percent or more of their constituents reside in the district. Anticipating correctly that the fire and police districts were not likely to have 60 percent of the county's population after the 1980 census, the Republican leadership had the statute changed in 1980, allowing the at-large members to serve on the special district councils regardless of their population.

Improvements in Leadership and Management

Indiana mayors are generally strong, both politically and administratively. But even in comparison with Indiana's other mayors, or with pre-Unigov mayors of Indianapolis, the power, prestige, and central position of the mayor have clearly been enhanced under Unigov. The mayor is now the dominant political figure, the chief spokesperson for both city and county. His control over the administrative departments has been greatly strengthened. Moreover, the mayor's strong role appears to have reduced the comparative significance of the role of party chair.

In short, the mayor is now at or very near the top of the community's power structure, which was not always the case. An experienced and perceptive journalist commenting on the 1950s and early 1960s reported that community power was largely in the hands of three men: William H. Book, executive vice-president of the Indianapolis Chamber of Commerce; Eugene C. Pulliam, owner and publisher of the *News* and *Star*; and Frank E. McKinney, chairman of the board of American Fletcher National Bank and leading figure in the Democratic Party.[4] Book and Pulliam were Republicans, McKinney a Democrat. While all three shared a politically conservative outlook, they were not necessarily always allies.

By contrast, in the post-Unigov years three separate efforts to identify the local power structure by asking knowledgeable people to name the most powerful and influential people in the community produced lists headed by Mayor Lugar and then by Mayor Hudnut.[5] Counterparts of the three earlier leaders are still prominent and appeared on the lists, although not at the top. (Pulliam and McKinney have been

4. Irving Leibowitz, *My Indiana* (Englewood Cliffs, N.J.: Prentice-Hall, 1964), pp. 64–87.

5. William Doherty, "Perceptions of Indianapolis," unpublished manuscript presented to Department of Political Science, Indiana University, Bloomington; and "Indy's Movers and Shakers: Who's Who in the City Power Structure," *Indianapolis Star*, November 28–December 10, 1976.

succeeded in the power structure by their sons and Book by Carl Dortch, his protégé and replacement at the Chamber of Commerce.)

Changes in management practices clearly have occurred, although they are neither highly visible nor easy to evaluate. Moreover, it is uncertain whether they are the result of Unigov or of the establishment of a Republican business-oriented regime, or both. But the Unigov reform does appear to have changed the government's managerial tone. Unigov's promise of dynamic and conclusive action, plus the personal persuasiveness of both Unigov mayors, have attracted a number of qualified professionals to the new government, including several executives on leave from local businesses. Consequently, management improvements have been introduced in the various departments, many developed and implemented under the planned variations federal grant that specifically allocated money for management improvement.

Improved Efficiency

Improved efficiency was sought by instituting such measures as an interdepartmental mail delivery system, a phone utilization program, a unified city-county duplicating services contract, and a combined office of property management for all city and county property. A comprehensive insurance program reduced the total number of policies from 56 to 18, with annual premium savings of $185,000. A combined city-county purchasing office was set up, and legal services for city and county agencies were consolidated. Useful but less noticeable was the adoption of new accounting and bookkeeping procedures in the finance division where staffing was held to 49 persons despite a rise in annual dollar transactions from $55 million to $166 million with the advent of unified government.

Legal Services

Consolidating legal services not only promoted efficiency but also gave the mayor's office considerable additional influence on policy. Before Unigov, legal interpretations were made by each department's attorney, at least in the first instance. As legal interpretation can affect departmental policy decisions, consolidating legal services in one office under the Department of Administration, which is subject to the mayor's direct or indirect appointment, gave the mayor added influence over a broad spectrum of governmental programs.

Streamlining Personnel Practices

There has been a major attempt to streamline and professionalize personnel functions. The combined Unigov agencies have seen significant payroll reductions, as compared with their predecessor city and county agencies, despite substantially increased salaries, particularly at the upper levels.[6] Admittedly, a large portion of the payroll reduction can be traced to Indianapolis's participation in federal programs, especially the Department of Labor's Emergency Employment Act (EEA)—subsequently the Comprehensive Employment and Training Act (CETA) Titles II and VI—which placed over 900 new public service employees under Unigov by 1973. Nevertheless, some of the savings can be attributed to good management.

Business influence on Unigov management can be seen in numerous other advances in personnel practices: a management training program for supervisory personnel was instituted; a systematic personnel performance review program was established; exit interviews are now held with departing employees; and five separate employment application procedures have been combined into one. Perhaps the most important change was computerizing a wage administration control book, listing each position by job description, title, labor grade, and salary. This process revealed salary inequities, most due to lower salaries for the county than for the city. The county salaries were adjusted upward.

Political Patronage

The Unigov administration is highly partisan, like the pre-Unigov city and county administrations and like most local government in Indiana. Most top appointments go to the mayor's political associates. Most appointees to city jobs need political clearance through the party machinery, and city employees at all levels are encouraged (at least) to participate actively in partisan campaigns. Probably such patronage practices—typical of Indiana politics—will continue to characterize the Unigov administration for some time.[7] Nevertheless, the business style of management of the first two Unigov mayors effected notable improvements in the professional status of mayoral appointees, particularly in the county offices. The number of outright patronage appointees is down while there is an increasing number of nationwide searches for trained professionals to fill an increasing number of impor-

6. City and county personnel services used 55 percent of the total budget in fiscal 1969, the last preconsolidation year. These services represented 40.3 percent of the 1973 budget.

7. The fire and police merit system and a recent state collective bargaining law for public employees should, however, reduce the number of patronage jobs. Most city positions are now covered by collective bargaining. Accordingly, many positions are filled by a bid process wherein openings are posted and bid for by workers on the basis of their qualifications for the job, and employees cannot be removed without cause when administrations change. Only management-level positions are filled at the discretion of the mayor.

tant Unigov posts. These improvements are likely to be retained, whatever party is in office.

Progress in Services, Planning, and Development

Service levels and quality are always difficult to evaluate. Partisans of the Unigov administration say they are clearly better since the reform, whereas opponents disagree. A reporter with long experience covering city hall summed up an early assessment this way: "Among other facts that apparently can be documented are those that show the administration is producing record numbers of streets paved, sidewalks built, condemned houses razed, junk cars removed, jobs found for unemployed, and low-cost housing units built and federal grants approved for various programs."[8]

Transportation

The most conspicuous service improvements related to transportation and downtown development. Creation of the Department of Transportation (DOT) was the most comprehensive of the departmental and service area mergers. Adding substance to transportation's organizational and functional changes was the reallocation of state-collected road and street monies to Unigov's DOT. The Unigov reforms enabled the department to implement areawide transportation plans with far fewer governmental or budgetary constraints than before. Moreover, its accomplishments are more easily measured than are those of other departments. Unigov mayors and other observers have emphasized the striking increases in the miles of streets and roads paved or resurfaced. For example, in the first three years of Unigov alone, the miles paved or resurfaced increased from 56 in 1969 to 150 in 1970, to 265 miles in 1972.

Another significant accomplishment was resolution of a major road and traffic problem at the General Motors (Allison Division) plant on the city's west side. A pre-Unigov attempt to provide access to the plant had been stymied by budgetary considerations, jurisdictional conflicts, and overlapping plans. One of the first actions of Unigov's Department of Transportation was to bring together the various county departments, the city of Speedway, and several old city departments, to complete the project. The effort was greatly facilitated by the consolidation and the centralized budget under the new department.

Completion of the inner and outer highway loops in Marion County cannot be directly attributed to the new government as it was federally funded, with matching state funds. Nevertheless, Unigov

8. "Unigov Making It? All Depends," *Indianapolis News*, April 8, 1971, p. 8.

must be given considerable credit for the ease and rapidity of the new highway system's completion: "Unigov as a single unit of government was greatly responsible for the completion of the inner and outer loops. Particularly, the Unigov system allowed for the development of a coherent plan for the completion of the transportation system way ahead of the normal time for these things."[9] The Unigov Department of Transportation can also justifiably be credited with building the appropriate connecting road linkage to coincide with the loop construction.

Indianapolis is on flat terrain with no major physical barriers, and its new interstate highway system is of "classic" design, often likened to a wheel, the inner loop being the hub, the outer loop the rim, and the bisecting thruways the spokes. The system's completion was crucial to Indianapolis's continuance as a regional center for trade and commerce. On the other hand, some critics argue that the travel convenience provided by the new highway grid will hasten the flight of the well-to-do to the suburbs.[10] While this may be true, it is not necessarily an argument that the transportation improvements should not have been done at all or that their facilitation does not represent a substantial Unigov accomplishment.

Planning and Community Development

Extensive community developments were completed in the 1970s but cannot entirely be attributed to the new governmental arrangement. The mayors and other community leaders had been committed to development for some time—in the case of Mayor Lugar, even before Unigov—and new federal dollars gave substance to many of their plans. Certainly some development would have occurred anyway, but probably not at the level it did under Unigov.

Unigov has probably been most effective in removing some of the institutional barriers to development. This is especially true of the Department of Metropolitan Development, which brought the basic elements of planning and development together in one agency.

Unigov mayors have been notably successful in using the Department of Metropolitan Development's authority to locate development projects in the central business district, using acquisition and development assistance to give the necessary impetus to new private construction. Federal dollars have been combined with state and local revenue and private trusts—for example, the Lilly Endowment and the Krannert Charitable Trust—to "leverage" private capital investment. As one close observer commented, this kind of private-public partnership has been a critical feature of Indianapolis's renewal effort: "But the bottom

9. Richard G. Lugar, interview with James Owen, Indianapolis, August 17, 1976.
10. Richard Hebert, *Highways to Nowhere: The Politics of City Transportation* (Indianapolis: Bobbs-Merrill, 1972), pp. 65–94.

The downtown Indianapolis skyline is framed by one of the area's several interstate highway interchanges that have contributed greatly to the city's claim to be the "Crossroads of America."
From: Division of Planning and Zoning, Indianapolis–Marion County.

line in Indianapolis is that the city is in the midst of an obvious revitalization and perhaps a more dramatic one than some comparable cities because in Indianapolis there are fewer restrictions, plus the city has a civic vision built on government-business teamwork."[11]

The reorganization of the Department of Metropolitan Development, incorporating all the essential public-sector mechanisms for development under one department, allows Indianapolis mayors to pursue their civic vision without crippling restrictions and roadblocks. The mayor's direct administrative control of the department allows him to make commitments on development projects to a far greater degree than was ever possible previously and to a greater degree than in most other large American cities.

Planning and Zoning. Before Unigov, a single planning commission and staff served the entire county, including all municipalities, but three separate boards handled zoning appeals: one for the City of Indianapolis, another for all the small municipalities, and a third for the county's unincorporated area. There was no appeal from these boards' decisions, except to the courts.

11. John Lyst, "Indianapolis: Economy Is Getting a Boost from Substantial New Projects on the Rise," *National Real Estate Investor* 23(12):109 (November 1981).

Under Unigov the functions of the previously combined county-wide Metropolitan Planning Commission were transferred to the Metropolitan Development Commission with no changes in authority or jurisdiction, but there were substantial changes in the zoning appeals process. Since Unigov, all zoning appeals—except in Beech Grove, Lawrence, and Speedway, which have their own zoning appeals boards—are heard in one or the other of three divisions of the Metropolitan Board of Zoning Appeals.

Appeals are assigned to the divisions by lot. The staff of the Department of Metropolitan Development provide opinions for all of the appeal boards—including those for the smaller municipalities. The director of the department, but not private petitioners or complainants, may appeal decisions by any of the appeal boards to the Metropolitan Development Commission (MDC). Private parties, on the other hand, may appeal to the regular courts decisions of a board of zoning appeals or of the MDC on a zoning appeal. The director of the department does not have this option. This arrangement apparently strengthens significantly the position of the central commission and staff. Thus, to ensure conformity with the county plan the commission has overruled decisions of appeal boards, and the staff seems much more satisfied with this arrangement than with the previous system.

An amendment to the original Unigov law further strengthened the authority of the department and its commission. Under the original act, zoning or rezoning actions passed by the Metropolitan Development Commission could be overturned by a simple majority of the City-County Council. With the new 29-member council, a member from a district affected by a rezoning could go to his fellow councilmembers and rather easily get support from enough of them to overrule the decision. In effect, councilmembers were becoming the zoning officers for their districts. Zoning supporters then got an amendment passed requiring a two-thirds council vote to override zoning recommendations by the MDC. It also now takes a council majority just to call such an issue up for a vote.

With these and other changes relating to planning and zoning, the government's capacity to plan orderly growth in Marion County seems substantially improved. What may be even more important under Unigov is the reinforcement of the planning process by the addition of certain general divisions; that is, the housing authority, code enforcement, building inspection, and—perhaps most important—the urban renewal divisions are all now in the same department.

Community Development. As mentioned, prior to Unigov, planning was a separate countywide activity and lacked a close connection to the operational functions of government, for example, parks, health, transportation, and urban renewal. Unigov forged a link between planning and operations and established centralized leadership to get things done. Michael Carroll, the department director during much of the period and later deputy mayor, put it this way: "It is clear to me that the Department of Metropolitan Development was the lead agent or catalyst for all of the public and private partnerships that developed during the 1970s to create new investment in downtown Indianapolis. Because of the power and control, and the nature of the statute responsibility the department and its commission had, it was the logical department to implement that basic policy."[12]

The effectiveness of the consolidated planning and community development process is most clearly demonstrated in the central business district and near downtown neighborhoods that constitute Center Township. In the 1970s this inner-city township represented a study in contrasts. While its largely minority population continued to decline and some of its neighborhoods deteriorate, Center Township also benefited from the most conspicuous commitment of community resources found in the entire county—some would say in the whole state.

There was a twofold approach to Center Township's problems. First, there was a public-private commitment to the development of the mile-square central business district, site of a major effort to reestablish the downtown as the metropolitan region's entertainment, commercial, and education center. Second, there was a complementary program to rehabilitate housing and revitalize neighborhoods in the near downtown area.

Visitors are impressed by vast recent changes in the downtown Indianapolis skyline. As a featured city in the *Nation's Business* "Salute to American Cities" series, Indianapolis was described in 1976 as a city of tremendous physical growth, most of the examples of such growth being in the mile-square downtown area.[13] These included Merchants Plaza (a combined bank and office tower and Hyatt Regency Hotel); the Market Square development, with an 18,000-seat sports arena; a new convention center; and several new large office buildings.

The entire block where the Merchants Plaza development is situated was purchased and developed using urban renewal powers. The mayor effectively employed the Department of Metropolitan Development in getting location plans accepted, securing the necessary rezoning, and assembling the funding required to complete the project. This was also facilitated by the extension of urban renewal bonding to a larger, nearly countywide base, thus involving suburban interests in

---

12. Michael A. Carroll, interview with James Owen, Indianapolis, December 19, 1977.

13. "A Salute to American Cities: Indianapolis," *Nation's Business* 64(11):46 (November 1976).

A view of the Indianapolis downtown skyline featuring Merchants Plaza in the foreground and the tall Indiana Bank building directly behind it. Much of the originally planned mile-square area was revitalized in the 1970s.

From: Division of Planning and Zoning, Indianapolis–Marion County.

the downtown development.[14] Unigov made it possible to mobilize governmental powers and financial resources crucial to the downtown program. As in many other cities, plans for improving the central business district had been in existence for many years and had undergone several major revisions, but very little of substance had been accomplished previously.

Charles Whistler, longtime president of the Metropolitan Plan Commission and author of the metropolitan development section of the Unigov bill, credits Unigov with the success of the downtown projects: "The Hyatt House and the Market Square Arena would not have gone without Unigov. The mayor was able to act almost as a business in putting together a $45 million package with the city's money pledged to its support."[15] The Unigov mayors' ability to "deliver" on projects of this magnitude has some spinoff effect in attracting business support for similar undertakings. For example, the business-government relationship was essential to the location of the downtown developments, as the director of the Chamber of Commerce noted: "The sports arena is located downtown for a simple reason: the

14. The four "excluded cities"—Beech Grove, Speedway, Lawrence, and Southport—were not included in the tax base for urban renewal.

15. Charles L. Whistler, interview with James Owen, Indianapolis, August 12, 1976.

The skyline of Indianapolis, featuring the domed sports arena, reflects the health and vitality of downtown.
From: City of Indianapolis, Mayor's Office. Michael A. Heitz, photographer.

developers who were attempting to attract capital had chosen a site out on the interstate at 59th street, in an open cornfield where they could acquire property. But some of the bankers, a large real estate firm, and Mayor Lugar said that if there was going to be any public funds involved, it's going to be located downtown. And that's the way it was; the developers had to have public participation, and to get it they had to go to the mayor."[16]

The use of public resources to support downtown development was not universally approved. The Democrats were particularly critical of the use of substantial general revenue sharing money to help finance the sports arena, as their priority was neighborhood development.

Despite some demonstrable results, the city's housing strategy has also drawn mixed reviews. Part of the blame rests on a strategy that gives top priority to large capital improvements, followed by housing rehabilitation. The Republican administrations under Unigov have contended that they have a two-part approach to housing, with downtown renewal as a central component. Using this strategy, they have attempted to stabilize and improve residential neighborhoods,

16. Carl R. Dortch, interview with James Owen, Indianapolis, August 18, 1976.

for example, in Center Township, through the "ripple effect" of large downtown projects that create jobs, improve the amenities of neighborhood living, stabilize housing conditions, and encourage further private investment. They have also employed such programs as the federally sponsored community development block grant to rehabilitate old houses and build new housing in blighted neighborhoods.

Two housing projects demonstrate why the city's housing strategy, overall, has brought mixed reviews. The most recent, Lockefield Gardens, is cited by both supporters and critics—either as an example of the ripple policy in practice or of the secondary importance of housing rehabilitation. There, because of major new developments in the adjacent area—including the $27 million sports center—the city has agreed to rehabilitate 175 of 275 low-income units abandoned two decades ago and to build an additional 250 private apartments on adjoining land in an attempt to encourage neighborhood stability.

The second housing project, in the Lockerbie Square of Center Township on the near east side, is a classic case of "damned if you do, damned if you don't" planning for housing. This project to restore a number of large nineteenth-century mansions *and* return middle-class residents to Center Township has brought complaints of "Negro removal" from the black community. Critics argue that the urban gentrification process converts multiunit housing used by blacks into single-family units for whites and that no new units are being made available nearby for the displaced black families. Instead, low-income housing units tend to be made available in other parts of the county, often outside Center Township. Thus, the city is caught in the inevitable position of wishing to encourage middle-class families to live in the central city and, at the same time, reduce the decentralization of Center Township population to the suburbs.

John R. Ottensmann, an Indiana University planning professor, claimed that a loss of inner-city population is the unavoidable consequence of housing rehabilitation: "Even the most favorable revitalization of the inner city would mean continued population decline. The dwellings in the inner city have been overcrowded. With rehabilitation, they are going to be reconverted into larger units to be occupied by smaller households, so there will be fewer people living in the center."[17] Ottensmann sees the decline in central-city population as an opportunity for "people who have been living in substandard housing to acquire better housing further out."[18]

One of the things contributing to Ottensmann's optimism is Unigov's authority to develop a communitywide housing strategy. "The

17. John R. Ottensmann, "Urban Development in Indianapolis: Prospects for the Future," *School of Public and Environmental Affairs Review* 3(2):20 (Spring 1982).
18. Ibid., p. 21.

Department of Metropolitan Development has done a very good job in zoning for moderate-income multiunit private housing development in suburban areas," Ottensmann said.[19] The fact that Unigov has planning and zoning jurisdictions in both the inner city and the suburbs greatly reduces the impact of the suburban exclusion experienced in other large metropolitan areas. This is notable in the private market as well as in the publicly subsidized sectors.

The Indianapolis housing strategy is designed to meet the needs of the larger community, although the department's record in placing subsidized housing in the suburbs has not been as good as the private-sector effort. This is definitely an improvement over the former arrangement, under which the county government had no public housing plan, and unified planning and zoning were impossible for both the city and the suburbs. But the debate continues over whether Center Township has benefited from the city's downtown development strategy. Opinions vary in substance and intensity. One interesting statistic that has emerged from the debate is the growth of the township's tax base during the 1970s. Center Township's pre-Unigov net assessment of taxable real property totaled $347,254,680 in 1969, increasing to $516,831,598 in 1982. While this 33 percent rise in 13 years does not represent spectacular growth—not even keeping pace with inflation—it is highly significant because the pattern of annual increases contrasts sharply with the deteriorating tax bases of core areas in most other urban regions.

Regionalization and Decentralization

Since the enactment of the Unigov bill there have been significant efforts to provide governmental institutions both for the wider metropolitan area and for local neighborhoods. But the Indiana Heartland Coordinating Commission, a regional planning agency for transportation, land use, and water quality, has experienced only limited success, and the quest for the formation of neighborhood governments never really got off the ground.

Regional Developments

The Indiana Heartland Coordinating Commission, established in the summer of 1972, is the principal effort to organize governmental institutions over a larger area. Unigov's primary jurisdiction, of course, was limited to Marion County. But the standard metropolitan statistical area (SMSA), expanded by the US Bureau of the Budget in 1967, now includes Marion County plus seven other counties. The

19. John R. Ottensmann, interview with James Owen, July 8, 1982.

desirability of certain kinds of mechanisms coordinating certain functions throughout this larger area has long been recognized. Nevertheless, governmental mechanisms extending beyond county limits are usually less acceptable and much more difficult to establish than single-county arrangements. While Unigov represents a marked improvement over the previous city and county arrangements, the movement for a more effective regional government has not fared nearly as well.

On the other hand, spurred by federal grants, a number of regional forums and coordinating agencies have been established. At the time of Unigov's adoption, the Comprehensive Health Planning Council of Central Indiana included all eight counties; it has now been supplanted—as have similar agencies in other states—by a larger agency, that is, the Central Indiana Health Systems Agency, encompassing about a third of Indiana. The Indiana Criminal Justice Planning Region Number Five also includes the eight counties, as does the Hoosier Heartland Association, established to consider soil and water conservation measures. All of these are loose, low-visibility associations for planning and coordination, with limited funds (mostly from federal grants).

For a number of years, many federal agencies, acting under Office of Management and Budget Circular A-95, have required local

The revitalization of historic Lockerbie Square, shown here before (left) and after (right) improvements, is an example of the city's program to tie neighborhood housing improvement with downtown development in Center Township.
From: Historic Preservation Division, City of Indianapolis. Allan Conant, photographer

applications for many types of federal grants to be cleared through a regional planning agency or council of governments. Marion County long had a countywide planning agency with substantial staff and extensive jurisdiction, so federal agencies had accepted clearance through this body as satisfactory A-95 compliance for all projects relating to Marion County.

When the SMSA was enlarged to include the eight-county region, the Marion County Planning Agency began making some plans and studies relating to the entire region, but the other counties were not represented on the single-county agency and could not get the requisite federal clearance through it. Under pressure from these counties for a clearance channel, the US Department of Housing and Urban Development notified Marion County and the other counties that after June 30, 1972, an agency would have to encompass the whole region, or at least a larger part of it, to be considered satisfactory.

For some time the state planning division—part of the Indiana Department of Commerce—had been actively promoting establishment of such regional planning agencies and had sponsored state-authorizing legislation, although there were no requirements for state grants to clear through such an agency. In any event, on the recommendation of its planning division, the state designated substate planning and development regions, the one involving Marion County coinciding with the eight-county SMSA. But there was no direct state financial assistance for these regional activities.

The existing Hoosier Heartland Association (largely representing the soil and water conservation agencies), plus the director of the state planning division, then took the initiative in trying to establish a regional planning agency for the eight-county Indianapolis region. Under the statutory provisions they were proposing to use, each participating county would have been given an equal voice. But Mayor Lugar and his associates in Unigov were not satisfied with this kind of representation. They were aware that Marion County had only one of eight votes in the Criminal Justice Planning Agency, and they felt they had received a disproportionately small share of the grants controlled by that body.

The Indiana Heartland Coordinating Commission

Marion County's consent was of course crucial to the formation of a regional agency. On the other hand, none of the other seven counties had a similar block of voting power, as federal practice apparently permitted the recognition of a regional planning agency that included representatives of more than 75 percent of the SMSA population. This criterion would be met if Marion County could get the participation of only one or two of the other counties. Partly because of this leverage, partly because of some unwillingness to accept state leadership and involvement—which the Hoosier Heartland Association proposal would have involved—and partly because Marion County offered to accept a proportional share of the costs of the regional agency (if it were given a similar proportion of the voting power in matters affecting Marion County), most of the surrounding counties agreed to participate in forming a new Indiana Heartland Coordinating Commission (IHCC) shortly before the June 30, 1972, deadline. Seven of the eight counties are presently full members of the IHCC, and three municipalities in the eighth county, which has no county plan commission, are also members.

The framers of the agreement did not use the special state statute authorizing a regional planning commission but instead acted under a more general law, commonly known as the Interlocal Cooperation Act.[20] They formed what they called a "multijurisdictional coordinating commission," whose sole purpose was "to function as an Areawide Planning Organization (APO) as defined by the Department of Housing and Urban Development (HUD) and the Environmental Protection

20. *Indiana Acts of 1957*, Public Law 118 (Indianapolis, 1957), pp. 2–3.

Agency (EPA) of the United States, and serve a similar role in the future with regard to other federal agencies."[21] The bylaws provide that each county shall have three representatives on such a commission (if a county itself is not a member, then a city or group of cities within that county that are members shall be entitled to two representatives).

Commission action is by majority vote, except that any action involving a specific recommendation for agreement between two or more participating units must have their approval as well as that of a majority of the commission. Moreover, on any matter relating to commission approval or comment on applications for federal grants or funds, any representative from a unit submitting the application shall have the right to insist on voting apportioned according to the population of the member units. Financial support is apportioned according to population. The proportional voting clause gives Marion County a decisive voice with regard to its own applications, if it wishes to use it, and on other applications as well. Another critical factor giving Marion County a strong influence over the emerging regional body in its incipient years was the use by the IHCC of county staff members, provided initially in lieu of cash contributions.

Early Years of Operation

The regional organization is now several years old, having in a short span grown considerably in size, budget, and activities. The first full-time director was hired in August 1973. Commission offices were opened on January 1, 1974, and the initial staff of seven was set up that year. The commission's early budgets, based almost entirely on member subscriptions—much of it paid in kind—and on matching HUD 701 comprehensive planning grants, were substantially increased in 1976 when the Environmental Protection Agency funded a $1 million water-quality study for the Heartland area. Consultants were retained for most of the research for the study, but the commission's role as the grant's prime sponsor increased its prestige and raised staff needs to a complement of twenty-one members.

Much of the work of the Indiana Heartland Coordinating Committee continues in the area of water planning and A-95 review for federal grant applications. Recent membership, budget, and staff gains, however, plus a 1975 amendment to its bylaws, have increased the commission's authority "to provide intergovernmental and multi-jurisdictional planning and coordination; and to provide technical assistance to the members hereof."[22] Its planning and coordinating

21. The wording is from the intergovernmental contract establishing the agency.

22. "Amended Agreement for Formation and Operation of a Multi-Jurisdictional Coordinating Commission," approved by the Indiana Heartland Coordinating Commission on October 7, 1975.

activities have also increased since 1975, especially with the establishment of the Agricultural Advisory Committee (AgAC) and the Business/Industry Advisory Committee (BIAC). The commission staff also provides Indianapolis's seven surrounding counties with technical assistance on grant application and implementation.

In spite of IHCC's early rapid growth, it does not appear that the pattern set in the first five years represents a trend toward forming an operational regional government in the near future. Nearly all of its early growth was in response to federal government requirements for areawide planning. As that need is met, the commission will probably reach an operational plateau. The commission's bylaws very explicitly limit its authority and jurisdiction: the sovereign status of all member units is stated as a paramount concern of the IHCC. Its services can only be rendered upon request, and even then are only advisory. But the IHCC does represent a significant attempt to provide a regional planning and coordinating agency capable of dealing with several functional concerns.

The IHCC has only low visibility politically. The staff makes some of the studies and plans required and encouraged by federal programs; it has been more active in assisting its constituent units to secure federal funds than in trying to veto projects, although it may have influenced the nature and design of proposals. There has been little or no controversy about the commission, although there is some grumbling about the amount of paperwork involved. Moreover, throughout the state there is a general rumble of discontent about federally imposed "regionalism."

Community Councils: Minigov

Some, not all, of Unigov's framers thought all along that the move toward countywide and regionwide structures should be balanced by the formal establishment of small, local community governmental institutions. A "Minigov" bill was introduced in the same legislative session that adopted Unigov and reappeared in the 1971 session; a modified version was adopted in the 1972 session.[23]

The original Minigov statute required the Department of Metropolitan Development to submit to the council for approval a plan to subdivide the consolidated city's area into small communities. Each of these communities would hold a referendum to decide whether it wished to organize a community council, with very limited powers.

When the department's plan was submitted to the council, however, it drew a good deal of criticism. The 1973 legislature, meeting

23. See also Elinor Ostrom and Nancy M. Neubert, "Unigov + Minigov = Multigov," speech presented to the American Society for Public Administration, Los Angeles, Ca., April 2, 1973.

soon thereafter, modified the law, calling for a new territorial plan with more attention to traditional township lines and making even clearer the community councils' complete subordination to the City-County Council, particularly relating to any financial activity. The Department of Metropolitan Development prepared a new plan, but it also was obviously not acceptable to the council, never even being brought to a vote. The councilmembers, most of whom were elected from single-member districts, were unenthusiastic about arrangements for neighborhood representation through channels other than their own City-County Council.

There seems to be no significant prospect of any such arrangement being implemented in the near future. A wide variety of voluntary neighborhood associations continue to flourish with varying degrees of activity, and they get some encouragement and staff assistance from the Department of Metropolitan Development, but they have no legal status or powers. Minigov now seems completely dead, although the statutory authorization is still on the books.

Nevertheless, the debate surrounding Minigov did have important consequences. Councilmembers now utilize the neighborhood associations to a greater extent than before. While this is especially noticeable among councilmembers chosen from districts composed primarily of downtown and near-downtown neighborhoods, it is certainly not limited to them. Moreover, at least one at-large councilmember, Republican Paula Parker, is closely identified with neighborhood programs. Other established councilmembers such as Rozelle Boyd (Democrat) and Steve West (Republican), who had strong party political bases before the neighborhood associations were established, became very active in the associations in the 1970s and advanced their electability by thus serving neighborhood interests. In short, although neighborhood accessibility to government was not institutionalized by the adoption of Minigov, in some degree the political process nevertheless helped fill the void.

Amendments and Modifications

The Indiana General Assembly regularly passes legislation affecting the government of Indianapolis and Marion County, just as before Unigov's passage in 1969. The Unigov statute itself was amended 17 times from 1971 through 1976, and several other statutes relating to Indianapolis and Marion County have been passed, making changes in the governmental structure. Despite these modifications, there has been remarkably little alteration in Unigov's basic structure as established in 1969. Nevertheless, in time the cumulative effect of these annual incremental changes may be substantial, underscoring the argument that Unigov is not a "completed project."

Clarifications and Amplifications

Some of the changes are only minor clarifications or amplifications of the original statute. These include spelling out in more detail the budget-making and ordinance-passing procedures or the arrangements for transferring property between units and districts, authorizing various activities to be shifted from one department to another, and recognizing Southport as an excluded municipality, while making sure that none of the other small communities could achieve that status. More precise regulations on the special service district councils were enacted to satisfy the federal district court's doubts about the constitutionality of a councilmember's voting on matters affecting a district if only a portion of the council constituency area was within the special service district.

Two amendments strengthened the mayor's position as chief executive. One amendment permits the mayor rather than the Metropolitan Development Commission to appoint the head of the Metropolitan Development Department. Another change divested the county commissioners of their remaining general executive authority, transferring it to the mayor. This change probably grew out of a dispute over some county-owned land the mayor wanted to use for a housing experiment by the federal Department of Housing and Urban Development. The county commissioners, relying on the old statutory presumption that they were responsible for county property, held up the project for a time, and the amendment was the response.

Two other amendments merely applied to Indianapolis modifications that were being made statewide. Thus, the 21-year minimum age for public office was removed, permitting 18-year-olds to serve. Another change provided for filling council vacancies by the precinct committee members of the party to which the retiring or deceased councilmember had belonged, rather than by the council itself. The newly appointed member serves the remainder of the unexpired term and may stand as the incumbent for the seat at the next election.

Some of the longer amendments dealt with police and fire department personnel. As in other major cities, the Indianapolis police department has been a special center of controversy, and the rules governing its personnel continue to be changed. These changes are lengthy and complicated but do not significantly modify the basic governmental structure.

One important amendment concerned zoning ordinances. As

noted above, the City-County Council now requires a two-thirds majority to override a Metropolitan Development Commission (MDC) zoning action. This places the MDC in a relatively stronger position on zoning matters than existed under the previously required simple majority for council to overrule a decision.

Three other changes continued the gradual adjustment of governmental function to an area that had been functioning in the region for decades. Thus, in 1972 the geographical limits of the urban renewal taxing district were extended from the old city limits to the new limits of the consolidated city. This change extended the tax base for renewal from the old city to the whole county area, minus the four excluded municipalities. It was a significant move toward resource redistribution, although in Indianapolis urban redevelopment has not been either massive or tremendously expensive.

A 1975 statute created a solid waste district, separating it administratively from the sanitation district of which it had previously been a part. For the time being, the geographic limits of the two districts remained coterminous; but enlargement of the solid waste district was made easier under the law than enlargement of the sanitation district, which continues providing sewage collection and disposal. This means that in the future the government can undertake garbage collection and disposal for a larger area than that receiving sewage service.

Public Transportation

As noted in the previous chapter, a public transportation corporation was formed after Unigov's passage to provide bus service in the Indianapolis metropolitan area. The transportation corporation, called Metro, is interesting not only for its increased territory and separate budget authority but also because of its administrative independence. The board of directors comprises five members serving staggered terms, three being appointed by the City-County Council and two by the mayor. The transit corporation is not subject to supervision by the Department of Transportation, giving it an independence that seems to conflict with the basic Unigov thrust, that is, to subject all or most of the local government activities to unified administrative control under the mayor's office. This may be attributed in part to the fact that a general state statute was used, but it may also be regarded as a new manifestation of the Unigov proponents' continued willingness to compromise organizational "purity" in meeting a particular need.[24] In practice, moreover, the new corporation has thus far worked closely with Unigov's established leadership.

24. It is interesting to note that the first president of the transit corporation was John Walls, former deputy mayor and one of the chief architects of Unigov.

Judicial Review

The Unigov legislation was subjected to court test as soon as possible after its original passage to resolve doubts about the reorganization's validity. Almost immediately after enactment, a general suit was brought by persons who were basically friendly to Unigov, filed in the name of Carl Dortch, chief executive of the Chamber of Commerce. There was a precedent for this, as chamber officials had from time to time previously sponsored such litigation for early resolution of doubts about governmental powers and authority. On January 26, 1971, the Indiana Supreme Court ruled unanimously that the Unigov legislation was valid, rejecting a large number of arguments and contentions against it.[25]

Agreement on the At-Large Council Seats

The composition of the council was the source of considerable discussion and controversy. While the Unigov bill was being developed and implemented, litigation was in progress on the legal arrangements for at-large election of all members of the Marion County General Assembly delegation. The federal district court had held that at-large election of the entire county's state legislative delegation deprived central-city minorities in Indianapolis of equal protection. Although this opinion was later overturned by the US Supreme Court,[26] at the time it caused some objection to electing any members of the City-County Council at-large. But Unigov proponents believed rather strongly that the party winning the mayoral election should normally be strengthened by the margin that four at-large councilmembers, presumably of the same party, would provide. The Democrats initially opposed this arrangement, but their opposition later diminished. They realized that regardless of how the individual district boundaries are drawn, the demographic pattern is such that Democratic voters will be a good deal more concentrated in a limited number of central districts than are the Republicans. Thus, without the potential of winning one or more of the four at-large seats, a small winning margin of Democratic votes countywide would be too heavily concentrated in a few inner-city single-member districts to secure a majority of Democrats on the council. Because the Democrats thus also stand to gain from the at-large elections, they have not pursued the matter further.

25. *Dortch v. Lugar*, 24 Ind. Dec. 357, 266 NE 2d 25 (1971).
26. *Whitcomb v. Chavis*, L. Ed 2d 363 (June 7, 1971) 403 US 124, 91 S. Ct. 1858, 29.

Seating on the Service District Councils

The composition of the special service district councils is another question that caused some constitutional and political controversy. Under the Unigov statute not all members of a council can participate in all decisions. Certain decisions affecting service districts are to be made by councilmembers who represent those districts. The original bill authorized a councilmember to vote on district matters if any part of his or her constituents reside within the service district. This portion of the act was challenged in federal court, and the judge ruled that to permit a councilmember to legislate for a particular area, when he or she had been elected in substantial part by voters outside the area, would violate the US Constitution.[27] The statute was promptly changed by the 1971 Indiana General Assembly. Under the amended statute, the percentage of the constituency that elected the member must be at least 50 percent (for single-member districts) or 60 percent (for members elected at-large) in order for a councilmember to participate in a special service district council action approving a district budget or in approving ordinances relating exclusively to such a district.

Later, in 1976 after the 1975 election reduced the council's Republican majority, the practice of the four at-large councilmembers serving on the police and fire service district councils was challenged. Dropping the four at-large members would give the Democrats a majority on the councils for those districts (which include only a little over 60 percent of the county's population). But if the at-large members continued to serve, the Republicans would have a majority. Presented with this fact and with figures indicating that the presently seated at-large councilmembers would have been defeated by their opponents if only the votes within the service district boundaries were counted, the federal judge ruled that the councilmembers elected at-large could no longer participate in matters exclusively affecting these areas.[28] But this decision was overruled by the US Court of Appeals, thus reaffirming the propriety of at-large members voting on district matters.

In 1980 the General Assembly amended the Unigov law,[29] probably anticipating that the 1980 census would show that the police and fire districts had less than 60 percent of the county population. The change allowed the four at-large members of the City-County Council to serve on the special service district councils without regard to their

27. *Bryant v. Whitcomb*, 419 F. Supp. 1290 (1976). Although decided in 1970, this opinion was not published until 1976 along with the decision mentioned in the following paragraph.

28. *Cantwell v. Hudnut*, 419 F. Supp. 1301 (1976).

29. *Indiana Acts of 1980*, Public Law 213 (Indianapolis, 1980).

constituent base. This may invite further legal action, although the Republicans gained nine of sixteen of the single-member seats on the police and fire district councils, a majority even without the at-large seats. The Democrats, thus far denied control of the unified government by Republican countywide victories, have more hopes of controlling the police and fire service district councils.

Unigov Tied to School Desegregation

A significant question about the reorganization's validity has come from a rather unexpected source. Indianapolis has been one of the major northern cities heavily involved in litigation over school desegregation. The story is complicated. The litigation began in 1968; the local federal district judge (S. Hugh Dillin, a very controversial public figure in Indianapolis largely because of his role in this litigation) issued four substantial opinions and sets of orders; four opinions were rendered by the court of appeals in Chicago; and several brief rulings were handed down by the US Supreme Court. The cases seem to have established firmly that the Indianapolis school district was guilty of de jure segregation and therefore has an affirmative obligation to take appropriate steps to desegregate the city school system. Under steady court pressure, the district has instituted some measures—reluctantly, at least at first.

While these highly controversial actions of the Indianapolis city school district did not in themselves directly affect the governmental reorganization, Unigov nevertheless came into serious question when Judge Dillin concluded that adequate and effective desegregation was not possible through actions limited to the boundaries of the Indianapolis school districts. The judge held, among other things, that the state had accentuated school segregation or at least inhibited desegregation by enacting the Unigov bill and thus consolidating most of the area's governmental functions, while leaving the school systems unconsolidated, although under Indiana common law and statute law, school district boundary changes had normally accompanied municipal enlargement. This action, he ruled, had been part of a pattern of governmental actions that furthered segregation or at least inhibited desegregation.

The judge ruled that it was not necessary to find the Unigov statute invalid, although he noted that its contribution to state actions that furthered segregation, taken with his conclusion that realistic integration was impossible within the existing school district limits, required him to order a desegregation plan applying to the entire metropolitan area.

After protracted litigation and controversy, a substantial amount of court-ordered cross-district busing began in 1981. The litigation and controversy are continuing, and some modification of school districts may occur, but the basic Unigov reorganization has survived.

Summary

The Unigov reform was clearly intended as much to streamline the previous governmental machinery as it was to realign governmental areas and jurisdictions. Critical elements of the Unigov reform include combining the executive offices of the city and county governments and the emergence of a consolidated City-County Council. Organizational shifts in the departments and in the mayor's staff were clearly intended to strengthen the mayor's executive power, clarify areas of responsibility, and draw lines of accountability more closely to the mayor's office. Contributing significantly are the mayor's powers of appointment and removal. Thus, six department heads are appointed by the mayor with council approval, serve for one-year terms, and can be dismissed by the mayor even in midterm.

In a further attempt to simplify administration, the Unigov law eliminated a number of small boards and commissions, whose functions were given to the new departmental boards. Membership on the departmental boards is also closely controlled by the mayor, who appoints a majority of the members of four of five boards; moreover, his appointed department head serves as board chair. The Department of Administration has no board. Changes in appointive powers under Unigov have aligned government more closely under the executive office of the mayor.

Unigov reforms were confined to governments within Marion County. The areawide Indiana Heartland Coordinating Commission was developed *outside* the Unigov concept and without much public visibility or impact. The Minigov proposal for the establishment of neighborhood governments was sponsored by some of the Unigov supporters in the state legislature, but it was not well received in the City-County Council and is no longer an active issue.

Although Unigov has been subjected to some litigation, it has not yet been stymied or seriously hampered. The immediate filing of a "friendly suit" by the Chamber of Commerce established the judicial integrity of the overall concept during its first year. Subsequent suits over specific applications of the law, notably the school integration question and the representation arrangement, have neither slowed Unigov's activities nor obstructed its political acceptance by the community. We now turn to community issues.

9

The Political Community:
Unigov and Beyond

Major modifications have been made since the original enactment of Unigov in 1969, and now, after a decade and a half, Unigov's
arrangements seem to be quite firmly established. Those who pushed
for consolidation are still in control of the government, although of
course there have been some changes in personnel, for example, the
principal instigator, Mayor Lugar, became a US senator in 1977.

The greater Indianapolis political community weathered the
merger, and many former officeholders of both parties have positions
in the government. The Democratic Party, thus far the minority under
the reorganization, has abandoned its thoroughgoing opposition to
Unigov and now appears fully committed to the struggle to control the
consolidated government. Following a lengthy and sometimes hectic
period of adjustment, governmental operations have settled into a reasonable, definable pattern.

Unigov's extended boundary was the principal cause of the jump
in Indianapolis's US census ranking of cities in 1970. In 1960 Indianapolis ranked twenty-sixth with a population of 476,215 and an area
of 82 square miles. In 1970 the city was ranked ninth with a population of 793,590 and an area of about 400 square miles.[1] Meanwhile,
the basic economic and demographic forces affecting the urban community have continued and have probably accelerated. The interstate
highway network in and around the city has been completed, unemployment is substantially below national or midwest regional levels,
and the downtown shopping and business district has undergone extensive redevelopment. Above all, Indianapolis has emerged with a
national reputation as a progressive, well-governed city.

There is no sure way to evaluate all the consequences of a complex institutional reorganization. Observers' perceptions differ widely,
and we can speculate on a variety of causes for most things that
happen. Thus, to what extent Unigov is responsible for Indianapolis's
successes is debatable. Nevertheless, Unigov appears to have made

1. Or eleventh place, with 745,739 people, if the four "unincorporated" communities, which are included for some purposes but not for others, are not counted.

substantial contributions to Indianapolis's emergence as a major US city in the 1970s. As noted earlier, Unigov was probably especially effective in transforming the city's internal and external "image," a change that may be of great importance.

Voter Reaction

The first real test of voter reaction to Unigov came in the 1971 mayoral election. Unigov, and particularly the failure to conduct a referendum on it, was the principal issue in a hotly contested campaign between Mayor Lugar, the Republican incumbent, and Democrat John F. Neff, his challenger. Mayor Lugar's decisive victory effectively silenced most critics who had argued that Unigov lacked public support. The victory not only kept Lugar at the helm during the early stages of Unigov but also put him in a strong position to complete a smooth transition to the new government.

The 1971 Mayoral Election

Richard Lugar had been a very active first-term mayor of Indianapolis, establishing a reputation as a willing and eager incumbent, and becoming the uncontested Republican nominee for mayor in 1971. Some party regulars supported Mayor Lugar because they felt that he had promised them that he would "see it through" if they would support the passage of Unigov. Since it was his program, they thought he should have to stand for election on its merits. As Unigov's most readily identifiable supporter and administrator, the mayor was committed to implementing the reorganization—a commitment he willingly assumed.

John Neff, the 34-year-old Democrat selected to run against Lugar, was a young attorney who had been a Rector Scholar at DePauw University and an all-star athlete at Arsenal Technical High School in Indianapolis. In the 1960s he served in the Indiana General Assembly and was, for a short time, an associate city and county attorney, but all of his recent predecessors had spent more time in the precincts and wards, and some regarded him as a newcomer to party activities. But the Democrats were looking for someone as young and vigorous as Lugar, who had waged a strong campaign in 1967 against "tired old John Barton." Neff committed himself to this comparison in his primary victory speech: "I'm going to knock not only once on doors but twice. I'm going to use my bicycle. I'm going to coffees. And I'm going to campaign against Dick Lugar the way he campaigned against John Barton."[2] Both candidates were closely identified with youth, scholar-

2. "Neff to Battle Lugar, Nixon," *Indianapolis Star*, May 5, 1971, p. 10.

ship, and athletic vigor. Their personal qualities seemed approximately in balance, making party strength and partisan issues more notable in 1971.

The Democrats' campaign strategy against Unigov and the mayor was not altogether unlike their campaign during the 1969 legislative debate. Neff focused on charges that Unigov was a partisan effort, passed without the support of the people, that failed to go far enough. Neff, who had backed the Democrats' so-called "power grab" bills in the 1965 General Assembly, supported the idea of governmental reform but told reporters he was against Unigov

> because it was misrepresented initially. They said it was going to reduce taxes and eliminate duplication in government and give better service. All of these things have not happened.
>
> It is not metropolitan government. If it were metropolitan government, it would include the Health and Hospital Corporation, Airport Authority, Capital Improvements Board, fire and police, schools and many others.
>
> It's nothing more than one political party grabbing votes. Keith Bulen called it his greatest coup ever, bringing in 85,000 Republicans to vote for the mayor of Indianapolis. Plus it was crammed down our throats without our right to vote.[3]

This approach was repeated throughout the campaign with emphasis on the referendum question. Neff pledged that if he were elected he would call for a referendum on Unigov at the following primary. Voters were often reminded that a vote for Neff was a vote for a referendum.

In Indiana campaigns seem to be waged, not conducted, and elections seldom hinge on a single issue. Nevertheless, Mayor Lugar was clearly identified with Unigov in 1971, and Unigov—as an issue—was widely argued before the electorate that year. Thus, Lugar's overwhelming victory, 153,047 to 100,552—said by the *Indianapolis Star* to be the largest margin ever achieved by a major candidate in a county race[4]—strongly suggests the lack of significant opposition to Unigov.

One could argue that the anti-Unigov position was not well articulated by the Democrats—they favored reform in general but opposed its details and the way it was adopted. Or perhaps the voters had grown accustomed to the new arrangement and did not want still another change. Whatever the reasoning, Democrats and Republicans agreed afterward that the 1971 election was a clear indication that the

3. "Lugar, Neff Give Views on Unigov, Its Future," *Indianapolis News,* October 22, 1971, p. 1.

4. "Mayor's Heavy Margin Seen Breaking Record for County Politics," *Indianapolis Star,* November 3, 1971, p. 1.

people had accepted Unigov. Accordingly, demands for a referendum subsided, and Unigov has not been a major issue in subsequent election campaigns.

Partisan Political Gains

Notwithstanding Unigov's popular acceptance, campaigns continued to feature allegations that Unigov was really not primarily a government reform, but "nothing more than a political party grabbing votes." Clearly, reform proponents recognized the partisan political implications of Unigov. Mayor Lugar said: "I'll be candid. I know this is good for the Republicans. That is how I sold it to the legislators statewide."[5] Republican Party chair Bulen's boast that Unigov was his "greatest coup" added substance to charges of a political takeover.

Undoubtedly Republicans gained from the change, at least in the short run. They won mayoral elections in 1971, 1975, and 1979, as well as the preconsolidation election of 1968. They had not won three consecutive mayoralty contests since the 1920s. A close examination of these elections and others seems to indicate that the Republicans established a clear electoral advantage through Unigov, but that the "takeover" was neither as comprehensive as zealous Republicans hoped nor as permanent as apprehensive Democrats feared.

Mayoral Campaigns: 1971 and 1975

Mayor Lugar's 1971 mayoral victory was too decisive in both the old city and the new city to be considered a Republican success based on straight party-line voting. Lugar actually increased his previous margin in the old city wards, especially the black wards. One of his aides estimated that in 1971 between 28 and 30 percent of the blacks who voted supported Lugar, compared with only 12 percent in 1967.[6] Since Lugar did not need the new suburban margin to overcome the usual Republican deficit of votes in the erstwhile Democratic inner-city stronghold, his 1971 win did not depend on the Unigov boundary. On the other hand, the returns demonstrated that there were enough Republican votes in the suburban township wards to offset a 40,000 vote inner-city deficit—if they had been needed in 1971. They were needed in 1975.

One of the more interesting political developments made possible by the Unigov reform was the residence of both 1975 mayoral-race candidates outside the old city limits. In nominating Robert V. Welch

5. Phyllis Myers, "Jurisdictions: Why Did Indianapolis, of All Places, Take a Step Toward Metropolitanism?" *City* 3(3):39 (June 1969).

6. "Behind Closed Doors," *Indianapolis Star*, November 7, 1971, p. 10.

the Democrats chose a candidate they hoped would cut into the normally large Republican suburban vote. Welch, a conservative Democrat, was one of eleven children from a native Indianapolis family, a graduate of Indianapolis Cathedral High School and the University of Notre Dame, and a self-made businessman whose estimated net worth was $7 million.[7]

Welch had never held public office and had a difficult time getting the Democratic nomination. He was not the regular organization's candidate in the May primary but built his own organization to upset William Schreiber, the county chair, in a bitterly contested battle. Schreiber had long been known as an opponent of Unigov and still campaigned against it, while Welch was clearly running for the mayor's post in the combined government.

The Republican nominee, William H. Hudnut, a Phi Beta Kappa graduate of Princeton University, a Presbyterian minister, and a former US congressman, had also been seriously challenged for the nomination by City Council president Thomas Hasbrook and others. These early bids were resolved in the "slating" process. The other serious candidates withdrew, and Hudnut appeared virtually unopposed on the Republican primary ballot. The ability of the Republicans to resolve their differences internally, thereby beginning their campaign with a unified organization, gave them an early edge that allowed Hudnut to succeed by a modest (124,000 to 109,761) margin in November.[8]

Welch's effort to consolidate the Democratic Party into a cohesive block was never completely successful. He not only ran behind predictions (based on presumed party strength) but fell nearly 3,000 votes behind his party's at-large candidates for City-County Council. The fact that their mayoral candidate did not lead his own ticket prompted some Welch supporters to accuse county chair Schreiber of conducting a personal vendetta. Volunteers leaving Democratic headquarters on election night charged that they had been "sold out" by their own people, who were "out to dump" Welch.[9]

A more plausible explanation for Welch's loss is that while reasonably well suited to appeal to suburban voters, he could not draw strong support from longtime Democrats in the old city. This millionaire had not politicked with them before; he was a stranger to them politically and ideologically. Compounding this was Welch's lack of

---

7. When Welch was pressed by political circumstances to declare his assets, he waited until late in the campaign before making a statement. Perhaps he waited too long, because many interpreted his delay as an attempt to hide something.

8. "Hard Work Won Election for Mayor-to-Be," *Indianapolis News*, November 5, 1975, p. 1.

9. "Fate of County Demos Uncertain," *Indianapolis News*, November 5, 1975, p. 7.

campaign experience. Unpracticed in speaking to neighborhood groups and large audiences, Welch often came off second best to Hudnut, who was in his sixth major campaign in four years. Moreover, Hudnut, a former minister, had a much more polished speaking style than Welch.

Despite intraparty squabbles and their candidate's lack of campaign experience, the really decisive factor in the Democratic loss to Hudnut was the change in Unigov's electoral unit boundaries. Welch carried the old city with a plurality of only 17,500, while his opponent carried the suburban area by over 31,000 votes, giving Hudnut a net winning margin of nearly 14,000 votes.[10] The central-city/suburban vote split clearly demonstrates the Unigov merger's political advantage to the Republicans. Nevertheless, Democrats were encouraged that they had substantially reduced the 52,000 vote margin that Lugar had received in 1971, despite the fact that they did not fully exploit their old-city strength. Encouraging for the Democrats was the small average difference in the votes between the major party candidates for the at-large seats on the City-County Council, only 7,000 votes, in a total count of 234,000 ballots. On the day before the election both newspapers were predicting good weather, a heavy vote in the area of 255,000 to 265,000, and a close race. The heavy vote did not materialize. Indeed, a substantial turnout normally benefits Democrats and could have made the race much closer.

The 1979 Hudnut Landslide

Every election has its own peculiar features, and the 1979 election may not be a good indicator of the relative strength of the two political parties in Marion County. Incumbent Mayor Hudnut, seeking reelection, had demonstrated early, in the spring surveys done by both parties, that he would be an almost unbeatable candidate in the fall. Given little or no chance to win, the better Democratic candidates chose not to enter the primary. The Democratic choice then went to Paul Cantwell, a longtime councilmember who had been a persistent antagonist of Mayor Hudnut, but who had not established a positive stand on issues or a constituency. Cantwell was unable to unite his party behind him and raised only $38,000 in campaign funds. Hudnut's well-oiled machine spent $278,000 in achieving the largest victory margin (83,000 votes) in Marion County history.[11] His victory was overwhelming in both the old city and suburban wards. Cantwell even lost in his own Southside precinct. Mayor Hudnut also won a convincing election in 1983 over Democratic challenger John J. Sullivan, a 34-year-old attorney and newcomer to campaigning. (The original

10. "Final Figures Given on Election," *Indianapolis Star,* November 6, 1975, p. 65.

11. "Hudnut Beats Cantwell, 3 to 1," *Indianapolis Star,* November 7, 1979, p. 1.

Unigov legislation limiting the mayor to two terms had been amended in 1982 to provide for unlimited terms.) Hudnut's sweeping victory (he gained 67 percent of the votes) also added another Republican to the combined City-County Council, resulting in a 23-to-6 majority.

These Republican mayoral successes under Unigov prompted some local Democrats to refer to the new government as "Unigrab." Clearly the Republicans have established a post-Unigov dominance in Marion County elections, benefiting from a shift in the political power base. Robert Kirch, an Indianapolis professor of urban government, described the Unigov mayoral elections as follows: "Given the result of these three elections, it becomes rather obvious that the Unigov consolidation design has proven itself as a workable political strategy. It has accomplished its basic goal, which was to displace the Democrats from city hall and take command of Indianapolis city government with all the privileges, patronage, and partisan benefits that go along with such political control."[12] Kirch adds supportive evidence: "Hudnut won the mayor's race [1975] by 14,300 votes. Since he lost the old city vote by 18,200 votes, Mayor Hudnut clearly needed the 32,500 vote margin he received from the county areas. Without the Unigov Consolidation, [Democrat] Robert Welch would have been elected Mayor of Indianapolis by more than an 18,000 vote majority."[13]

Since political advantage was a part of the Unigov strategy, Hudnut's 1975 win over Welch upholds the thesis that the Republicans gained from the redistricting. But the advantage cannot be explained solely in terms of a territorial expansion of the political district. Redistricting does not explain the three Republican victories where their mayoral candidates carried the old-city districts by safe margins. These victories were the result of the presence of highly qualified Republican candidates and a higher level of party organization and funding than was generally seen under the previous arrangement.

The strengthened office of mayor is now a far more attractive post, sought both as a place where things get done and as a forum for national recognition. Despite their other electoral successes in county elections (discussed below), Democrats have not as yet been able to organize around a mayoral candidate who can win in a countywide constituency. On the other hand, the Republican Party does not have a monopoly on such candidates, and Democrats are gearing up for the next mayoral race, many of them anticipating that Hudnut will then succeed in his rumored quest for higher office. Thus, the next mayoral contest should be a very good test of the durability of the Republican advantage gained under Unigov.

The Republican advantage is also being challenged by shifting

12. Robert V. Kirch, "Unigov Stratagem Revisited: 1979 Indianapolis Election," *Indiana Academy of Social Sciences, Proceedings*, 3rd ser. 15:106 (1980).

13. Ibid., p. 105.

voter patterns as urban decentralization continues. Kirch notes: "Local conventional political wisdom says that the great majority of these people leaving Marion County are Republican voters. L. Keith Bulen, a highly respected Republican political observer, estimated that 9 out of 10 migrants are practicing or potential Republican voters."[14] So it appears that while the Democratic Party is organizing to extend its voter rolls to obtain countywide parity with the Republicans, they are being assisted by a decline in the size of the potential Republican vote.

In sum, Kirch is correct in his assessment of the political advantage Unigov redistricting gave to the Republicans. Elsewhere in this book, however, the authors dispute his contention that the political strategy to displace Democrats from city hall was the *basic* Unigov goal. Moreover, they maintain that he should have given greater emphasis to other important factors, such as the Republicans' quick and forceful exploitation of their advantage, outpacing the Democratic efforts to challenge them.

Also, as noted, the demographic trends of the past decade and a half may work to the advantage of the Democrats in the 1980s. Finally, critics who use the *Unigrab* term as a reproachful reference to the Republican electoral successes under Unigov generally neglect to note that these same elections are a fair measure of the community's acceptance of the new government.

City-County Council Elections

The 1971, 1975, 1979, and 1983 elections for the combined City-County Council followed the pattern of the mayoral elections. Republicans, relying heavily on suburban votes, secured large majorities of the twenty-five single-member seats and took all four at-large seats each time. In 1971, Lugar-led Republicans won seventeen council district seats to the Democrats' eight. The Democrats won all eight of their victories in contiguous districts in the old city's Center Township (see Map 8).

In the 1975 Hudnut–Welch race, election results in the single-member districts favored the Republicans fifteen to ten. The Democrats picked up two seats, including one in Decatur township, their first suburban win. With their four at-large seats, the Republicans still had a commanding council majority in 1975.

The coattail effect of Mayor Hudnut's overwhelming 1979 victory boosted the Republican council advantage in the single-member district seats to eighteen to seven. With the four at-large seats, the Republicans gained an overall City-County Council margin of twenty-two to seven, including a thirteen-to-seven majority on the fire and police special service district councils.

14. Ibid., p. 106.

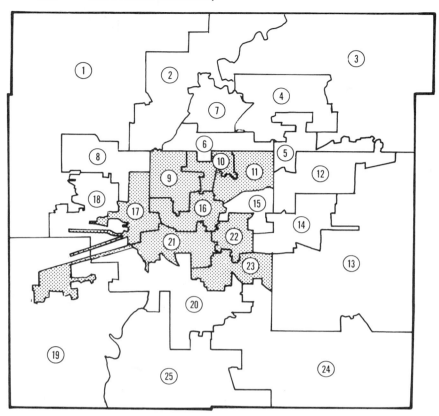

	District	At-Large	Total
Republican won	17	4	21
Democrat won	8	0	8
Total	25	4	29

Map 8.

1971 City-County Council Election Results

Source: *Indianapolis News*, November 3, 1971, p. 65.

Hudnut also led the ticket in 1983, when the Republican major-ity in the City-County Council increased to 23 to 6.

Other Elections

In other post-Unigov Marion County elections, the Republicans won convincing victories in the presidential years, 1972, 1976, 1980, and 1984, but the Democrats swept the county in the 1974 campaign for state and local offices. The Republican wins in the presidential elections—Presidential candidates Nixon, Ford, and Reagan carried Marion County with large margins for four successive campaigns— were determined in very large measure by their heavy suburban vote, more than compensating for close Democratic wins in the old-city wards. The only countywide Democratic candidate to break the GOP's near monopoly since 1974 is two-time sheriff James L. Wells, who secured convincing wins in 1978 and 1982. In 1974 the national impact of the Watergate affair was compounded in Marion County by two scandals, one involving a Republican Party kickback scheme, the other, charges of a police cover-up.

Although the scandals were considered to be mostly "city politics" and the traditional county officials were not directly involved, the impact was felt in the county campaign. Following that year's trend, the Democrats won every administrative and judicial office in Marion County, including the posts of sheriff and prosecuting attorney, and provided large margins for most Democratic state candidates. This was only the fifth time in this century that the Democrats had done so well. Perhaps the biggest reversal was Lugar's failure to carry his home county in his race against incumbent US senator Birch Bayh (he did carry it later, in his successful 1976 campaign against Democratic incumbent R. Vance Hartke). The Democrats did not, however, see the 1974 sweep as a major turning point for their party, viewing the upset as an exception. In the words of William Schreiber, Democratic county chair at the time: "The only time we can win around here is during an Eisenhower recession, a Goldwater debacle, or a Watergate. It will be two more elections before we can compete on a regular basis with the Republicans."[15]

One little-noted aspect of the 1974 election suggested a possible future advantage for the Democrats. Unigov has tied the city and county governments closely together, and city problems of politics and government will have a more immediate effect on county elections. Thus, the Republicans not only brought the suburbs into city elections but also made the city's affairs of immediate concern to the suburban voters. It follows that any scandal, such as the police cover-up in 1974, will cost the party in power voter support. Furthermore, if past ethnic and class political alignments continue, gradual demographic changes may increase Democratic strength. The county's black population is increasing more rapidly than the white, whereas some of the newer middle- and upper-class suburban development is now beyond the county line.

15. William M. Schreiber, interview with James Owen, Indianapolis, November 1976.

Minority Representation

A very interesting but rather elusive aspect of the Unigov reorganization is its relationship to the black minority's political effectiveness. At the most obvious numerical level, it is clear that black voting
strength has been diluted. Most of the black leaders recognize this and
are unhappy about it. In 1970, about midway between the law's enactment and the first post-Unigov election, the population of the old-city
area was approximately 27 percent black, whereas the entire county
was only 17 percent black. If the old city had continued as the basic
political constituency, the blacks would have still been a minority,
but they were developing a good deal of political leverage, especially
in the old city's normally victorious Democratic Party. This leverage
was reduced when Unigov extended the boundaries countywide.

The most prominent blacks opposing Unigov are those who have
been Democratic officeholders. The current proportion of blacks *countywide* is at about the level it reached 20 to 25 years ago in the old
city, and black leaders see this as a significant setback. On the other
hand, Unigov does incorporate features considered favorable to
blacks, and this, plus a trend toward increased black political activity,
has weakened their opposition to Unigov.

A More Prosperous Community?

Some of the more thoughtful supporters of the reorganization,
sensitive to the criticism that Unigov reduced the black proportion of
the effective electorate, suggested three factors that offset the reduction
of the black electorate. One factor often mentioned is that although
blacks have a somewhat smaller share of the power, they are a part of a
more prosperous and more effective community. A relatively smaller
slice of a bigger pie, the argument suggests, may in reality be better than
a larger slice of the old pie that seemed to be rapidly deteriorating.

This argument would be much more persuasive if it were based
on stronger evidence that these augmented resources were actually
being shared. Admittedly there have been some gains in the resources
supporting central-city needs, that is, the police district now includes
some adjacent industries, the urban renewal and sewage treatment tax
bases have been extended, and some of the costs of general government, and of streets and roads, may be shared more equitably now.
Perhaps more important, but difficult to measure, Indianapolis has a
larger share of federal funds, and these are being used in substantial
measure to help the central city where blacks are concentrated.

Aside from these factors, a basic postulate of the Indianapolis
reorganization scheme is that costs of services should be allotted as
nearly as possible back to the areas receiving the services. This is what

some black leaders are referring to when they say they might have accepted the Unigov political losses if there had been compensating resource gains achieved by spreading the cost of municipal services countywide. But they see the gains that were made as much too small.

Direct Representation of Black Districts

Another argument suggests that black political representation via single-member districts is more effective than the previous system of at-large city elections. Before reorganization, each party was allowed to nominate no more than six candidates for the nine at-large City Council seats, assuring a degree of minority party representation. To get a balanced slate, each party would almost always include blacks among its nominees. But these black candidates, if chosen by the usually influential preprimary slating process, were selected by a primarily white leadership. Moreover, if they were actually elected in the pre-Unigov citywide primary, they would in effect be chosen by white voters. Allegedly, they would be less likely to represent the "true" interests of the black areas than if nominated and elected directly from black districts, as they now can be under Unigov.

On the first Unigov council, with its single-member districts, four of the eight Democrats and one of the twenty-one Republicans were black. The second Unigov election also returned five black councilmembers, with the same party breakdown. A black was elected by Republicans at-large as in 1971, and four black Democrats were elected from districts, setting a trend that continued in the 1979 election. In the pre-Unigov arrangement, usually only one black served on the City Council. Thus, in aggregate numbers at least, blacks gained in representation under Unigov, and in fact the black percentage of the council is almost identical to its percentage of the population. Moreover, there is significant evidence that party activists from the districts have a greater voice than previously in the slating and nominating procedure,[16] an especially effective way of increasing black political influence in the party and in the council.

In post-Unigov elections, black council candidates still depend on the party slating process for nomination and election, but their real voter strength is based in large measure on their own communities, outside the party structure. This is particularly true of elected councilmembers such as Glenn Howard (Democrat) from the heavily black ninth district. During the late 1960s and early 1970s, Howard estab-

16. Robert V. Kirch, an Indianapolis professor who was somewhat critical of Unigov, concurs with the above argument, saying that through the single-member system in "those districts with a majority of Negro voters, the district can select its 'own man' "; see Kirch, "Unigov: Metropolitan Reform or Partisan Politics," *Indiana Academy of Social Sciences, Proceedings*, n.s. 4(4):156 (1969).

lished a reputation as a community organizer by his work with the Black Radical Action Party (BRAP), the Southern Christian Leadership Conference's Operation Breadbasket, and the UNWA Neighborhood Association (the Unified Northwest Association of former model cities and community development neighborhoods). His party nomination came after, presumably because he had developed a personal following in the black community.

Like Howard, but perhaps to a lesser extent, the other black councilmembers owe a large measure of their support and political independence to constituent ties with black community organizations. On the other hand, the party's importance should not be underestimated, as was demonstrated by the failure of Reggie Jones, a black community activist in the black fifth district, to unseat the slated white incumbent in the 1979 spring primary. Jones's close defeat by 24 votes is attributed to his lack of an organization to get out the vote.

Their political independence and skill in legislative politics have given the five black councilmembers an incisive minority voice in the extended political community. They have been most effective in gaining control over issues relating to neighborhood development and employment opportunity programs. This has been especially apparent at budget time when the council's majority leadership has had to solicit Democrats' votes to offset the opposition of a dedicated conservative Republican faction.

The minority leadership had generally been able to deliver the black votes after receiving certain concessions.[17] As one black Republican councilmember commented: "The five of us [four Democrats, one Republican] work together on items that are generally identified as black issues—issues such as CETA, multipurpose centers, and the Community Development Block Grant come to mind. There are always votes we can trade off on. This is especially true when the Republican Caucus breaks down. As a result of this I am sometimes not consulted by the Republican Caucus."[18] Thus, with full awareness of the rules and risks of the political game, blacks have been able to trade votes and gain support for programs of greatest importance to their constituents.

Black political influence has not been restricted to central-city

17. The Unigov council is organized each year with new officers and committee assignments. The chief offices are council president, majority leader, and minority leader. There are twelve standing committees, six matching Unigov departments (metropolitan development, parks and recreation, transportation, administration, public safety, and public works), four other substantive committees (economic development, municipal corporations, community affairs, and county and townships), and two organization and procedural committees (rules and public policy and the committee on committees). Five of the Unigov councils have had minority leaders who were black: Rozelle Boyd, 1972–1975, and Glenn Howard, 1978.

18. Paula Parker, interview with James Owen, Indianapolis, June 19, 1979.

issues. The combined vote of the black councilmembers was also necessary to get a majority vote for a nearly countywide extension of the territorial jurisdiction and tax base of the sanitary district. Five of the 16 favorable council votes (13 were opposed) came from blacks who welcomed suburban participation in paying the capital cost of sewer extension. Prospects for further black influence are promising. If the Democrats should gain control of the police and fire service districts— a likely prospect—blacks will have a decisive vote on these two critical services.

More Blacks in Government Offices

Reorganization proponents also suggest that the Republicans, especially with their new and more "enlightened" leadership, may actually be more responsive to the needs and interests of the black population than the Democrats, who previously dominated the city government. This effect might be augmented if more blacks shifted their allegiance to the Republicans, as some did, at least temporarily, in the 1971 election. (Table 8, showing the vote in the three most heavily black wards in recent mayoral elections, demonstrates how the black votes that shifted to the Republican Party in the two Lugar campaigns returned to the earlier Democratic voting pattern in 1975. Note also how blacks increased their support for Lugar after Unigov when he was clearly identified as its chief proponent.)

In their 1971 campaign literature the Republicans said: "More blacks currently are involved in administrative positions, boards, and advisory committees than have been involved during any previous administration." The Democrats also complained that Lugar had co-opted some of the black leadership. Thus, Mayor Lugar appointed two blacks to high administrative posts: Ray Crowe, to head the Metropolitan Park Department, and Dr. Eugene McFadden, coordinator of federal funds. Republican Mayor Hudnut appointed minority persons to high office, naming a black, Joseph Slash, as the city's first deputy mayor in January 1978. The Lugar and Hudnut administrations were also probably more active than their Democratic predecessors in supporting and promoting efforts to deal with central-city problems.

In effect, this argument holds that the Republican Party, whose majority is white and lives outside the old-city limits, has—through a sense of civic responsibility and enlightened self-interest—actually done more for blacks and others in the old city than the Democratic Party, in which blacks were much more numerous. Mayor Lugar made these comments on racial divisions soon after Unigov's enactment: "Indianapolis has approximately 130,000 black citizens who comprised approximately 25 percent of the old city's population and 17 percent of the new city's population. We are not immune to severe

Table 8– *Votes for Mayoral Candidates in Heaviest Black Wards*

Ward	1967		1971		1975	
	Barton (DEM.)	Lugar (REP.)	Neff (DEM.)	Lugar (REP.)	Welch (DEM.)	Hudnut (REP.)
3	2,615	654	1,989	648	1,884	199
6	4,000	852	3,691	1,206	4,765	325
23	3,312	781	2,939	1,231	3,399	393
Total	9,927	2,287	8,619	3,085	10,048	917

Source: Compiled by authors from official election returns, recorder's office, City-County Building, Indianapolis, 1978.

disagreements between major racial groups but we were determined to effect a unified government, racially as well as functionally and geographically before dreary polarization sapped the will or the idealism of those who believe in a pluralistic society as opposed to a segregated one. We still retained time to act but not much time in my judgment."[19]

But many blacks are not convinced. While it would be presumptuous for observers to suggest definitive conclusions about the net gains or losses of black citizens, it does seem clear that blacks have accepted Unigov, perhaps begrudgingly, and are actively seeking to advance their public interest through the restructured system. Warren Stickles's study of black political participation in Indianapolis concludes that although the blacks' political power was diluted, "they have not exhibited the frustration, alienation, and the apathy that many scholars have associated with blacks in the central cities. In fact, in Indianapolis black political participation at the same socioeconomic level, and especially so for income and educational levels, is about equal to that of white political involvement."[20] Comparing the voting records of blacks and whites in the same socioeconomic class, Stickles finds no measurable drop-off in black political participation because of Unigov.

Summary

In summing up this review of minorities (blacks) and Unigov, we want to highlight two facts. First, blacks did not play a decisive role in the Unigov debate. They had not been an important part of the political process in Indianapolis since before the heyday of the Ku Klux Klan, and the fast pace of Unigov's passage did not give them time to organize, either for or against the proposal.

19. Richard G. Lugar, speech to Robert A. Taft Institute of Government, New York, May 21, 1970.

20. Warren E. Stickles, "Black Political Participation in Indianapolis, 1966–72," *Indiana Academy of Social Sciences, Proceedings*, 3rd ser. 7:113–120 (1973).

Second, it is apparent that blacks have gained an increasingly important presence in the political arena in the past 10 years, as they have in most sectors of the greater Indianapolis community. We can only speculate how much of the improved political status can be attributed to Unigov and how much is due to general trends of the civil rights movement. Certainly, however, blacks have gained a substantial political power base under Unigov, power that operates through the mechanism of the reformed structure.

A Communitywide Council

Unigov's single legislative body for the city and county gives some governmental policies and programs areawide impact, although the individual tax and service districts persist.

To what extent has the council become a truly communitywide legislative body? Although the Unigov principals and others claim a sense of community as a major Unigov accomplishment, they sometimes question the council's role in this development: "One aspect that is not clear from our experience at this point is the role of the council: whether, in fact, those 25 who are from single-member districts, each representing about 36,000 persons, will be parochial as opposed to seeing the good of the whole."[21] One thing is certain, the council serves as a community forum where urban and suburban problems are regularly debated and decided. Moreover, the public feuding that accompanied most previous attempts to resolve differences between the county and the city governments under the old arrangement is much less evident now.

The treatment of housing and building codes provides an illustrative example of the council's communitywide impact. Thus, a sentence added to the Unigov measure while in the legislature states that existing city ordinances should continue to apply only in the same territory where they were effective before, unless specifically extended. Some blacks charged that this was done largely to prevent the city's open housing ordinance from applying in the suburbs. The bill's authors denied this, noting that without the change, some existing central-city ordinances might prohibit ownership of a cow or a pig, even in the rural portions of the consolidated city-county. This potentially troublesome issue was resolved when the combined City-County Council passed an ordinance extending the housing ordinance to the entire county as its first major act. A further example of the combined council's communitywide impact was another first-year ordinance establishing a countywide uniform building code.

21. Richard G. Lugar, in National Association of Counties, *Consolidation: Partial or Total,* transcript of the National Conference (Washington, DC, 1973), p. 11.

At budget time the council's continued deliberations on communitywide issues are perhaps most notable and effective. That is when
the public forum is most visible and effective program priorities are set.
Also at budget time nearly all of the community's programs are assem-
bled and reviewed by a single governmental body. Although the consolidated city and county budgets are first compiled separately by the
controller and auditor, respectively, they are presented to council in
combined form. This is done when the budget is written in legal form
by the corporate attorney for presentation to the council. The attorney,
who represents both the consolidated city and county, works with the
controller and auditor to present a single integrated tax ordinance to
the council. Also included in the integrated budget are the budgets of
several formerly independent boards and commissions, for example,
the Health and Hospital Corporation (1985 budget $27,151,879). Before
Unigov, the health and hospital budget was passed by the corporation's
board, without executive or legislative review.

Unigov Impact Statewide

The Indianapolis experience with metropolitan government has
generated much national interest, but perhaps the greatest interest has
been in Indiana where since Unigov's advent citizens in each of the
other metropolitan cities have proposed some form of governmental
reform.

From 1905, when the Indiana Municipal Code was written, until
1969, governmental reform was not widely pursued by Indiana cities.
An incipient movement toward city manager government ended when
Indianapolis's manager system was declared unconstitutional in 1929
and subsequently was not tried again. Numerous special service districts were formed in the post–World War II era, always on a piecemeal basis. An interlocal Government Cooperation Act was passed in
1957 but has seldom been used.

Prior to Unigov, larger cities had made modest reform efforts, but
since Unigov, activity has increased considerably in response to the
Indianapolis success. The typical intercity rivalry for new industries,
federal dollars, or increased population is intensified in Indiana by
the widely held belief that Indianapolis consistently benefits more
from state legislation than any other city. This feeling was reinforced
when Indianapolis gained national prominence in the 1970s. Stimulated by the Indianapolis reorganization, in several areas chambers of
commerce, leagues of women voters, legislative study committees,
and other civic groups increased their reform efforts, and a number of
spirited campaigns advanced as far as the legislature. Despite the activity, most of these recent reorganization attempts have failed.

Evansville: Vandigov

The reform effort in Evansville–Vanderburgh County was probably the most prominent. Evansville, Indiana's fourth largest city, is on the Ohio River in a small county in the state's southwestern corner, halfway between Indianapolis and Nashville, Tennessee. Evansville is the only incorporated city in Vanderburgh County. Its population of 138,764, largely old American stock, comprises over 80 percent of the total county population (168,722). Evansville experienced two severe economic declines in the 10 years following World War II, prompting a communitywide effort to stabilize the industrial and business communities.

The fragmented city and county government was often cited as needing reform. The merger idea was first propounded publicly in 1959 by Evansville's Future Inc., a citizens' group like the Greater Indianapolis Progress Committee formed to study the community's problems and devise solutions. The first measurable accomplishment did not come until 10 years later in 1969 when the same state legislative session that created Unigov also approved a six-member local government study committee to draft merger proposals for Evansville and Vanderburgh County.

A draft proposal of a legislative bill for local government reform was completed, endorsed by Democratic Mayor Frank McDonald, and submitted to the 1971 General Assembly. The bill failed to pass, but a new and more broadly based study committee was approved. This 11-member committee sponsored a revised bill, introduced in 1972. The 1972 bill was drafted by newly elected Mayor Russell Lloyd's city attorney, John C. Cox, who had been a member of the previous study committee. Both Lloyd and Cox were Republican, as was State Senator Robert Orr, one of the bill's sponsors. The bill retained its nonpartisan status when Democratic Senator Philip H. Hayes agreed to cosponsor it. This bill died in a House committee where a Marion County Republican cast the tie-breaking vote to defeat it eight to seven.

During the remaining months of 1972 Mayor Lloyd and attorney Cox pursued a dual course toward reform. One approach would achieve functional consolidation by means of city and county ordinances to merge the city and county departments of purchasing, traffic engineering, building control, weights and measures, city and county garages, and property maintenance. Had ordinances merging all six functions passed both the city and county councils, they would have constituted a fairly comprehensive merger of functions. The other course would have effected an actual governmental consolidation through state legislation similar to that setting up Unigov. There was some initial success—four of the ordinances passed the City Council, and one of them, dealing with purchasing, became effective when it also received county approval. But a third attempt at total merger through state legislation was introduced in the General Assembly, causing further consideration of the functional mergers to be abandoned temporarily. Several key supporters of the functional merger ordinances, who supported this approach in part because they saw it as a substitute for total merger, lost interest when they learned that total merger was still being pursued.

Undeterred by their failure to secure General Assembly approval for a Unigov type of government reform in 1971 and 1972, the proponents of Vandigov[22] submitted a third bill in 1973. Vandigov resembled Unigov in several ways. The Evansville reformers had established regular contact with several of the original Unigov supporters and tried to pattern their bill after Unigov. The Vandigov proposal was no more comprehensive than Unigov: schools, township government, and the courts were omitted, the constitutional county offices were not to be changed, and there was to be no major redistribution of the tax base. Despite its similarities to Unigov, the mood of the legislators had changed. The legislators' decision requiring Vandigov—unlike Unigov—to go through a referendum for approval was the deciding factor that caused the proposal's defeat.

Although Vandigov's proponents were better organized and funded than their opponents and enjoyed the support of the Chamber of Commerce, the League of Women Voters, the city administration, and both major newspapers, as well as other media, the proposal lost overwhelmingly, 36,971 to 13,177. The new government was defeated most conclusively in areas outside the city where it lost by a proportion of ten to one. But it also lost in the city, failing to carry a single ward.

Many reasons are given for the defeat, but those noted most often were (1) the assumed taxation disparity it would have created between those receiving services and those paying for them, (2) the allegedly excessive powers it would give the mayor, and (3) the belief that the Republicans would gain the most politically. The taxation issue was highlighted by the United Taxpayers Association, a county-based group organized expressly to combat unified government. Other groups opposed included the volunteer firefighters, township trustees, the Farm Bureau Federation, and the Teamsters Union.

The partisan political issue was probably not very important. Although some Democratic organization members and a number of officeholders were opposed and anti-Vandigov materials were in-

22. It is not certain when this popular term for the Evansville–Vanderburgh County consolidation legislation was coined, but it became most popular during final legislative hearings in 1973 and the subsequent referendum period.

cluded in their election precinct materials, the party was generally split on the issue. For some time Democrats had been successful in countywide elections, and the threat of a Republican suburban take-over was not a real issue. Moreover, the bill had the support of a number of Democrats, including former Mayor Frank McDonald, but it failed in Republican and Democratic wards alike. Blacks were also generally divided on the issue and did not mount a well-organized effort against it. Probably the pervasive element contributing to the defeat was a deep-seated fear of bigness and change. The opponents concocted a monster from a local magic store and had it parade downtown and at public functions throughout the campaign. The monster image, as a symbol of bigness and oppression in government, was a distillation of most voters' fears.

In conclusion, the Vandigov debate was substantially influenced by the Indianapolis experience. Although the Evansville–Vanderburgh County merger idea had been formulated at least 10 years prior to Unigov, the actual merger campaign spanned the five years immediately following Unigov's passage. Many of the Unigov strategies were used. The form of government, with adjustments for the political realities of the area, was to be nearly identical to Unigov. Evansville's campaign to secure citizen support was intensified by the addition of a referendum, but many of the same Unigov campaign techniques were employed. Evansville's lobbying program, closely patterned after Mayor Lugar's, was largely responsible for the bill's passage in the General Assembly.

The reform effort clearly benefited from Unigov as a forerunner but also inherited a share of its negative legacy. Consolidation opponents across the state—feeling they had been caught unaware in 1969 when Unigov passed without requiring a referendum—were now vigilant and insisted on a referendum. They would undoubtedly try to add a referendum requirement to any future consolidation bills. Local officials in Indiana are aware of the typical fate of referendums. Accordingly, subsequent local reform proposals have been much less comprehensive than either Unigov or Vandigov.

Less Comprehensive Reform: St. Joseph County– South Bend

St. Joseph County and the city of South Bend (the St. Joseph County seat) have made the most substantial governmental changes in the state since Unigov. In parallel but separate acts, the city adopted a cabinet government, and the county restructured its council districts and made certain functional changes in the duties of both the County Council and the County Commission. The timing of these reform debates was approximately the same (1970 to 1974), and there was some membership overlap among the supporters, but the city and the county sought unrelated goals, steered separate courses, and employed distinctly different methods.

The county reform process was more overtly organized than the city's, included greater citizen involvement, and took longer. The debate about county reform began with the appointment by the mayor and county commissioners of a St. Joseph County Government Committee to study the question of a metropolitan government. Although consolidation was discussed, reform of the county government evolved as a more immediate need and a more attainable goal. The committee's first completed report, submitted to the 1971 General Assembly, recommended in addition to the typical reforms that the proposal would replace the three county commissioners with a single executive. The controversy over this issue was the main reason the legislators added a referendum requirement to the enabling act. The referendum on adoption was held during the 1972 fall general election, defeating the measure by a large margin. Shortly after the defeat, a smaller group of the original study committee submitted a new bill to the General Assembly, identical to the previous year's measure, except for retention of the county commissioners. Thus amended, the bill passed the 1973 session of the General Assembly without a referendum requirement. The first commission and council, elected under the reformed system, were chosen in November 1977, and the new government began operating on January 1, 1978.

The county reform bill was a twofold measure.[23] First, new electoral districts were formed so that all nine members of the County Council and the three county commissioners are elected from single-member districts. Second, the three-member County Commission was retained, but its powers were substantially reduced; many were transferred to the council, whose powers had previously been limited to taxation and finance. With these changes, the county governmental arrangement now more closely resembles an executive-legislative system of checks and balances. Electing councilmembers from districts has had the intended result of reducing the traditional rural dominance of the membership and agenda. Urban interests are now clearly represented by three districts in South Bend, one district in the neighboring city of Mishawaka, and a fifth district shared between the two cities.

Unigov's significance to the South Bend–St. Joseph County reforms was mostly indirect. As in other Indiana cities, reformers there were generally impressed with the General Assembly's generosity to Indianapolis and were eager to be granted the same consideration, but

23. *Indiana Acts of 1973*, Public Law 163 (Indianapolis, 1973).

for their *own* reform plan. It was also inevitable that the first mention of local government reform would provoke arguments for and against "what happened in Indianapolis" with the Unigov law. Views varied as to exactly what this was, and debate continued over its applicability to St. Joseph County, but the most important consequence of the 1971 hearings was that they alerted the opponents to merger, enabling them to keep reform discussions on an incremental basis, and to attach a referendum requirement to the bill they did not like.

The city's reform debate developed in the midst of the St. Joseph County government committees' deliberations when the Democratic candidate for mayor, Jerry Miller (a former County Commission and study committee member) campaigned in 1971 on a platform of bringing a cabinet form of administration to the mayor's office. After his election he had little trouble selling the cabinet reform proposal to the Democratic St. Joseph County legislative delegation. They in turn carried the bill to the General Assembly as a voter-approved reform— inasmuch as the newly elected mayor had made it an issue in his campaign—that had unanimous delegation support. Following its usual custom of also acceding to the wishes of a united local delegation, the General Assembly passed the bill virtually without opposition, 80 to 3 in the House and 39 to 2 in the Senate. Also contributing to the large majority was the fact that the legislators saw the bill as of minor scope and applicable to only one city. (Although later in the session the city of Gary agreed to be included in the bill, no local ordinance has since been passed in Gary to establish a cabinet government.) Support for the bill was so broad that it was not necessary to remind the majority Republicans that three years previously two St. Joseph County Democrats had provided critical Senate votes for Unigov.

The new South Bend city government[24] is largely a realignment of existing governmental entities into six major departments, each directly responsible to the mayor, following very closely the administrative restructuring that accompanied Unigov. The mayor's appointment and removal powers were increased; previous quasi-independent agencies were made more accountable to department heads and thus to the mayor, and lines of budget control were drawn more closely to the mayor's office. After many years of operation, the new arrangement in South Bend appears firmly established. Although the police and fire departments have successfully resisted being brought under the administrative control of the public safety director, the mayor now has greater budgetary and administrative authority over parks, planning and development, public works, and personnel.

24. *Indiana Acts of 1972*, Public Law 130 (Indianapolis, 1972).

Home Rule

In addition to reform efforts in individual cities and counties—via a general state statute drafted for a particular local government—increased attention in the post-Unigov years has focused on more home rule for all Indiana local governments.

Home rule is not a new idea in Indiana, as 16 home-rule resolutions were presented to the General Assembly between 1937 and 1969, and two constitutional home-rule attempts came close to passage in 1943 and 1953. Only recently, however, has some modest success been achieved, partly through the efforts of a Constitutional Revision Commission in the late 1960s.[25] The commission recommended that the General Assembly change strategies, to seek home rule by statute rather than by constitutional amendment. Following the commission's recommendations, the 1971 General Assembly passed a fairly comprehensive home-rule effort. The basic home-rule law as amended in 1973[26] did essentially two things: (1) it organized most municipal laws into one chapter and enumerated the powers already established, and (2) it gave cities broad general and residual functional home-rule powers. But the General Assembly's attempt to clarify the municipal law was only partially successful, as many local government laws were omitted. With respect to home rule, the power clauses were explicitly designed to reverse the presumption of Dillon's rule, granting cities powers not expressly denied them or vested in another governmental unit. These same powers were conferred on counties in 1975 and on towns in 1977.

Most observers agree that the General Assembly's intent was a liberal extension of cities' corporate powers. But mixed opinions by the courts and the state attorney general have caused a certain amount of uncertainty. The problem is not so much the law itself but the context of other state laws within which it must be used. Established state laws respecting municipal concern are numerous and often unclear. Many are outdated but never repealed. Since the home-rule law states that the powers exercised under it may not conflict with established law, most attempts to use home-rule powers are thus subject to litigation. The resulting lawsuits and confusion have weakened the law in ways that were not intended. Further, local governments are also governed by numerous state agencies whose regulations often obstruct local attempts to exercise home-rule authority.

The 1978 Indiana General Assembly established a Local Government Study Commission to consider the functions of local govern-

25. Indiana Legislative Council, Indianapolis, "Report of the Constitutional Revision Commission," September 1970, p. 21.

26. *Indiana Acts of 1971*, Public Law 250 (Indianapolis, 1971), p. 955; and *Indiana Acts of 1973*, Public Law 171 (Indianapolis, 1973), p. 866.

ment and how services might be rendered more efficiently and economically.[27] Home rule was a central part of the commission's legislative package presented to the 1980 General Assembly.

In all, the General Assembly passed 14 commission-sponsored bills, each relating in varying degrees to home rule or to the commission itself. Four bills comprised the heart of the legislative package, the thrust of the legislation being found in House Enrolled Act 1001, which restates the home-rule principle, recodifies the existing municipal law under a new title of the Indiana Code (Indiana Code 36–1–3), removes irrelevant statutes, and includes a list of general powers for local units. The commission was careful not to add any new authority to the statutes, the sole aim being to make the existing law usable; they seem to have been successful. The recodification will remove some of the legal hindrances to the implementation of existing home-rule authority. Local administrators will now have a clearer understanding of the legislature's intent to grant home rule. This in turn should help the courts reach greater consistency in their home-rule decisions.

The General Assembly included the unusual provision that the home-rule legislation would not go into effect until September 1, 1981— 16 months after enactment. This was done in part to allow administrators and others sufficient time to become familiar with the law and to amend it if necessary. But the most significant reason was to give the Local Government Study Commission time to prepare draft legislation that would give charter-making powers to local governments.

Although a bill to give local governments extensive charter-making authority was included as the featured item of the 1981 home-rule legislation package, the measure (House Bill 1005) died on the House floor without much debate. The two principal reasons given for the bill's failure are (1) no one actively supported the bill's city manager provision, and (2) many representatives opposed the section that would have permitted local governments to adopt a countywide system of government by referendum. Although the bill did not specifically mention Unigov or unified government, a considerable amount of the opposition was based on anti-Unigov sentiment across the state.

Unigov's notoriety was not always detrimental. Two 1981 changes—increased administrative powers for mayors and a provision to allow the state's remaining counties to adopt the St. Joseph County government system—can be traced to the reform spark ignited by the Unigov debate.

It is still too early to predict how local governments will adapt home-rule authority to their needs. It is clear, however, that if local officials choose to use it, a broad range of substantive home-rule powers are now available for their administration.

27. *Indiana Acts of 1978*, Public Law 160 (Indianapolis, 1978), p. 222.

10

Conclusion

After 15 years of operation it is still too early to report the definitive lessons from the Unigov experience. Nevertheless, enough time has elapsed for a reasonable evaluation of the administrative and political arrangements producing the reorganization and to draw some general conclusions about Unigov's applicability elsewhere. The central questions relate to how the restructured government has been able to respond to urban problems and what conditions led to the adoption of Unigov without a referendum.

The Restructured Government

The evidence indicates that Unigov is an accepted political reality, evoking among its supporters a sense of accomplishment and self-esteem that now extends to most of the community. Its critics no longer seek a return to the former arrangement, working instead for more favorable positions or larger voices in the new system. Carl Dortch, retired executive vice-president of the Indianapolis Chamber of Commerce and one of the principal Unigov proponents, said about the Unigov reform: "This [the previous arrangement] patchwork additional layer of local government has been expensive and often unsatisfactory. And even Unigov provides no quick, complete remedy for our ills. Compromise with varied objections and pressures has resulted in exemptions, exceptions, and a clutter of advisory boards and committees. But Unigov is a fresh start. To many of us, with all its limitations, our new consolidated city concept is a worthy experiment."[1]

This definitely favorable but modest statement from the Chamber of Commerce executive suggests, as does this study, that Unigov has successfully clarified and simplified matters but is not as comprehensive a reform as the unified government acronym might lead one to believe.

---

1. Carl R. Dortch, "Consolidated City-County Government, Indianapolis–Marion County, Indiana Style," unpublished manuscript, January 1971, p. 6.

Characteristics of Unigov Reform

Although the Indianapolis–Marion County consolidation was less comprehensive than several other recent consolidations elsewhere in the United States, most municipal functions were extended countywide and placed under a combined City-County Council and a single elected city and county executive.[2] The merger strengthened considerably the mayor's budgetary and administrative authority, an important indication of the business community's involvement and a reflection of the sponsors' intent to incorporate business principles into the new government. Unigov mayors enjoy a closer balance between what they are held accountable for and what they have authority and responsibility to do than the balance under the previous arrangement or that in most other large cities.

Development. The Unigov mayor's ability to commit public resources to projects having a far greater degree of authority and conviction than before has pursuaded local businessmen and outside investors that Indianapolis is a good place for development. In just one decade Indianapolis has to be recognized for its large population and size as one of the nation's great cities and for its reputation as a politically and economically sound city, as well as a good place to live. At this time no one can say for sure how much of the success can be attributed to the reformed governmental structure, how much may be due to the renewal of spirit and morale that accompanied the reform movement, or how much the national trend in city improvement may have contributed. Some experienced observers of metropolitan reform, for example, Vincent Marando, while acknowledging the difficulty of establishing the existence of close cause-and-effect relationships between structure and performance, maintain that structure does have significant consequences. Thus, Marando says: "Whether the structure of local government actually causes or is merely one symptom of societal urban problems has not yet been determined; nevertheless, there is a relationship, and one of crucial importance, between local government structure and what has come to be called the 'urban crisis.' "[3] We contend that a large portion of the community development in Indianapolis–Marion County—whether applauded or criticized—can be attributed in a clear and significant way to the mayor's office restructuring done under the Unigov reform.

2. The Unigov plan omitted schools, townships, the courts, and three incorporated municipalities and continued the status of existing special service districts. Thus, it is clearly less comprehensive in the number of units merged than the consolidations of Jacksonville–Duval, Nashville–Davidson, and Lexington–Fayette.

3. Vincent L. Marando, *Local Government Reorganization: An Overview* (Washington, DC: National Academy of Public Administration, 1972), p. 1.

The Unigov mayors have been aided and supported in developing and legitimizing their policies by the existence of the combined City-County Council, which provides a forum for debate and decision on many programs involving both the central city and the suburbs. The council's role in establishing communitywide policy was perhaps most notable in its lead role in extending the service of the sanitary district to a nearly countywide jurisdiction. Prior to Unigov, this would have required approval by the mayor and the City Council along with the county commissioners and County Council—four separate competitive entities that had no effective working relationship.

The most visible community development projects during the 15 years of Unigov have been in downtown development. Concentrated in the mile-square central business district and projecting an imposing presence against the skyline, projects such as the Market Square Arena (where the National Basketball Association's "Pacers" play), a $4.7 million renovation of the City Market, a $46 million Merchants Plaza hotel-office complex, and the new American United Life Insurance building (with 600,000 square feet of office space over a parking garage) provide clear and obvious evidence of Unigov's effectiveness. The combination of the strengthened mayor's office and the unified planning and redevelopment authority under the Department of Metropolitan Development has given Indianapolis one of the nation's strongest community development programs.

Business and Economic Growth.   Less visible than the altered downtown skyline, but no less important in its significance for the community, has been the business and economic growth under Unigov. The *Wall Street Journal* recently reported that, despite its "Indian-No-Place" or "Naptown" image, Indianapolis is one of the few frostbelt cities that grew in the 1970s: "In recent years though, Indianapolis has done something that few of its putatively more cosmopolitan Northern neighbors can match: It has held its own against the Sun Belt in the war for population and jobs. It has even gained a bit."[4] The article attributes the Republican mayors' special success to their ability to interest the Indianapolis business community in Unigov's development plans and also notes: "One big reason Indianapolis has been able to do what it has in the last dozen years is its unusual Unigov system, the partial consolidation of city and Marion County Government that took effect in 1970."[5]

The increased recognition Indianapolis received because of the *Wall Street Journal* coverage and its earlier designation by the Na-

4. "Star of Snowbelt, Indianapolis thrives on Partnership of City, Business, Philanthropy," *Wall Street Journal*, July 14, 1982, p. 1.
5. Ibid.

tional Council on Municipal Performance as the nation's healthiest economy are evidence that Unigov has both real and symbolic value. The central theme of this study is that Unigov created a structure that focused real authority in the mayor's office to provide for more efficient government. In addition, Unigov has also inspired a sense of community accomplishment that has helped coalesce private-sector leadership. These two elements must be taken together to account for Indianapolis's economic growth in the 1970s. It is impossible to say with any precision which of the elements is the more effective in promoting the synergistic and mutually beneficial private-public leadership that has emerged. Certainly, however, Unigov provided the necessary focus for the community to rally around in removing its long-enduring "Indian-No-Place" image.

Internal cost savings under Unigov are notable but not extensive. There have been economies of scale that have saved money on such items as central purchasing, legal fees, and comprehensive insurance and trash collection plans. While the prospect of such savings was not a major concern in the development of the Unigov plan, they have since become an important part of management practice.

The key economic issue in the Unigov debate occurred on the revenue side of the budget process. The reform proponents pledged not to raise property taxes or to charge for services not received. They have effectively complied with the pledge through 15 years of Unigov experience. This has been made possible by a statewide property-tax freeze and the availability of additional revenue sources, especially transfer funds from the federal government. Indiana ranks last among the states in the amount of federal dollars returned to the state per capita, but Indianapolis–Marion County has fared exceedingly well with its allocation. In 1980 Marion County received $631,752,000 in total federal grant funds, while the other Indiana county closest in population, Lake, received $212,765,000. In short, Lake County, with a population of approximately 525,000, received $405 dollars per person, while Marion County, with approximately 700,000 persons, received $902 federal grant dollars per capita—more than twice Lake County's proportion.[6] Similar contrasts can be made with other large urban counties such as Allen, St. Joseph, and Vanderburgh.

The uniqueness of the Unigov structure is only partly responsible for Marion County's advantage in obtaining federal funds. Unigov mayors have been prominent national spokesmen for federal urban assistance—both are past presidents of the National League of Cities. Moreover, as Republican mayors, they found favor with Republican

6. Data compiled from *Geographic Distribution of Federal Funds in Indiana, Fiscal Year 1980* (Washington, DC: Community Services Administration, 1980), which may be obtained from National Technical Information Service, Springfield, Virginia.

administrations in Washington, DC. In addition to these factors, the Unigov plan facilitates unified planning and administration in ways that are attractive to federal agencies, and the mayors regularly emphasized this in their grant proposals—the Indianapolis Model Cities programs and Planned Variations award are good examples.

Black Involvement Under Unigov.

Early evaluations of Unigov by black leaders were divided. Some supported it because it would bring suburban resources into the city. Others opposed it because their voting strength in the old city would be diluted. Still others, unsure of what Unigov would do, preferred to wait and see. Blacks now play significant roles in the new government. The number of participating blacks is proportionately greater than before, and their voice in public policy certainly does not seem any less effective. Blacks have held and continue to hold high administration posts under Unigov, for example, the deputy mayor and department and division head positions, which they did not hold prior to Unigov.

Blacks elected to the City-County Council from inner-city districts through the single-member district system now have a voice in suburban affairs, sometimes giving them voting leverage that can be used to bargain for support for their own programs. They have gained a leadership position within the Democratic minority on the council and at the same time have acquired an added presence in Unigov's Republican administrations. Thus, under Unigov black political influence has been extended to suburban and political environs where they previously had little or no voice. Not everyone sees these new developments in a positive way. William Schreiber, a former Marion County Democratic Party chair and prominent critic of Unigov, concluded that Unigov had an adverse effect on the influence of blacks and especially on their influence wielded through the once-dominant Democratic Party. He noted: "Finally, consolidation dilutes minority group, especially black, voting power. Whether it does so as a side effect or primary purpose is difficult to determine, although there is cogent evidence that it may be the latter. In the case of Indianapolis, at least, the crucial dimension of this dilution relates to minority influence not in the total community but in the dominant political party. Insofar as consolidation dilutes the power of the dominant political party in the pre-consolidation city, that party is the primary victim of consolidation."[7]

Despite the compelling logic of these arguments, blacks in Indianapolis–Marion County have generally not opposed Unigov with as much fervor or commitment as the Democratic Party, which was "the

---

7. William M. Schreiber, "Indianapolis–Marion County Consolidation, How Did It All Happen?" unpublished manuscript, n.d., p. 29.

primary victim of consolidation." The dilution of the black vote on the Democratic ballot has also been influenced by an overt Republican Party effort to court the black vote. While the results have not been spectacular, the larger black vote that Republican mayoral candidates got in the 1970s, contrasted with the three previous decades, suggests a substantial level of black acceptance of Unigov.

The large population base of blacks had only given them the *promise* of majority influence. They had not capitalized on their voting strength in the old city in the preconsolidated government and had no recognizable voice in county government. While the restructured government may not have fulfilled the *promise* that the preconsolidation arrangement held out for blacks, they now have a prominent political voice as an accomplished fact under Unigov. They have a considerably larger voice than ever before.

The prospect of political advantage was an important motivation behind the Unigov decision, and the benefit was clearly seen in the harvest of the large Republican mayoral and council victories in the 1970s. Although Unigov's contribution to these wins is usually attributed to the redistricting, equal consideration must be given to the camaraderie and excitement generated among Republicans by passage of the reform. It is also generally believed that the Democrats could win control of the new government if they could spark the same degree of enthusiasm for their leading candidates (especially the candidate for mayor). This is the strategy they have adopted. Democrats no longer campaign against the Unigov plan as such but seek instead to control the new government themselves. Should Democrats succeed, observers will have new evidence and a wider perspective on which to base a fuller evaluation of Unigov and especially of the most frequent critical allegation, namely, that it is designed to favor business and economic interests and physical development over people-oriented programs. It would be interesting to evaluate Unigov's performance under a Democratic mayor and council.

Summary. To sum up, Unigov has had definite successes and has received some criticism. It is too early, however, for a definitive evaluation. Moreover, successes during the 15 years are not so clearly the product of unified government that they justify the marketing of Unigov as a reform model for widespread adoption elsewhere. On the other hand, metropolitan areas beset by problems and crises may find some important lessons in the Unigov experience. Melvin Mogulof's assessment of consolidated government in Jacksonville, Miami, the Twin Cities, and Toronto, written 13 years ago, could well be extended to Unigov's first 15 years: "They have generally done well the things they set out to do—they almost always seem to have done them with more skill than was displayed in the metropolitan area prior to the restructuring. This is not to suggest that these achievements could not have been accomplished under the previous governing structure of the area. But they were not. The fact is, in each of the operating metro areas, the new structure has brought a sense of governmental competence and buoyancy, which is a rare commodity on the American governing scene."[8] Borrowing from Carl Dortch's assessment, Unigov has been a "worthy experiment" for Indianapolis–Marion County.

The Reform Process

Other cities are more likely to consider trying to adopt features of the Unigov consolidation plan than of the reform process by which it was adopted. The special conditions in Indianapolis–Marion County, the only US metropolitan consolidation achieved without a referendum in the twentieth century, seem most unlikely to be repeated elsewhere. Despite the Unigov debate's unusual features, there are interesting parallels to and contrasts with other mergers. Perhaps the most helpful finding from such comparisons is that the similarities in referendum and nonreferendum mergers are more notable than the differences. Most of the same actors participate in both kinds of mergers, and the state is a crucial partner in the process. Furthermore, political considerations are critical to the approval of the reforms, and realistic political negotiations militate against a fully comprehensive structural consolidation.

Unigov: A Model for Reform?

Unique or unusual factors have contributed to the success of each of the recent consolidations that have occurred. For example, a 10-dollar "green sticker" tax on all automobiles using city streets and the announcement of an aggressive city annexation program contributed to the Nashville–Davidson County consolidation in 1962.[9] The transient nature of Miami's population, many people having arrived during the two decades before the merger referendum, was an unusual factor in the Miami–Dade consolidation.[10] A major political scandal and the local schools' loss of accreditation contributed to the successful vote to consolidate Jacksonville and Duval County.[11] Unigov watchers tend to

8. Melvin B. Mogulof, *Five Metropolitan Governments* (Washington, DC: Urban Institute, 1972), pp. 136–137.

9. John C. Bollens and Henry J. Schmandt, *The Metropolis: Its People, Politics, and Economic Life*, 4th ed. (New York: Harper & Row, 1982), p. 392.

10. Edward Sofen, *The Miami Metropolitan Experience* (Bloomington: Indiana University Press, 1963), p. 74.

11. Richard Martin, *Consolidation: Jacksonville, Duval County* (Jacksonville, Fla.: Crawford Publishing Co., 1968), pp. 35–42.

focus more on the merger process than on the changes it brought about, and they tend to emphasize that the absence of a referendum vote is the exceptional factor in Indianapolis and Indiana. They conclude that this precludes the Unigov process from being used as a model elsewhere. Subsequent merger proposals in Indiana (Evansville and South Bend) both required referendums. This and the recent state supreme court invalidation of the legislative-mandated merger of Las Vegas and Clark County, Nevada, tend to support the assumption that use of the Unigov nonreferendum process elsewhere is unlikely. The constitutional and political conditions that prevailed in Indianapolis (and Indiana) at the time of Unigov's adoption are unlikely to occur again in the same alignment as observed in Indianapolis in 1968–1969.

In constitutional terms, Indiana was a traditionally governed state, as it had not adopted the reforms many states accepted at the turn of the century. Thus, the initiative, recall, and nonpartisan ballot were unknown in Indiana. The referendum was rarely employed, and when used, the results were considered only advisory. Home rule had been a persistent topic of legislative discussion in Indiana, but local self-determination never materialized. Dillon's rule prevailed, and local governments regularly went to the General Assembly for even the most modest substantive and structural changes. The state legislature had become accustomed to serving as a kind of giant city hall for the state's municipalities. Consequently, when the Unigov bill was presented to the 1969 General Assembly, neither legal precedent nor customary practice prevented the legislature from acting unilaterally in putting the merger into effect. In short, Indiana was able to act more like a Canadian province than the typical American state when it mandated Unigov.

Political Strategy.   Throughout the debate, Unigov's proponents operated on the premise that consolidation was the exclusive province of the state legislature. Their strategy focused on using their political power to get the merger plan through the General Assembly. Marando has taken specific notice of the importance of the political process in consolidation attempts where a referendum vote is required: "The reform process is important, but quite limited in its effect upon reorganization adoption. A metropolitan area includes 'environmental' and 'political system' conditions that have a large and immeasurable impact upon the probability of local government reorganization acceptance."[12] Marando states further that "when metropolitan reorganization is pursued . . . the probability of controlling the political process to result in reorganization is severely limited."[13]

12. Vincent L. Marando, "The Politics of Metropolitan Reform," *Administration and Society* 6(2):256 (August 1974).
13. Ibid., p. 230.

Our study emphasizes that politics was also a critical factor in the nonreferendum Unigov debate. If the Republicans had not controlled the process at all key points from the Indianapolis mayor to the state governor's office and if Marion County's political leadership had not been determined to push Unigov as their sole high priority item in the legislature that year, it is unlikely that the reform bill would have passed. But Indianapolis is notable for the high level of partisan political activity in support of Unigov. In fact, Unigov reversed the customary reform process wherein proponents draw up a reform proposal and then seek political support. The Unigov principals recognized that they had an advantageous political position in the state, determined that they would use that power to reform local government, and proceeded to draft the main elements of the plan they hoped to implement.

Political Leaders' Role. While duplication of the Indianapolis–Indiana political circumstances elsewhere seems unlikely, there are valuable lessons to be learned from the Unigov debate.[14] The important element of leadership and the role of the state in resolving a metropolitan government problem are two generally applicable ones.

Bollens and Schmandt note how incumbent officeholders usually oppose consolidation and how political parties rarely take official positions on merger proposals, but they cite Indianapolis as a notable exception.[15] In general, local officials tend to defer to the leadership initiatives of civic reform groups, for example, the League of Women Voters, the Chamber of Commerce, the media, and university faculty. In Indianapolis, however, the initiative and direction came from the established governmental and political leadership. Mayor Lugar emphasized the importance of taking such a lead role in reform efforts: "But the solid factor lacking in most county governmental modernization discussions has been the search for votes, majority votes in the appropriate forums of decision. As practical politicians or county statesmen, we have been reluctant to stake our political lives on unifying the people we serve. We have noted correctly that a great many people are trying to diligently fragment local government; too often we have tried to justify these divisions and thus ride the crest of discontent."[16]

The exercise of their political leadership gave Mayor Lugar and the other Unigov proponents certain advantages as compared with re-

14. The one-man, one-vote redistricting of the Indiana General Assembly in 1972 makes the likelihood of another unified delegation, such as the slated delegation elected at-large in the legislature during the passage of Unigov in 1969, extremely remote.

15. Bollens and Schmandt, *Metropolis*, pp. 384–386.

16. Richard G. Lugar, "The Need for County Leadership in County Modernization," speech to the thirty-fourth National Conference of the National Association of Counties, Portland, Oregon, July 28, 1969, p. 4.

form sponsors elsewhere. The most important difference is the impetus their commitment brought to the Unigov debate. Getting public officials' support for consolidation is traditionally one of the most difficult tasks for reforms initiated by civic groups and the business community. This was already evident over 100 years ago in the case of Philadelphia's nineteenth-century nonreferendum consolidation: "The imperial growth of our cities has always required their political partnership with the state legislatures and the courts. In the case of Philadelphia, it took the business community five years of effort to secure the election of enough sympathetic Pennsylvania legislators to vote the consolidation in 1854. Generally the initiative on behalf of annexation comes from the commercial interests of the central city; the task is then to secure legislators to vote approval of the design."[17]

The governmental-political leadership pushing Unigov did not, however, act autonomously. A major emphasis of their reform campaign was directed at securing public support for the merger, but their appeal was directed toward groups known to be receptive to reform proposals. Operating from within the official decisionmaking process, they were able to influence some key variables in ways that favored Unigov's adoption. For example, they were able to control the timing of the public debate to coincide with the start of the General Assembly and at the same time keep potential opponents off stride. The attorneys who drafted the legislation were selected for their experience in local government legal work, their political savvy, and their personal ties with the leadership. Thus, they were able to act with greater dispatch than most officially constituted study commissions that develop merger proposals. The leadership's style of close management and direction was also evident in the way they demonstrated public support for Unigov. This was particularly notable in the work of the mayor's task force, whose membership and agenda were closely monitored to produce a legitimate grass-roots supportive statement.

Despite the political advantages and management style of the Unigov principals, they were not able to ramrod their merger plan through to adoption without effective opposition or substantive amendment to their original proposal. Most of the same sources of opposition to mergers seen in referendum elections also emerged to oppose Unigov, albeit in a different forum. Elected county officials, the opposing political party, radical conservatives, racial minorities, representatives from special district boards, labor leaders, and suburban communities all obtained concessions during the negotiating process over the Unigov proposal. The strategy of negotiating and compromising on issues large and small was used by the principals to

---

17. Milton Kotler, *Neighborhood Government: The Local Foundations of Political Life* (Indianapolis: Bobbs-Merrill, 1969), p. 22.

"obtain an end product," as Charles Whistler put it, "rather than a lot of sound and fury."[18]

In fact, the political process was very demanding in Unigov's nonreferendum merger. Opponents were able to extract important concessions that weakened the original proposal, but the nonreferendum process and the proponents' compromise strategy prevented them from defeating the entire plan on the basis of their opposition to a single issue. The result was a merger that embodies more decentralization than in consolidations elsewhere.

Another important leadership factor in the Unigov debate was the willingness of the elected officials to take full ethical and political responsibility for the objectives and substance of the reform plan. They campaigned for it openly and persuasively, knowing that their future political fortunes would be affected by their success or failure. While their efforts were also supported by the media, the business community, the Republican Party, and others, the elected officials were the most visible proponents and thus the most directly vulnerable to possible negative citizen reaction. The state legislators were somewhat less visible but certainly no less responsible, especially the Marion County legislators who saw the bill through to passage.

The State's Role. Because Unigov was a legislatively mandated consolidation, the state's role might mistakenly be seen as greater than it actually was. Mogulof, for example, has emphasized the role of the state: "The state is not simply another factor in reorganization—it is the central factor. It is the 'gatekeeper' of the whole decision process because none of the political subdivisions has powers beyond those granted to them by the state through laws or charters."[19]

The state was as important in the Unigov debate as it was in the five other metropolitan governments studied by Mogulof.[20] The key issue, however, is not the state's *legal* authority but the way the state's authority is brought into play. Mogulof points out that all of the five metropolitan areas he studied were "highly visible to their state houses," and three of these cities (Portland, Toronto, and Minneapolis–St. Paul) were each "potentially the tail wagging the state dog."[21] Indianapolis fits this metaphor very well.

As the largest metropolitan area in the state and the site of the state capital, Indianapolis had traditionally enjoyed a strong bargaining position in the General Assembly and the political party conventions. The Unigov principals acted decisively through the Indianapo-

18. Charles L. Whistler, interview with James Owen, Indianapolis, June 14, 1972.

19. Mogulof, *Five Metropolitan Governments*, p. 26.

20. The five were Jacksonville, Florida; Miami, Florida; Minneapolis–St. Paul, Minnesota; Portland, Oregon; and Toronto, Ontario, Canada.

21. Mogulof, *Five Metropolitan Governments*, p. 27.

lis legislative delegation and Republican Party leadership to secure the passage of Unigov.

Gatekeeper seems an appropriate term for the state's role as a rather passive partner in a locally initiated and managed reform effort. Because Unigov was manipulated through the state decisionmaking process in a very forceful power play, the state cannot be regarded as the reform's initiator or sponsor. Unigov was not a product of enlightened state activity. Observers such as Patricia Florestano and Vincent Marando comment that "prior to Unigov's passage Indiana was not a state that evidenced responsibility for cities and their problems."[22] On the other hand, the Unigov experience did spark an increased state awareness of local government and its problems. Our study shows that Unigov stimulated increased state concern in the 1970s with the restructuring of governments in Evansville and South Bend. Moreover, the state passed comprehensive home-rule legislation and property-tax relief measures.

While urging greater state participation in metropolitan area affairs, Florestano and Marando note that the "states may move in the direction of their own choosing" but also add: "They may choose not to move at all [or] continue with current patterns of relationships and nonrelationships."[23] Unigov demonstrated that the state of Indiana could act decisively in metropolitan areas, thereby whetting local officials' appetites to petition the state more forcefully for other assistance.

Robert Wood's oft-quoted comment that government reorganizations are the "result of accident, not design"[24] is a telling criticism of metropolitan reform efforts of the last two decades. His statement is basically true, but Indianapolis clearly departs from the pattern. There was more design than accident in the process that created Unigov. The leadership consciously chose to subordinate everything else, including their future electoral prospects, to secure the reform they sought. The proponents' willingness to compromise on many issues, seeking what they considered attainable, is a valuable lesson for other reform activists. In conclusion, the significant features of the Unigov experience lie in the nature of the local leadership and the willingness of state officials to resolve a local problem. Indiana's constitutional and political environment at the time allowed the Unigov principals to try for a more comprehensive reform than is usually possible. Cities and metropolitan areas that are willing to settle for less may find Unigov an excellent case study of the ways political power can be used to effect reform.

---

22. Patricia S. Florestano and Vincent L. Marando, *The States and the Metropolis* (New York: Dekker, 1981), p. 3.

23. Ibid., p. 54.

24. Robert C. Wood, "Contributions of Political Science to Urban Reform," in *Urban Life and Form*, ed. Werner Z. Hirsh (New York: Holt, Rinehart & Winston, 1963), p. 113.

Appendixes

Appendix 1: The Mayor's Task Force on Improved Governmental Structure for Indianapolis and Marion County

William A. Brennan, Jr.
President
W. A. Brennan, Inc.

H. Prentice Browning
President
American Fletcher National
Bank

John Burkhart
President
College Life Insurance
Company

George P. Cafouros
Spotlight Publishing
Company

Eldon Campbell
Vice-President and General
Manager
Time Life Broadcast-WFBM

Robert N. Davies
Baker and Daniels

Henry F. DeBoest
Vice-President of Corporate
Affairs
Eli Lilly and Company

Carl R. Dortch
Executive Vice-President
Indianapolis Chamber of
Commerce

Robert Early
Managing Editor
Indianapolis Star

Roy C. Echols
Chairman of the Board
Indianapolis Water Company

William H. Hardy
Davidson, Hardy, and
Associates

Thomas C. Hasbrook,
President
Indianapolis City Council
Eli Lilly and Company

William H. Hudnut, III
Second Presbyterian Church

James E. Knott
Plant Manager of
Indianapolis Plants
Allison Division of General
Motors

Robert B. McConnell
Vice-President
WISH Television

William Pace
General Manager
North Side Topics

Walter H. Pagenkopf
General Manager
Western Electric, Inc.

Wendell A. Phillippi
Managing Editor
Indianapolis News
William T. Ray
W. T. Ray Realty Company
Jack E. Reich
Chairman of the Board
American United Life
Insurance Company
William D. Ruckelshaus
Ruckelshaus, Bobbitt, and
O'Conner
Raymond W. Saxon
Vice-President
Consumer Products Services
Radio Corporation of
America
William G. Schneider

Beurt SerVaas
President
Marion County Council
Review Publishing, Inc.
Marcus Stewart, Jr.
Publisher
Recorder
Wendell D. Vandivier
Carpenter's Apprenticeship
Training Program
Charles L. Whistler
Baker and Daniels
William E. Wuerch
Vice-President and General
Manager
AVCO Broadcasting
Corporation
Mrs. Carl Zimmer

Members of the Marion County delegation to the Indiana General Assembly were all considered ex officio members of the Task Force and were invited to all meetings of the Task Force.

Appendix 2: Form Letter from Mayor Lugar Directing Formation of Task Force on Indianapolis–Marion County Reorganization, November 1968

(on letterhead of the City of Indianapolis)

RICHARD G. LUGAR, MAYOR
November 6, 1968

Name
Title
Organization
Street Address
Indianapolis, Indiana

Dear _____:

    I would like to invite you to participate as a member of a task force to give policy direction toward the development of improved governmental structure for Indianapolis and Marion County. The task force will be cochaired by Mr. Thomas C. Hasbrook, President of the Indianapolis City Council, and Mr. Beurt SerVaas, President of the Marion County Council. The task force will have three specific assignments:

1. To direct the preparation of legislation for presentation to the 1969 Indiana General Assembly by a committee of lawyers who will prepare the actual bill.
2. To work with the members of the General Assembly and the public in promoting this legislative program.
3. To give guidance to the Mayor and other public officials in establishing the governmental structure following a successful legislative effort.

    I am appointing this task force within the structure of the Greater Indianapolis Progress Committee in order that many representative groups and organizations can participate in this important assignment. Government reorganization for the purpose of improving the efficiency and services of local government within the Indianapolis area is perhaps the most important single task facing this community. If successful, the positive impact on the development of Indianapolis will be felt for many years to come.

I hope that you can accept this assignment. Please let me know as soon as possible if you will be able to participate. If you have questions, please contact Deputy Mayor John W. Walls at 633-3165.

Sincerely yours,

Richard G. Lugar
Mayor

RGL:bjk

Appendix 3: List of Members of County Task Force as Reported in Memorandum by Judge John L. Niblack, Chair, County Task Force, December 19, 1968

Judge John L. Niblack, Marion Circuit Court
Judge Frank A. Symmes, Jr., Superior Court
Judge John T. Davis, Criminal Court, Div. I
Judge William T. Sharp, Municipal Court
John T. Sutton, county auditor
Marcia Hawthorne, county recorder
William Mercuri, county assessor
E. Allen Hunter, county clerk
Beurt SerVaas, president of County Council
Noble R. Pearcy, prosecuting attorney, Marion County
Walter Hemphill, county commissioner-elect
Lee R. Eads, sheriff, Marion County
Bonnie Stephenson, assessor, Perry Township

Source: Files of the Greater Indianapolis Progress Committee.

Appendix 4: Editorials on Unigov, 1968–1969

"It's a Grab"

The *Indianapolis News*, in its December 31, 1968 issue, printed an editorial comparing Mayor Lugar's quest for Unigov to the Democrats' "more guarded" 1965 consolidation plan, which the *News* had labeled a "power grab." The thrust of the editorial was aimed at the mayor's task force report and said that the Unigov proposal was not designed to make governmental boards and commissions more accountable to elected officials, as Lugar claimed. It was instead an attempt to concentrate power in the hands of the mayor.

A specific case mentioned was the Metropolitan Planning Commission, which was then a powerful nine-member agency, four of whose members were appointed by the mayor, two by the County Council, two by the county commissioners, and one by the City Council. The *News* favored the existing arrangement as one responsible to a wider segment of the community compared with Lugar's unifying proposal to place all these appointments in the mayor's office. The task force report, the editorial concluded, was a "power grab" and "bad government" and should therefore be rejected on both counts.

Consolidation Will Come*

The question of consolidated government for Indianapolis and Marion County to deal effectively with problems and functions the city and county have in common is not unlike, on a small scale of course, the issue of union confronting the colonies after the American Revolution.

There is little doubt consolidation will take place. In time even its now most zealous enemies are likely to demand it to rationalize the governing of what in many ways is now a single community split only

Indianapolis Star, January 23, 1969, p. 6.

by outdated boundary lines whose irrelevance is plain to anyone who travels along them.

Consolidation will be demanded to eliminate duplication and overlapping, waste, conflict, confusion and pointless expense—in short, to bring better government, more effective government, more responsible government, more responsive to the needs of the community and people.

Consolidation will come. The only question is how and when.

Hostility to the Uni-Gov bill pending in the General Assembly centers on certain points. One charge is that the changes are complex and messy and would do more harm than good. Another set of charges accuses the bill of promoting tyranny. Another group says the bill will favor one political party at the expense of the other. Interestingly, both some Republicans and some Democrats are expressing strong hostility to the bill.

We agree that the original Uni-Gov proposals concentrated excessive power in the hands of the mayor. But revision has removed this feature.

The claim that one party will profit at the other's expense is weakened, if not invalidated, by the fact that members of both parties are making it. It is founded, moreover, on the assumption that party loyalty and makeup are static, which history disproves.

As for the charge that the changes are complex and messy and would do more harm than good, this assumes that the present system—or lack of system—is superior. No rational individual familiar with the present setup can believe this.

The county commissioner system is an antiquated, ill-conceived, three-headed monstrosity combining executive and legislative functions which should not be combined. Its failures and weaknesses and the scandals surrounding it are persistent and notorious.

It is in effect the top governing factor of a metropolitan population of 276,000. It is totally unfit for the job. It should be scrapped.

Continuity of metropolitan problems is a pressing reality. Traffic is one example. Building and upkeep of streets and roads is another. Crime is another dramatic one. Bandits and rapists from the city do not stop at the city limits, but the law enforcement agency charged with controlling them does.

The makeup of the 25-member City-County Council representing all districts in the area, will provide essential checks and balances to guard against any threat of "one-man government" by the mayor . . . particularly if the terms of office are staggered, and elections are held in the off year as city elections now are.

School systems and existing municipal governments will not be affected. But outside cities would have free choice in asking for extension of countywide services.

The Uni-Gov Bill is 162 pages long. It is complex. It is certainly no cure-all. Its critics may be prompted by the highest of motives. Yet it offers a chance to make a real beginning in doing a complicated task that is going to have to be done not only in Indianapolis–Marion County but in other large metropolitan areas.

Not only the Marion County delegation but other members of the legislature and responsible citizens of Indiana should consider this.

Its realization is certain to bring an outcropping of now-unforeseeable problems. Such complex undertakings always do. But they can be faced and dealt with as they arise. Officials and voters and taxpayers of Indianapolis–Marion County, and of the entire state, could profit from these experiences.

It may be tempting to postpone some consolidation of city and county government in Indianapolis. It can be postponed. The complicated and fast-growing problems of metropolitan life cannot.

In the Balance*

The recent move by Mayor Lugar's task force on metropolitan government to get more balance into the plan for countywide voting here is an encouraging one. The task force has taken a step in the right direction and we trust that other such initiatives will be forthcoming.

Among several efforts to modify the "strong mayor" concept is a proposal that five members of the Metropolitan Development Commission be appointed by the council and board of county commissioners. The original plan had all nine board members being appointed by the mayor alone. This change is a good one.

Other moves have also been taken to infuse greater balance into the plan, and these will bear examination when the proposals are embodied in bills before the General Assembly. There are many further details which need discussing—such as the question of who will appoint and direct the staff of the development agency. Hammering out these items and gaining full agreement on the kind of changes to be enacted are yet to come.

We hope that these labors will provide still more emphasis on the need for checks and balances. Proper countywide solutions to problems of government in Indianapolis can be achieved without putting too much power into the hands of a single person or subjecting civic services to complete political turnover every time a new administration takes office. The News has historically favored a countywide executive and council. It does not favor setting up a system in which the countywide executive would have all power concentrated in his hands.

*Indianapolis Star, January 14, 1969, p. 4.

The current attempt at countywide solution provides, in our opinion, a chance to restore balance to local government rather than to distort that balance even further. Agencies put under the thumb of the mayor by the 1965 "power grab" bills can now be restored to equilibrium, with appointive authority distributed among the countywide executive, the council, and other county officials. In this way rationalization of services could be combined with safeguards against excessive political influence.

We commend the members of the task force for their willingness to take another look at these matters and to move toward a more balanced system. This willingness suggests a solution can yet be arrived at which will command broad support and enable Marion County to have government that is efficient in performance yet protected from unbridled power.

Uni-Gov—Let's Look at the Charges*

If the Legislature approves Uni-gov—the merger of Indianapolis and Marion county governments—would the county mayor be a "dictator"? Would Uni-gov do away with needed "checks and balances" on the mayor's powers?

Some Uni-gov opponents say the answers are "yes." We do not agree.

The county mayor would appoint most department heads in his administration. Through these appointees he would direct a major part of local government. But he could do only what the Legislature and the city-county council permitted. His appointments would be subject to council approval. Both mayor and council would face elections every four years. If the county mayor would be a dictator, then so are the Governor of Indiana and the President of the United States.

As for "checks and balances," this term usually refers to the controls exercised over each other by the two houses of a legislative body. Supposedly, because of differences in makeup or length of service, they assure that needed changes will be made, but not recklessly or too rapidly.

The county mayor would be an executive, not a legislator. An executive's function is not to decide a course of action, but to get the job done.

In recent years, each new government task in Indianapolis and the county has been handed to a new board, commission, or authority. The mayor is able to indirectly control a few of these agencies through his appointive powers. But appointments to others are divided among

*The WFBM Stations, Time-Life Broadcast, Inc., Indianapolis, January 22, 1969.

the mayor, city council, and various county officials. We now have a swarm of departments entrusted with vital and costly government functions, but not really answerable to anybody—the voters least of all.

The result—not surprisingly—has often been a maximum of confusion, power struggles, wasteful duplication, and bickering—with a minimum of cooperation in the interest of the community. In our opinion, this governmental jumble must be blamed for many failures to deal with our most urgent problems.

We urge that critics of Uni-gov forget for a few moments their personal ambitions and chronic opposition to change. We urge them to take a long look at our city and county. How much more of this kind of government can they stand?

Unigov*

"Unigov" is not the answer to all of the many problems that plague city and county government. Neither is it a monster that puts officeholders in positions of unchecked power, as some would have us believe. Simply, Unigov is designed to make city and county government work better.

Indianapolis and Marion County presently are fragmented into many governmental jurisdictions. Services now overlap in some areas and are not complete enough in others. The many police and fire departments in the county, to name only two services, operate independently of each other.

Under Unigov, or United Government, the city and county would be governed as one unit. The mayor would be the highest executive officer. There would also be a countywide elective council. In the future, there would probably be one police department, one fire department, one highway department. In short, one department for nearly every service a modern city provides. Schools will not be included. These changes will take place gradually, but even at the outset, coordination among the various groups would be improved. The object of the Unigov plan is not to dilute the quality of services by spreading them too thin, but to make them more efficient by weaving together the crazy-quilt pattern of agencies we have now. Hospitals, libraries and airports in Marion County have already realized the benefits of countywide management. All three have their own "Unigov-type" metropolitan boards.

There are those who fear Unigov is a bid for power by Mayor

*WISH-TV8, Indianapolis, a Corinthian station represented by Blair Television, January 21, 1969

Lugar and the Republican party. The Mayor has said he will relin-
quish his office and run again when and if Unigov becomes a reality.
No matter who is Mayor under Unigov, the voter must demand a good
performance and use the power of the ballot box to insure it.

Suburbanites feel their taxes will go up if Unigov is enacted.
They are right. The taxes will increase only as services in their area
increase.

Black leaders are afraid that the voice of the Negro living in the
central city will not be heard under Unigov. It is likely, however, that
improvements and programs made possible by a broader tax base will
benefit central city residents most.

The decision lies with the state legislature, where the Unigov bill
was put before the Senate today. We believe there is much merit in
having our growing metropolitan area served by the plan for United
and more efficient government.

Appendix 5: 1969 Marion County Legislative Delegation

Senate

(R) Walter H. Barbour	Real Estate Developer
(R) Lawrence M. Borst	Veterinarian
(R) Charles E. Bosma	Sec.-Treas. Bosma Dairy
(R) Danny L. Burton	General Insurance Agent
(R) Leslie Duvall	Attorney
(R) Joan M. Gubbins	Homemaker
(R) George A. Rubin	Attorney
(R) John M. Ryan	V.-P. and Counsel American Fletcher National Bank

House

(R) David L. Allison	Trust Officer American Fletcher National Bank
(R) Harriette B. Conn	Attorney
(R) Ray P. Crowe	V.-P. Summit Laboratories
(R) Doris L. Dorbecker	Homemaker
(R) Choice Edwards	Marketing Dept. Indiana Bell Telephone Co.
(R) Wilma J. Fay	Homemaker
(R) John C. Hart	Builder and Developer
(R) Robert L. Jones, Jr.	Educational Consultant
(R) E. Henry "Ned" Lamkin, Jr.	Physician
(R) Morris H. Mills	Farmer, Partner in Mills Brothers Farms
(R) John M. Mutz	V.-P., Circle Leasing Corp.

(R) Donald T. Nelson — Industrial Psychologist, Eli Lilly and Co.

(R) Arthur T. Northrup — Asst. City Attorney of Indianapolis

(R) Raymond E. Sanders — Pres., Sanders Automotive Supply Co.

(R) Otis M. Yarnell — Yard Conductor on Railroad

Appendix 6: Roll Call on Senate Bill 543

Roll Call 196

Yeas	N-V	Nays
● Andrew		
Augsburger		●
Bainbridge		●
● Barbour		
● Biddinger		
● Bloom		
● Borst		
Bosma	●	
● Burton		
Christy		●
Conrad		●
● Duvall		
● Edwards		
Fair	●	
Fanning		●
Frazier	●	
● Frick		
● Gardner		
Gubbins		●
● Gutman		
Harrison	●	
● Helms		
Kizer		●
● Kleinkort		
Konrady		●
● Kramer		
● Kruse		
LaMere		●
● Lundquist		
● Mahowald		
McCormick	●	
McDaniel		●
● Nash		
O'Bannon		●
● Orr		
Plaskett		●
Rogers		●
● Rubin		
● Ryan		
● Schmutzler		
● Shawley		
● Sheaffer		
● Snowden		
Stanish	●	
Sullivan		●
Swisher		●

Yeas	N-V	Nays	Yeas	N-V	Nays
●Ullrich _____			__Young _____		●
●Wilson _____			__Mr. President _____		
●Wise _____					

Bill Number__543__ Yeas:__28__ N-V:__*__ Nays:__16__

Source: Journal of the Indiana State Senate, Ninety-Sixth Session of the General Assembly (Indianapolis: C. E. Pauley & Co., 1969), p. 1240.

*"No votes" were not tallied in the original.

Appendix 7: Closing Remarks of E. Henry "Ned" Lamkin, Jr., on Passage of SB 543— Reorganization of Government in Marion County—Before Indiana House of Representatives, March 5, 1969

Mr. Speaker, Ladies and Gentlemen of the House, it is the responsibility of each of us here to listen to and represent the feeling and desires of the people whom we represent. In our community the people have both supported and opposed this legislation. I have attempted to listen to both of these points of view. I have given a great deal of time and thought to this legislation myself since I have had sincere concerns about it. I probably could not have supported it in its original form. While I rise today to support this bill, I believe I have a responsibility to present some of the objections which have been raised to this legislation and to try to answer them.

The objections have come from two sources. First, the people living outside of the current city limits have objected to the extension of city controls out into the county, and they have objected to the possibility of increased taxes which might flow out from the city. The bill does neither of these things. What it does do is give to these people a vote for the legislative and executive branches which will oversee those boards and authorities that already have jurisdiction over these parts of the county and over which these people currently have no control. No taxes will change until such time as these areas become urbanized and demand additional services at which time the taxes will go up to pay for these services as they are extended. The suggestion that expansion of the city be done by annexation would extend taxation and disrupt existing services. In many instances a corresponding extension of city services would not be possible.

A second area of objection is from the inner city where the objection is that the legislation does not do enough—that it does not extend

Source: From the personal files of E. H. Lamkin, Jr.

all services and all taxes countywide. The answer is simply that the city cannot provide all these services countywide at the present time and that people will be taxed only for the services they actually receive. Tax relief for the city is, however, possible through efficiency of administration which is contemplated through this legislation.

But, as with any other legislation, it is important to listen not only to the arguments and objections, but to listen behind the objections to the more fundamental reasons for them. For instance, behind some of the objections to this bill are motivations which are purely political—both between the two principal parties and within our party. In reality the differences between the two parties are somewhat manufactured since the two parties have split evenly in the last half dozen countywide elections.

But more important than these motivations are those which I sense derive from a feeling of fear—fear of change, fear associated with vested interests (jobs that people fear may be abolished, contracts that may shift), fear that the problems of the city such as crime and poverty will automatically be extended out into the county (although artificial boundaries bear little relation to these. For instance, in January of this year crime within the city increased 0.3% while crime in the county outside the city increased 48% compared with January of last year). There is a fear of integration and, on the other side of the coin, a fear of increased discrimination, increased oppression by the majority, and a loss of personal identity. There is a fear of elected officials—and even a fear of representative government.

This kind of fear sows the seeds of decay in a city; this is how a city dies. Indianapolis is a fine city; it has the potential to be a great one. But the seeds have been sown here. As urbanization proceeds, it spawns certain problems in the inner city; and as they develop, people begin to flee to the suburbs, industry moves out, investment dries up. And we find ourselves tracing the same paths that other cities have trod toward that kind of donut existence characterized by the suburban circle around a dead or dying core. And as this happens, we find that our ability to find solutions for these rising problems is leaving too—not just financial, but more important, the interest and involvement of people who have the ability and can give the effort that it takes to come up with the answers. And we move further toward that kind of split society that the Kerner report talked about—filled with fear, and alienation, and hostility. And defeat (or delay of this legislation for a referendum), in this climate and with the misinformation that has been both mistakenly and purposefully introduced into this community, would merely accentuate these feelings.

But the important thing is that it doesn't work. You can't run away. We are all part of the same community; and sickness in one part affects all of the others. Crime in the city is crime in the county, a poor economic climate in the city will discourage growth throughout the county, alienation in the city fosters fear in the county. And conversely, a healthy city means a healthy community—more jobs, better education, greater investment—for all. Indeed in this period of time, no man is an island.

That's what this bill is all about. It doesn't do everything; it's not intended to. You can't solve all the ills of our community with one bill any more than you can solve all the problems of the state with one session of the legislature. It is precisely because they attempted to do too much that previous attempts to move the same direction as this bill have been unsuccessful in the legislature. But, as Peter Marshall said, small things done are better than great things planned. We can't do everything, but that's no reason why we shouldn't do something.

What this bill does do is to bring all the diverse boards and authorities which have jurisdiction in the city and the county and are nearly autonomous under an elected administration and make this administration and all these authorities responsible to a strong, elected, representative Council—with absolute authority to direct policy, review all budgets, approve all ordinances, and allow bond issues.

But more importantly, this Council—which is the heart of the legislation—gives every member of the community an equal voice in his government. The districts are small enough that the people can know their councilman, and he can understand and be responsive to their needs and desires. It says to all of our citizens, "Let us come together as equals and talk together. Let us learn to communicate and understand one another and work together for our mutual benefit"— what the church calls "reconciliation."

And to those few in our community who are like the registered nurse who called me quite early one morning, filled with fear, and anger, and misinformation, who refused to listen to the facts or acknowledge the truth when it was presented to her, and who threatened to destroy not only my public life, but my private medical practice as well, this bill says, "Either you will now learn to live together with your neighbors in this community and learn to bear your fair share of the burden in meeting its problems, or you will have to move elsewhere, where your prejudices, your pocketbooks, and your consciences can again be protected from the responsibilities required by the realities of our day."

The theme of President Nixon's inaugural was "Bring us Together." I'd like to share with you some comments from his nomination acceptance speech.

He said, "None of the old hatreds mean anything when you look down into the faces of our children. In their faces is our hope, our love and our courage. Tonight I see the face of a child, he lives in a great city, he is black or he is white, he is Mexican, Italian, Polish. None of that matters, what matters is he is an American child. That child in that great city is more important than any politician's promise. . . . For most of us the American Revolution has been won. The American dream has come true. What I ask you to do is to help me make that dream come true for millions to whom it's an impossible dream today."

The only answer to fear is faith. This is a bill of faith—faith in representative government, faith that people can communicate with and understand one another, and trust and help one another.

Franklin D. Roosevelt said, "The only limit to our realization of tomorrow will be our doubts of today. Let us move forward with a strong and active *faith*."

I ask your support for this legislation.

Appendix 8: Roll Call on House Bill 543

Roll Call 663

Yeas	N-V	Nays	Yeas	N-V	Nays
● Achor			● Chase		
● Allison			● Cloud		
Anderson		●	● Coblentz		
Arredondo		●	● Coleman		
Babincsak		●	● Conn		
Bainbridge		●	● Coppes		
Bales		●	● Cox		
Baran		●	● Crowe		
● Barber			● Deckard		
Barker		●	● Donaldson		
● Bauer, B. C.			● Dorbecker		
Bauer, F. T.		●	● Dunbar		
● Bays			● Edwards, Choice		
Beneville		●	Edwards, W. C.	●	
Benjamin		●	● Fay		
● Boehning			● Ferguson		
Bolerjack		●	Gardner		●
● Borst			● Gaylord		
Bowen			● Hamilton		
● Brand			● Hart		
● Breeden			● Hayes		
Bruggenschmidt		●	● Heath		
● Burrous			Heeke		●
Bushemi		●	● Heine		

Yeas	N-V	Nays
● Hibner		
● Hillis		
Hric		●
● Humphrey		
Jessup		●
● Jones		
Kesler		●
Lake	●	
● Lamb		
● Lamkin		
● Lapar		
● Latz		
Lesniak		●
● Lewis		
Loughlin		●
Maloney		●
● Mauzy		
● McComb		
● McIntyre		
● Mertz		
● Mills		
Mullendore		●
Murakowski		●
● Mutz		
● Nelson		
● Northrup		
Pearson	●	

Yeas	N-V	Nays
● Peterson		
● Pratt		
Rainbolt		●
● Rea		
● Richardson		
Rickard	●	
● Riggin		
● Robison		
● Rogers		
● Roorda		
● Sanders		
● Shank		
● Shick		
● Sinks		
● Slenker		
Smitherman		●
Spanagel		●
● Telle		
● Thomas		
● Thompson		
● Ulmer		
White		●
● Williams		
Yarnell		●
Zaleski		●
Mr. Speaker	●	

Bill Number __543__   Yeas: __66__   N-V: __*__   Nays: __29__

Source: *Journal of the Indiana House of Representatives, Ninety-Sixth Session of the General Assembly* (Indianapolis: C. E. Pauley & Co., 1969), p. 1682.

*"No votes" were not tallied in the original.

Appendix 9: News Release from the Files of the Greater Indianapolis Progress Committee

(no date)

For Immediate Release
Contact: Don Foster or Thomas Lyons
       243–3521   787–5005

Phone Survey Shows 69% Favor Unigov

A scientific phone sampling of public opinion in Marion County conducted by the Indianapolis Jaycees and Jayncees shows 69% of citizens familiar with the Unigov proposal are in favor of it.

The survey was conducted by 40 callers under close supervision of Thomas E. Lyons, director of qualitative analysis for Herron Associates, an Indianapolis consumer market research firm.

More than 1,500 calls were completed from a random sampling of the Indianapolis phonebook. To qualify to register their opinion, citizens must be 21 years of age, must live in the household that was called, and must have said they were familiar with the Unigov proposal now before the General Assembly.

There were 281 qualified votes, or 19% of those called. Of these, 171 lived inside the Indianapolis City limits; 138 were for, and 33 against for a 78% positive response.

Outside the city limits, but within Marion County there were 110 qualified votes—57 for and 53 against for a positive response of about 52%.

Figured on a combined city-county average, the total qualified response measures 69% in favor of Unigov.

Indianapolis Jaycee president, Donald Foster, said, "The Jaycees took on this project to determine how the people of Marion County felt about this important change in their governmental structure. We believe that the methods used in the survey are sound and that the results are accurate; and we therefore urge the members of the General Assembly to act on Senate Bill 543 without delay."

Professor Shou E. Koo, of the Indiana University Statistics Department, confirms that a random sampling of 275 or more from Marion County is "an easily acceptable figure" to provide a valid accurate result. A copy of the list of people called has been preserved with their names, addresses, and phone numbers for verification.

INDEX

Compositor: Huron Valley Graphics
Text: 10/12 point Melior
Display: Machine Bold Roman and Melior Bold
Printer: Braun-Brumfield, Inc.
Binder: Braun-Brumfield, Inc.